A Practical Guide to Teaching Creative Writing

A Practical Guide to Teaching Creative Writing

Supporting Inclusive Pedagogy

Bronwen Tate and John Vigna

BLOOMSBURY ACADEMIC
LONDON • NEW YORK • OXFORD • NEW DELHI • SYDNEY

BLOOMSBURY ACADEMIC
Bloomsbury Publishing Plc, 50 Bedford Square, London, WC1B 3DP, UK
Bloomsbury Publishing Inc, 1359 Broadway, New York, NY 10018, USA
Bloomsbury Publishing Ireland, 29 Earlsfort Terrace, Dublin 2, D02 AY28, Ireland

BLOOMSBURY, BLOOMSBURY ACADEMIC and the Diana logo are
trademarks of Bloomsbury Publishing Plc

First published in Great Britain 2026

Cover design: Gita Kowlessur

A catalogue record for this book is available from the British Library.

A catalog record for this book is available from the Library of Congress.

ISBN: HB: 978-1-3504-2771-6
PB: 978-1-3504-2772-3
ePDF: 978-1-3504-2773-0
eBook: 978-1-3504-2774-7

Typeset by Integra Software Services Pvt. Ltd.
Printed and bound in Great Britain

For product safety related questions contact productsafety@bloomsbury.com.

To find out more about our authors and books visit www.bloomsbury.com
and sign up for our newsletters.

Contents

Interviews

Sample Assignments

Acknowledgments

Ideas for this book first sparked during conversations we had as participants in the *Integrating Library, Archives and Special Collections into Creative Writing Pedagogy: An Experiential Symposium* hosted by the University of Calgary in May 2021 and the *Anaphora Arts DEI Symposium* in December 2021. As we spoke about ways to apply new ideas in our classrooms and discussed teaching practices we'd already developed, we realized that—although we'd studied and taught in different countries and contexts—we'd gravitated toward similar approaches and come up with similar strategies. While we found our pedagogy largely aligned, we were also intrigued and stimulated by the complementary differences we encountered (based on teaching across genres, levels, and institutional contexts).

We began to see the contours of the book and gained momentum in the weeks and months that followed. Our practice as teachers is fundamentally in conversation with other teachers. We don't teach alone and we didn't want to stand alone in this book either. We're still learning every day, inspired and challenged by the ideas of others, and we saw this book as a chance to keep learning. We're deeply grateful to the writers and teachers who shared their experience and insight through interviews for the range, nuance, and expertise their voices bring to this book. Having a diversity of voices representing different genres and approaches from post-secondary institutions across the world was, we felt, necessary to offer a full range of possibilities in teaching.

We brainstormed and outlined many chapters at Storm City Coffee in Vancouver, BC. It turns out that having to write tens of thousands of words over four years with a writing partner is a great way to write a book, especially when momentum flags due to respective family illnesses and loss, one of us riding the Tour de France as a fundraiser for leukaemia (John), one of us clearing the necessary hurdles and paperwork to get tenure (Bronwen), teaching schedules, writing and professional duties, holidays, and so on. We're grateful to our editor at Bloomsbury, Lucy Strong, for her infinite patience and direction throughout the project.

So much of this project involved conversations with colleagues, friends, and family; we thank them for listening and offering their perspectives. We're grateful for the support of the UBC School of Creative Writing, especially Alix Ohlin, Annabel Lyon, and Sonia Dhillon.

We also appreciate the support and recognition of the Dean of Arts Educational Leadership and Innovation Award, the Arts Undergraduate Research Award, and the Undergraduate Program Evaluation and Renewal Grant.

Thank you to PJ Rayner for their insights and to Micah Favel for going over and above their duties.

We'd also like to express gratitude for our anonymous reviewers at Bloomsbury for their helpful suggestions, and also to the following writers/instructors who offered timely suggestions: Lucy Alford, Adrick Brock, Brian Castleberry, Paul Dhillon, Holly Flauto, T. Eleanor Fuller, Elee Kraljii Gardiner, Jordan Hall, Anna Farro Henderson, Jillian Hess, Kristin Horrigan, Hannah Hudson, Thommy Hutson, Isabeau Iqbal, Shelly Kawaja, Barbara Bruhin Kenney, Marita Dachsel-Kerr, Cole Klassen, Tena Laing, Becky Richardson, Erika Thorkelson, and Bridget Whearty.

Profound thanks to the teachers and mentors who inspired and supported us and to all the students over the years who have taught and continue to teach us so much.

John would like to send immeasurable gratitude and love to Nancy and Rudy the corgi, his two favorite teachers.

Bronwen sends tremendous love and thanks to Round Table for phone walks and text-coworking; to Austen for Yvonne time; to Elee for cold swims, to Sophie, Theresa, and Matthew for encouragement and support; and to Caleb, Gen, and Vesper for patience, hugs, and keeping her world in balance.

1 The Narrative of Your Course

Getting started

A creative writing course can be many things. It might gather six students around a shared table or fill a lecture hall with three hundred. It might take place in person, through video conference, via online discussion boards, or through some combination. It might dip a toe in a range of genres, go deep into a single sub-genre, or trace a question or thread across multiple genres. A course might gather experienced writers with published books or raw beginners. Or it might include a tricky mix of both. Research, collaboration, literary history, group critique, experimentation, professionalization, revision, or performance may or may not play a significant role. A creative writing course can be almost anything. But it can't do everything.

To design a compelling course, we must consider the teaching context and identify priorities. Deciding what we're *not* focusing on is just as important as deciding what we *are* devoting our time to. Even when concentrated on a single genre, an effective course goes beyond the generic and identifies a *purpose*. A story. A mission. An angle. Clarity of purpose then informs the shape of the course: the key terms, the major assignments, the structure, and the flow from first class to final due date.

But course design is rarely a linear process. Full of ideas and enthusiasm, we seek to narrow, refine, and focus over time. Along the way, an exciting reading, assignment, or activity gets cut because it doesn't serve the main goal of this particular course. (Fortunately, these cut materials often germinate new courses.) Beyond that narrowing, we've also noticed that purpose can swerve. New insights about our students or about structure might shift our priorities and send us back to the beginning to start over. A confronting encounter with a calendar—and a reminder that students need breathing room to do deep work—always leads to further focusing. Like writing itself, course design is iterative, unpredictable, and inventive.

Know your teaching context, your students, and yourself as a teacher

Designing an effective course means grappling with paradoxes and challenges:

- How do we invite students to claim agency and do work they find meaningful? How do we do this in a way that helps them feel supported rather than anxious?
- How do we create a space where students are free to explore and take risks? How do we do this without creating a scenario where other students encounter triggering or offensive material not knowing how to respond?
- How do we balance the need for clear expectations with the need to extend grace and flexibility?
- How do we respect and make space for different writing processes while also helping students let go of habits they may be attached to but that don't serve them (like last-minute writing, reluctance to revise, or defensiveness around feedback)?

There are no one-size-fits-all answers to these questions. To make sound decisions about course design, we need to consider:

1. Where am I teaching?
2. Who are my students?
3. Who am I as a teacher?

Where am I teaching?

Each different teaching context comes with particular opportunities and challenges. Across our careers, we've encountered wide variation in class size, student experience, skill level, capacity for out-of-class work, and institutional policies and expectations. The **Institutional Information-Gathering Sheet** features all the questions we wish we'd known to ask when we first got started.

Institutional information-gathering sheet

1. How does this course fit into a larger curricular context?
2. How does the course fit into the department, the institution, the profession?
3. Do students have prerequisites for the course? Is this course a prerequisite for any subsequent courses?
4. Determining size and context:
   - **a** What is the enrollment cap? Is the course likely to reach that cap or not?
   - **b** What are the weekly contact hours?
   - **c** Is the course held in-person? Hybrid/blended? 100% online?

   - **d** Where is the class held? Check the physical space and/or virtual space (video call platform) or learning management system (LMS) in which the class will be hosted.
   - **e** What are the strengths and potential challenges of these spaces?

5 What are the institutional norms around:
   - **a** How much reading/writing students might be expected to do outside of class.
   - **b** Instructor availability to students outside of class (i.e., office hours).

6 Is the class supported by Teaching Assistants? If so, what mentoring or support do you need to provide?

7 What other systems or structures might you need to interact with (i.e., a different platform for submitting final grades or a system for alerting advisors when a student is struggling)?

8 What is the course schedule (start date, end date)? Holidays such as spring break can vary from place to place.

9 What resources does the institution offer to support students and how can you connect students with these supports? (Mental health, food insecurity, legal representation, immigration support, etc.)

10 What else do I need to know? You might, for example, review an instructor handbook or inquire about:
   - **a** Expectations around assessment and grading (i.e., a target GPA, how number grades correspond with letter grades, the range of practice around when and how assessments are shared with students).
   - **b** Policies and contact people for things like academic integrity and absences.

11 Syllabus template language or department policies around issues like content policies, academic integrity, and accessibility.

Who are my students?

The central question we ask ourselves and return to repeatedly in planning our courses is: **Who are we in conversation with?** We're in conversation with students, yes, but who are those students, and what brings them to our course? We might start with two simple but profound questions:

- Why is this particular course being taught?
- Why are students taking it?

The first question takes the point of view of the institution or context. Is this an introductory elective aimed at giving non-majors a chance to explore creative writing? Is it a senior seminar that serves as the culmination of a Creative Writing Major?

The second invites us to decenter our own perspectives and wrap our minds around the many reasons students sign up for a creative writing course. Asking "why are students taking this course?" raises other questions. Channeling our own student voices, we might ask: What's in it for me? What will I learn? How will this help me?

As much as we might like to think our students are there simply to learn how to write screenplays or deepen a love of songwriting, each classroom holds a plurality of motivations and questions from the pragmatic (will an intro to creative writing course raise my GPA for med school?) to the personal (will writing poetry help me process my breakup?) to the professional (will this MFA fiction course help land me a publishing deal?).

For students to care about a course, they must find the material relevant to their lives and know that they are connected and belong. Students have big, complex questions that take up a lot of their mental space:

- Am I okay?
- Who are my people?
- Am I smart?

In a creative writing course these questions are joined by others:

- Can I write?
- Am I creative?
- Do I have anything original to say?
- Does my voice matter?

Often, though, those aren't the questions students ask out loud. Instead, they're asking what's the policy on late assignments, or what's the course average, or how much further over the word count can I go? To bring their real questions, students need to be recognized and valued as people who share knowledge, not just receive it. They need to believe that they're in the right place and that the course is *for them.*

To design effective courses, we need to make the imaginative leap to consider the perspective of students. This takes effort. We need to set aside the "curse of knowledge" (Nickerson, 1999) where we think something is obvious or easy because we have a lot of experience with it, and remember what it was like to read and write without the craft knowledge and critical lenses we bring to our work. We also need to wrap our heads around people different from ourselves with different needs and ways of learning. We must imagine the struggles students might encounter while keeping a watch out for implicit bias (based on race, age, sex, class, ability, or anything else) that might obscure our vision.

Throughout the course design process, we need to interrogate our structures, terms, materials, and activities from a student's point of view. Along with asking an experienced friend or colleague to review an assignment sheet and point out potential sources of confusion or alienation, we recommend this thought experiment: identify an individual (a cousin in college, your past self, a former student) and imagine how this person might experience your course. Reflect on questions like:

- **What brings them to your course?** Is it a requirement or a choice? What do they really want to learn?
- **What are they anxious about?** What past experiences might they be carrying with them that could affect how they approach your course?

- **What materials or activities (even course terms) might make this student feel alienated or excluded?**
- **What steps might you take as an instructor to mitigate these feelings?** How might you introduce the material/activity, structure the course, or find ways to connect to the student's previous knowledge or feelings of competence and connection?
- **What materials or activities might make this person feel connected, curious, or excited?**
- **What might change for this person from the beginning to the end of the course?** Fill in the blanks: "At the beginning of the course, this person thinks (or feels or believes) … At the end of the course, they will think … "

Pre-course surveys

After we've drafted our syllabi (more on syllabi creation later in this chapter), we sometimes invite students to respond to a brief survey prior to the start of the course. This gives us an opportunity to get to know our students, give them a sense of what to expect in the course, and encourage them to weigh in, establishing that their opinions and thoughts matter. In our pre-course surveys or emails, we ask questions like:

- What are you reading? What areas/genres of writing interest you the most?
- Why are you taking the course? What do you expect or want to learn?
- What concerns or questions do you have about the course?

Pre-course surveys or check-ins not only offer insight into our cohort of students but also create an early opportunity to establish rapport and build community with them, immediately foregrounding multiple perspectives that can be built upon as the semester progresses.

Who am I as a teacher?

Finally, it's key to reflect on who we are individually as teachers. What are our specific commitments, aptitudes, and challenges in the classroom? Just as we ask about student motivations, we might do well to spend some time reflecting on our own: Why do I care about my discipline? About my teaching?

While some aspects of sound pedagogy are broadly applicable, others are individual. As Parker Palmer writes in *The Courage to Teach* (1997), "knowing my students and my subject depends heavily on self-knowledge. When I do not know myself, I cannot know who my students are" (3). In supporting graduate students interested in learning how to teach, we remind them not to focus on being "the best teacher" but instead on being the most authentic version of *themselves* as teachers. One student worries that his energy is too high and students might find his enthusiasm overwhelming, another wonders if students will find her initial deep-breathing exercise and emotional check-in too earnest, while a third student wonders if she can even be a teacher if she doesn't have a strong grasp on all of the latest tech. While we all have room to grow as teachers, we also have strengths to work from, and they're often the things we might find worrying or embarrassing: our energy, our obsessiveness, our goofy humor.

It's worth taking time to ask ourselves: what will play to my strengths? What do I have to offer as a teacher and as a writer? This might mean performing a quick audit on not only our strengths and values but also on areas where we might struggle. Defensive course design gives us an opportunity to identify these areas—perhaps we're not as strong at incorporating technology in our courses, or marking efficiently, or facilitating close readings—and determine where to focus our efforts. It's important to continue to grow as a teacher, but it's also crucial to determine what we have the time and capacity to manage effectively. Each semester brings a new set of challenges that impact our course design and teaching effectiveness.

One pleasure (and frustration) of both writing and teaching is that there's always more to learn. When we start questioning why we do what we do, we may notice a rise in our anxiety as we identify gaps in our knowledge, background, and preparation. Imposter syndrome or doubt can creep in. But effective teachers don't need to know everything, nor can they know everything. We only need to take seriously the responsibility of creating a space where learning is possible. We're often best served by embracing a sense of ourselves as lifelong apprentices. If we start from our enthusiasms and curiosities, consider student perspectives, pay attention, and keep revising from a place of humility, we can build courses that students will find meaningful.

Who are you as a teacher? Identifying guiding values

Whether you're a beginning teacher or someone with years of experience, it's worthwhile to consider the experiences that have shaped your approach and articulate the values that guide your decisions.

- Where are you coming from as a writing teacher? What are your values and priorities? What events and encounters have shaped the way you think about writing? About teaching?
- What light-bulb moments inspire you as a teacher? What examples and models are generative for you?
- What challenges inform your teaching? Reflect on difficult moments as a learner and as a teacher. How did you respond? How might you respond differently?

Intentional reflection like this shapes our teaching philosophy, which we can continue to revise each time we teach.

The narrative of your course

Out of all of the possible things a writing course could be or do, how do we decide? We need to commit to "a bold, sharp purpose" (2018, 1), as Priya Parker writes. "When we don't examine the deeper assumptions behind *why* we gather," she explains, "we end up skipping too quickly to replicating old, staid forms of gathering. And we forgo the possibility of creating something memorable, even transformative" (3). This is all too frequently the case when it comes to teaching. In education, as elsewhere, many choose "the template—and the activities and structure that go along with it" (4) before getting clear on purpose.

A category, like "Introduction to Screenwriting" or even "Climate Writing," is not the same thing as a purpose. The more we assume that the purpose is obvious without taking the time to think it through, the more likely we are either to teach a bland course, or to teach a course that's somehow in conflict with itself and pulling in multiple opposing directions.

Parker lays out "the test for a meaningful reason for coming together: Does it stick its neck out a little bit? Does it take a stand? Is it willing to unsettle some of the guests (or maybe the host)? Does it refuse to be everything to everyone?" (17). This might feel risky for us as instructors. Aren't our courses meant to be accessible and inclusive? If we pause to reflect, though, we can see that a course can't succeed at being everything to everyone, and that students are, in fact, best served when a course clearly announces its purpose and allows them to make an informed choice about whether that purpose aligns with their own.

Designing a course is similar to designing a piece of writing: there's a unity of purpose, often invisible, that holds it together and gives it shape. We like to think of our courses as a space of shared endeavor driven by a big idea or central question.

Described by Grant Wiggins and Jay McTighe (2005) as powerful ideas that promote insight and meaning-making, big ideas offer a structure for making connections and get to the heart of expert understanding of a subject.

Big ideas typically contain these elements (69):

- They have enduring value beyond the course.
- They are core to the discipline and revisited over the duration of the course.
- They require "unearthing," bringing to light the subtle, non-obvious, misunderstood, problematic, and controversial aspects of a concept.
- They engage inquiry.
- They are subject to refinement and iteration as students learn more.
- They have strong transfer value; applying to other inquiries across disciplines or subjects over time.

To arrive at a purpose, Parker recommends taking the initial reasons that come to mind and asking "why" until you "hit a belief or value" (22). Likewise, Wiggins and McTighe offer the following guided questions specifically keyed to educational experiences:

- Why study ....? Why should we care about ... ?
- If this course was a story, what's the moral of the story?
- What's the big idea underneath the skill or process of ... ?
- What larger issue, problem, or concept underlies ... ?

- What couldn't we do if we didn't understand … ?
- How is … used and applied in the world?
- How would we be changed if we understood … ?

Understood as a statement of purpose or central focus that connects all pedagogical decisions, a big idea guides our course design from the macro level (key concepts and assessments) down to the micro-level (class-by-class readings, activities, writing exercises, etc.).

John's big idea for a large lecture course in fiction for beginners stems from a common thread that he's observed across the stories his students are interested in writing and where they draw their inspiration from (often their own lives). So, his central question is simply: Are we the stories we tell/write?

Whatever statement of theme or central idea you settle on to guide your course design, remember that you are making a version of the course, not the platonic ideal of that genre or topic (which doesn't exist). Instead of asking, "What is the ultimate ideal short story course?" ask yourself, "What's a version of a short story course that draws on my strengths and interests and offers something particular to students?" Allow the course to focus on some things and let go of others.

We share the big idea with the students on the first day of the semester. Across levels, we make every attempt to be transparent with students and offer them a "why" they are doing this and "how" they are going to do it. The transparency helps students feel included and connected as co-authors of the course. At the end, we return to the big idea and show students visually how far they've traveled by illustrating a narrative of their learning across the semester, as writers and as human beings.

Pause and project into the future

As you get caught up in the nitty-gritty of due dates and word counts, step back and think about the long game.

1. Imagine it is two (or five or ten) years from now and you've run into a student who has taken the course you're currently designing. They're telling you that the most important thing they learned in your course was X. What do you hope the X is? Try to give an immediate response. Write it down.
2. Consider what came up in response to the previous question. What might that look like in practice? What needs more space and what can be reduced or cut?

Let this clarity of purpose help you make decisions about what's essential and what's a cool idea to explore sometime down the road.

Felicia Rose Chavez on inclusive course design

Why is it crucial to take an explicitly anti-racist approach from the very start of designing a course?

Because it invites our students to hold us accountable to the work.

Key terms convey our values and expectations to students. Can you give an example of this from your own teaching practice?

Guiding Principles are a favorite. We're responsible for a set of traditional learning objectives, true, but how would we like our students to grow as people during our time together? I identify a set of 2–3 guiding principles per course (elevated alongside my learning objectives) to challenge the norm of what's rewarded in the classroom. Maybe it's confidence, or risk-taking, or vulnerability, or empathy. Students reflect on these principles as they relate to their progress throughout the course, highlighting successes in a final reflective portfolio.

When you're designing a new course, how do you move from all of the possible approaches, activities, and assignments to a coherent set of things that fit the time allocated?

I could talk about this all day. A new course is a journey, so I plot it out like a roadmap. I start with a rubric for "real" learning. From start to finish, what are the steps of my students' learning journeys? Are they exercising agency by taking risks? Are they navigating within uncertainty? Are they testing new ideas and embracing failure? Are they cultivating change, maybe through a newfound sense of openness, or receptivity, or creativity? Are they reflecting on their challenges and successes, and documenting how they (and their work) have changed over time? I end on something like: risk, vulnerability, experimentation, growth, and change. Then I hold that rubric up to my activities and assignments to determine what best supports students when along the journey.

Across your work advocating for inclusive and anti-racist creative writing pedagogy, where have you seen the greatest resistance to change? If you could transform one underlying belief, what would it be?

That educators, in risking an anti-racist practice, will do it wrong, and that failure is a bad thing. The emotional experience of failure is awful because it has clinging power. A lesson goes wrong. An assignment bombs. A conversation is clumsy. So we carry that pit-of-the-stomach feeling home, judge ourselves, then retreat back to the safety of the tried and true. What if instead we used failure as a launchpad for learning? Because there's no getting it right the first time, no award for being Officially Anti-Racist. We fail constantly. Which means that we evolve constantly.

What can creative writing courses offer self-avowed "non-writers"? What do we need to do as teachers for this to be possible?

Provide them the space and time to reflect on their relationship to writing. My second-grade teacher told my mom I lacked an aptitude for writing, and you better believe I've never forgotten it. Our students embody their writing legacies, the good stuff and the bad. They carry that burden into our classrooms. I want them to face head-on what they need to heal from, and so on day one I ask them to write a list of their writing fears. To each fear we answer, "But I will write anyway."

FELICIA ROSE CHAVEZ is an award-winning educator and author of *The Anti-Racist Writing Workshop: How to Decolonize the Creative Classroom*. Originally from Albuquerque, New Mexico, she serves as an educational consultant in Seattle.
Image credit: Amy Barber, Bluegrass Bebe Photography

Structuring a course

Okay, say we've figured out a statement of purpose or big idea. How do we move from that concise statement to a coherently structured course? It can be tempting to start from a list of books or films or plays we feel excited about. Or maybe from a cool assignment we've been wanting to try. And these can both be great places to start. If you're anything like us, however, you'll soon end up with a tangled sprawl of books, supporting essays, interview videos, key concepts, neat things to try, possible assignments, really important principles and questions, possibly spread across two or three notebooks, notes scrawled in the margins of books, and/or computer documents and phone apps. How do we get from the sprawl to the syllabus?

If you're a new faculty member at the University of British Columbia (UBC), where we both teach, and you sign up for a Course Design Intensive, they'll show you a video about backward design proposed by Wiggins and McTighe (2005). Basically, designing your course backwards involves three steps:

1. Identify desired results (i.e., knowledge and skills).
2. Determine acceptable evidence (i.e., assessments).
3. Plan learning experiences and instruction (i.e., learning events, discussions, exercises).

The gist is that you begin by getting clear on what you hope students will get out of the course (learning goals) and then work from there to assignments, readings, activities, and so on.

Identifying learning goals

Some education contexts distinguish between learning goals, learning objectives, and learning outcomes. This can be useful at an institutional level, but for many instructors, it's enough simply to focus on what students will be able to do at the end of a course as a result of having taken the course. Important distinction: not just what students do in the course, but what they'll be able to carry with them after the course. The framing "Students will be able to … " is helpful here. The goals that follow should:

- **Begin with a present tense verb** (i.e., identify, take risks, analyze, create, craft, describe, complete, apply, locate, recognize, perform, communicate, assess, situate, articulate, judge, navigate, formulate, evaluate).
- **Be specific and measurable.** If a goal is "Get better at reading poetry," how will you know when students have achieved this goal? In contrast, if the goal is expressed as "Interpret poems with attention to diction, syntax, and figurative language," you can measure progress.
- **Be demonstrable.** If we want students to "know the difference between scene and exposition," that's fine, but how will we know if they know? How will they demonstrate this knowledge? A goal might be: "Identify examples of scene and exposition in a published short story and talk about how they come together to make meaning." Or it might be "Write a short story that makes use of both scene and exposition and explain these narration strategies in a short introduction."

As Felicia Rose Chavez makes clear in *The Anti-Racist Writing Workshop* (2021), learning goals can be repositories of uninterrogated concepts of value—often inherited and implicit—that perpetuate hierarchies of race, class, and status. Keep an eye out for terms like "mastery," "the classics," "literary," and "expert" and make sure the language you use is inclusive and aligned with your values. **Chapter 5** offers an in-depth discussion of keywords and craft terms and the need to interrogate and contextualize them.

How to write a course description when you're still figuring out the course

A course description gives potential students key details to help them decide if the course will be a good fit for them. The course description is usually due weeks or months (or even a year!) before we actually teach a course. So course descriptions involve hedging our bets: how can we give a sense of our vision for the course without binding ourselves to things that might still change? As we teach the same course multiple times, of course, we get more clarity about how to describe it clearly and succinctly.

A course description is typically in the range of 75–250 words and might address any of the following, as appropriate to context:

- Title
- Goals (what will students learn?)
- Major assignments (what will students do?)
- Framing for the course (is it centered around a genre? A topic? A process?)
- Delivery mode (in-person, online, synchronous, asynchronous)
- Experience level of students, any prerequisites

- Readings (often a few suggestive names to give students a taste of what to expect)
- Pedagogical approaches

Remember, the course description is the first place students get a sense of your voice and persona as a teacher. Use language that gives a sense of who you are and what it's like to work with you.

Back-and-forth design: from learning goals to syllabus

When we think hard about our course design process, we realize that it's not exactly "backward design," but rather something more like "back-and-forth design." It's iterative, just like our other creative projects. We find ourselves returning to those big questions: What is the purpose of this course? Who are the students who sign up? What are my guiding values as an instructor? What is central and what can be cut? Sometimes the big idea becomes clear early in the planning process, but often it takes a while. We get ideas when we read things, when we talk to friends, when we cook a meal, take a walk, spend time with the dog or kids. And then we go back and forth between the core guiding purpose/goals, the accumulating ideas/possibilities, and what actually fits in a given term. We return to big ideas and learning goals again and again, revising and sharpening them as the course design becomes more clear and stable. This can feel like pushing the material through a huge funnel to see what's absolutely essential from all the big-picture blue-sky thinking.

As we work under the umbrella of our big idea, we return to four key questions that back-and-forth design helps us navigate.

One: What fits in the time we have available?

To do anything well, a single course can't do everything. We have to make choices. A course might focus on generative work and invite students to create an abundance of new material. A course might dedicate time to "workshopping the workshop" and have recurring meta-conversations about how critique works and why. A course might have a reading list entirely sourced by students. A course might involve reading out loud or a collaborative assignment or a community-based component or a big research assignment or a project involving publishing or performance. So many beautiful and worthwhile things a writing course can include! But we cannot do all of them at once. Over and over, we have to ask ourselves: How much time will it take to do this well? How do these plans map onto an actual calendar? How much time is sufficient for students to build capacity and consciously apply what they've learned? How does one thing build into another?

Table 1.1 Course Sequence Planning Guide

Week's Focus*	Out-of-Class	In-Class	Reading/Resources

**Should relate to core ideas, key concepts, or essential questions that are required for understanding/working with big ideas and achieving learning outcomes.*

Table 1.2 Three-Column Course Planning Worksheet (courtesy of the Centre for Teaching and Learning Technology at UBC)

Learning Outcomes	Evidence/Assessment	Learning Activities
What will people **gain or learn** as a result of participating in your course? What will people **know how to do** as a result of learning in your course? *(consider outcomes that will have enduring value beyond the course)*	How will they **demonstrate or apply** this learning? How will work be **assessed or evaluated**? *(consider alignment with outcomes and relevance beyond the course)*	What activities or opportunities will help learners **build the capacity** for demonstrating or applying this learning? *(consider learning that scaffolds and aligns with outcomes and evidence)*

At this point, it can be useful to start capturing gathered material, readings, potential assignments, class activities, and discussions and testing them on a week-by-week **Course Sequence Planning Guide** and/or a **Three-Column Course Planning Worksheet**. These worksheets can help you see the big picture of the course, organize it thematically, decide where assessments might be incorporated, and more, as you map the spine of the course.

In mapping out the week-by-week pace of a course, we keep in mind our own capacity and pace as well as that of students. For example, we might deliberately stagger the due dates for all the courses we teach to avoid potential log-jams of reading/grading work. For students, we review breaks, holidays, and mid-terms and assign major assignments with an eye to providing some relief in their schedules. Reflecting on assignment design **(Chapter 2)** and workshop approaches and alternatives **(Chapter 7)** also helps us make informed choices about pacing and schedules.

Two: Does the course offer students what they need to succeed?

This is where the need to work back-and-forth really comes in. Let's say we decide that a learning goal for Introduction to Writing Poetry is: "Revise a workshopped draft into a more fully realized draft based on the synthesis of peer feedback and your own growing sensibility and aesthetic."

That means we need to give students opportunities to encounter and practice all of the skills explicit and implied within that statement. And we need to introduce the more complicated ones gradually, not all at once. We should ask, "What am I assuming that students already *know*? What am I assuming that students already know *how to do*? Are these reasonable assumptions?" Usually, students require practice focused on building capacity.

Unpacking all of the implicit skills and knowledge our assignments require allows us to build an assignment progression that will support all students, not just those with previous experience or high motivation. The unpacking process might look something like this:

- **Revision**—Students need to see examples of poems at different stages of revision so they can see how radical revisions can be. Maybe that article where Dwight Garner and Parul Sehgal walk through multiple drafts of Elizabeth Bishop's "One Art"?
- **Revision**—Students need to practice revision in small ways early on. Maybe some little assignments where they're invited to return to an earlier draft and expand or fine-tune it in some way?
- **Revision**—Revision is slow and messy. How can I help students play here rather than feel a need to be product-driven and efficient? How about a revision log where they document what they try out and what they notice? When in the course could I put this? How much time would it take? What kind of feedback would students need to be able to learn from it?
- **Workshopped draft**—This means students need to engage in a workshop process. What process will I use? Given the size of the course, does verbal or written feedback make more sense? How many peers need to comment on a draft? How much structure will be needed for this to work? Maybe I should include a session on how to ask good questions of your readers.
- **Growing sensibility and aesthetic**—Are those terms a student will connect to or should I change them? I could assign some reflective writing where students talk about work they find meaningful, what audience they're interested in reaching, and how specific formal choices come together to create a mood or tone.

Any goal can be unpacked this way. And then we start to see what it means to offer students the support they need to reach their goals. And how much time it takes to do this well. Again, we might need to make some hard choices about what to include.

Universal Design for Learning, accessibility, and access friction

In the early stages of course design, we must remember that students have different learning pathways. There's no one-size-fits-all approach. Instead, an integrated, thoughtful approach to course designing acknowledges and supports the diverse needs of students. Universal Design for Learning (UDL) foregrounds three core principles of providing multiple means of:

1. **Engagement**—connecting to different interests, learning motivations, and ways of engaging (routine and novelty, solo work and group work).
2. **Representation**—sharing course materials via text, audio, video, slides, and so on, with attention to how groups and identities are represented.
3. **Action/expression**—inviting different ways to demonstrate learning.

UDL reminds us that access points that may be essential for some students—like the audio recordings and screen-reader-accessible text formats absolutely necessary for a blind student—also offer valuable support for other students, who find they connect emotionally with poems they hear read out loud.

Although UDL is an important step toward accessibility, sometimes a thoughtful decision that leads toward greater access for some students can create barriers for others. Access friction can occur when individuals have opposing access needs, as when one student thrives in a high-involvement conversational environment while another struggles to follow overlapping voices. As instructors, we need to remember that we can't anticipate all possible needs or meet all needs at 100%. For example, an instructor and students with good vision may be comfortable with moderate lighting in the classroom, whereas one student with reduced vision requires bright lights and another student with migraines or sensory sensitivity needs low lighting. Each student's access needs are valid. When access needs, including those in friction, are taken seriously, instructors and students have an opportunity to work together toward a solution. Despite inevitable access friction, UDL offers a necessary baseline for designing an inclusive course.

Working with accessibility, advising, and other support offices

Our work with students brings us into contact with support offices, such as a center for accessibility or student advising. We may be asked to flag struggling students early in the term so that they can receive support, or students may share an Accommodation Letter. Some frequent accommodations include:

- Extended time for exams (the most common request).
- Permission to audio-record lectures.
- Access to lecture notes or slides or notetaker support.
- May occasionally miss class for medical reasons.
- Instructor consideration for occasional extensions on coursework with advance consultation.

These letters can be the start of a conversation, even if the specific accommodation doesn't apply to your course. For a large course, we might send a brief email confirming that the course doesn't include exams and inviting the student to get in touch if there's anything we can do to support their learning. For a smaller course, we might invite the student to meet with us to discuss the structure of the course and how they can set themselves up for success with our support.

When the accommodation includes "consideration for occasional extensions," instructors may struggle to decide how best to support a student in a workshop course with a high degree of reciprocal exchange of drafts and feedback on a tight schedule. We've often found that repeated or lengthy extensions for draft submissions or peer feedback letters can lead to students feeling out of step with the course, missing out on the chance to have their work discussed, requiring an "Incomplete" for the course, or attempting to write multiple feedback letters in the final weeks of the course (which can mean rushed work that suffers in quality and doesn't serve peers who have already moved on with their revisions). While flexibility is important to student success, so, too, is clarity.

If a key learning goal for your course involves giving and receiving feedback on work in progress, discuss with students which deadlines are open to extensions and which deadlines are firm (perhaps workshop drafts and/or peer responses). If you anticipate that these deadlines might present a hurdle for students, consider ways to lighten the load for everyone (by using small groups, designating some students to write full responses and others to bring a single question, etc.). We also understand that access to an accommodation letter might depend on a student's ability to afford designation testing, access to family advocacy and support, or cultural attitudes toward mental health. Keeping this in mind, we aim to design courses with policies that support many different kinds of learners so that those with undocumented accessibility needs also have a chance to succeed.

J. Logan Smilges on rethinking accessibility

How would you say teachers tend to conceive of disability and accessibility? What reframing might you offer?

I think it's fair to say that the dominant perspective among a lot of teachers is:

1. That there is no disability in their class. Like, it's just absent until they are informed otherwise, and
2. When they are informed that disability is in their class, they see it as isolated to a particular student and something to be dealt with through an added accommodation recommended by a disability service office, with the primary purpose of getting rid of the disability and effectively realigning that student with ostensibly non-disabled peers.

My recommended reframing would be to suggest:

1. That disability is all around us, whether we're aware of it or not.
2. That the purpose of access and accommodation should not be rehabilitation, where we take what we believe to be wayward and the correct course. Instead, the purpose should be to expand our collective sense of what we're doing in a given space.

I think there's something beautiful about approaching access as an invitation to reimagine how we're occupying space together and how we can support one another in our individual and collective goals.

There will always be obstacles for students accessing what we're doing in a course that exceed any person's capacity to accommodate because the institution itself was designed not merely without disabled people in mind, but on their explicit disavowal. So there is no accommodation that is going to create a just, equitable form of access.

With that recognition, I, as a teacher, am reminded that my work does not stop at the classroom door. Our work as teachers asks us to reimagine what learning is and where learning can take place and to offer students opportunities to demonstrate growth and learning in ways that are not premeditated by the curriculum or are perhaps immeasurable by the forms of evaluation and assessment that a university deems effective. To be a teacher is to constantly recognize the limits of teaching as we've come to understand it and to honor and amplify the ways students are growing on their own or even in spite of the teaching they're receiving through normative institutions.

Given this, when you sit down to craft policies, what are some key principles you keep in mind to at least reach toward true access?

True access requires a culture of access, not just a checklist. The phrase "culture of access" is something that I learned from Ada Hubrig and Ruth Osorio. For me, a culture of access refers to a collective understanding shared by the teacher and students that we are all responsible for creating a space where people not only are able to physically, mentally access the material, but also feel welcome and invited to engage.

It's an affective project, right? How are we feeling about access? How are we feeling about one another? But then, of course, there are also more practical things. I let students know ahead of the semester that I welcome multiple forms of participation, for example. For some students, that might mean participating verbally. Other people don't like to talk as much. So I have a series of designated roles that people can take on to allow them to engage participation:

- **Note takers**
- **Translators** (people who take others' notes and re-make them into other media, like a podcast, a comic, or something that allows broader access).
- **Re-vocalizers** (people who will ask other people's questions so that everyone's perspectives can still be shared).

Before we even meet for the first time, I make sure students know "There's a space for you here. Even if you don't see yourself in the roles that I've outlined, what you do see is effort, intention. You see an invitation." A culture of access requires the collective work of imagining new roles. Not every role is going to work for every class. So I work hard to invite students to work with me on allowing them access.

There's a way the language of universal design has done a real disservice to how we think about access because it suggests that there is a world in which everyone already has access. And that's just not how bodies work, right? Bodies are dynamic. So our needs are dynamic. What one class needs is not what another class needs. What one student needs in Week One might not be what they need in Week Three. That's just being human. Going into a semester knowing that a culture of access demands flexibility takes a lot of stress off of the instructor for getting everything right. It's a process. It's a negotiation. We do the best we can.

J. LOGAN SMILGES is an Assistant Professor at the University of British Columbia. Led by commitments to transfeminism and disability justice, their scholarship and teaching lie at the nexus of queer/trans disability studies, rhetorical studies, and the history of medicine. They are the author of *Queer Silence: On Disability and Rhetorical Absence* and *Crip Negativity*.

Image credit: J. Logan Smilges

Three: What do structure and accountability convey to students about course priorities?

Many students are obliged to be ruthlessly pragmatic about their learning. A course reveals its true priorities in where it places accountability (often in the form of grades). If students are assigned reading but their engagement with that reading doesn't show up anywhere in the course marking scheme (or is captured in a vague catch-all "participation mark"), it's understandable that students might choose to focus their attention elsewhere. If we tell students that low-stakes writing is important and valuable but assign it no more than 5% of the overall grade, we aren't conveying a consistent message. Likewise, if peer feedback or workshop contributions form a key part of the course, these skills need to be taught, and performance in these areas should form a substantial part of the final grade. (More on grading and assessment in **Chapter 10**.)

Four: Where and how am I supporting student agency?

Reading about learning objectives, some instructors might think, "But it's not about my goals. It's about the students' own goals for the course. I want to design a course that is flexible and responsive to students, not come in with predetermined notions of success." We hear you. Yet, even a course that invites students to identify their own goals needs a structure to support students in considering possible goals, selecting tentative goals, revising those goals as the term goes on, and reflecting on their growth at the end. If the class is going to work together as a group to identify and collaborate on a big group project, they still need some sense of what's required, what's open, and what's negotiable. The class will need to dedicate time to process and decision-making, which needs to be scaffolded and supported, especially if we want to avoid a scenario where the most confident/vocal students dominate the class.

In contrast, an instructor may design a course where parameters and goals are largely determined at the program level. In this case, the challenge may be how to create opportunities for students to make choices and exercise agency.

What about a context where the goals are more emotional than intellectual? Emotional goals need to be unpacked and questioned as well, especially to avoid scenarios that are emotionally coercive or open up traumatic memories instructors are not prepared to deal with. Bronwen's friend Matt, who taught in prisons, investigated the counseling available to inmates before he began a course and made clear to participants what their options were as writers and what was expected of them when receiving the work of others. As we teach across academic and community contexts, we need to make sure we don't carry unexamined assumptions that make sense in one context but would be counterproductive in another. We keep all of these concerns in mind as we begin to map out a course syllabus.

Anatomy of a syllabus

Course title. In some contexts, the title is pre-set or doesn't really matter, but in many contexts, the title is the first place a student makes a decision about whether to take a closer look. Consider the difference between Poetry I and Poetry is Not a Luxury: Reading and Writing Poems that Matter.

Course details. Instructor name, instructor email, scheduled office hours, any course pre-reqs, meeting days/times for course.

Land acknowledgment and/or mission statement

Course description. Often copied from the initial course catalogue. A 75–250 word description of the focus, purpose, and key assignments of the course.

Learning goals/objectives/outcomes. What students will be able to do by the end of the course as a result of taking the course.

Required texts. If full books are required, list them. You can also include a note saying that PDFs or a course reader will be available.

List of learning activities/assignments. What will students *do* in the course? If the course involves credit/grades in any capacity, you'll also need to think about what each assignment group is worth and how you'll assess it. A chart or table can be useful here.

Descriptions of learning activities/assignments. A tight paragraph per assignment group that says something about what the assignment involves and why the class will be doing it.

Course policies. This is where the boilerplate template language can really kick in, depending on the institutional context. Setting that aside, are there expectations *you* want to communicate to students about accessibility, content, technology, attendance, due dates, or anything else?

Course schedule. What is happening week by week? When are assignments, drafts, readings due? Does the course break down into discrete modules that you want to signal on the schedule?

Claire Donato on the art of the syllabus

Tell us about the philosophy guiding the care and attention you bring to crafting syllabi.

A syllabus can function both as an art object and a pedagogical tool. These aspects of a syllabus actually enhance one another and thereby the course itself. For example, the course schedule for my *Poetry and Psychoanalysis* course tried to both visually and textually represent free association and the wilderness of the unconscious. My *Twin, Double, Doppelgänger, Diptych* course was designed in two columns. My *Small Worlds, Miniature Forms* course schedule took the form of a textual dollhouse and included a miniature version of the entire course syllabus. And my *Silence* course schedule deployed caesuras and negative space to represent course themes. These visual explorations are really important to me as a teacher: I feel like I'm literally crafting a course container when I build these documents.

When I began teaching, I grew curious about the syllabus as a formalized document containing institutionally requisite component parts. I wondered how syllabi might be loosened, subverted, transformed. My course schedules desire and reach toward a sense of freedom and a form of research that comes from visual/spatial/design thinking. They are also direct extensions of my heart and possibly cast spells.

Instructors can be reluctant to give much detail on syllabi because they want to remain open to changes. How do you approach planning and flexibility in your course design?

Building out a detailed course schedule actually brings me a sense of freedom, but that sense of freedom only comes with the acceptance that a detailed course schedule—or my best laid plans—may need to be adjusted along the way. I'm thinking now about the Covid-19 pandemic, which required me to totally re-adapt all of my courses. A course whose final six weeks were focused on medieval mysticism became wholly devoted to the creation of a collective zine, and a considered study of the show *Love Is Blind*—including a visit from the show's producer, who was also in lockdown in his Hollywood basement.

In general, I try to give myself grace and space with regard to planning and flexibility in my course design, but I always want my students to feel anchored, and for them to know that I have carefully considered and am committed to the course they're taking, with the desire that they will be too.

A syllabus is one of the first contact points students have with a course. What messages are you hoping to convey through your syllabi?

A few messages I hope to convey are:

> *This course is a poetics laboratory, which I crafted with love.*
> *There are also expectations here, and "expectations" is a complicated word.*
> *My expectations come from a generous space.*
> *I put care into class and am excited about it and hope you will be too.*
> *I want you to succeed in this course, and to do so by being peculiarly you.*

I explicitly state all of the above to the groups I teach, whether on the syllabus itself or aloud in class as we read over the syllabus on the first day of class. I also try to reiterate these messages throughout the semester, both implicitly and explicitly.

CLAIRE DONATO is an Assistant Chairperson at Pratt Institute, where she received the 2020–2021 Distinguished Teacher Award. She is the author of three books, most recently *Kind Mirrors, Ugly Ghosts*.
Image credit: Claire Donato

Setting the tone

A syllabus needs to convey to students:

- What they can expect from your course.
- What will be expected of them if they choose to take the course.

Yet, the syllabus in higher education has increasingly become a contractual legal document with a whole swath of template language required by institutions. We understand why this is happening, but more and more we feel a need to repeat anything we want students to know elsewhere, as we understand why a student might skim or ignore a long, formally worded syllabus. The more students are able to get a taste for the big idea of a course early on, the more likely they are to choose the course in an informed way and give genuine consent to learning together. Along with a syllabus, then, we might welcome students (or potential students) to a course with:

- A video trailer that gives an overview of key questions and assignments.
- A pre-course survey.
- A page of real or imagined "Frequently Asked Questions."

Where a syllabus might read:

> You will engage in multiple learning activities, including reading and listening to poems, writing short sketches, revising poems, writing reflections, and engaging in peer feedback.

An FAQ page can say:

> **This course seems like a lot of work! How much time should I put in each week?**
>
> It is a lot of work! You will be turning in writing most weeks and will likely devote 1–3 hours/week to some combination of reading, writing, and watching micro-lecture videos beyond our class meeting time. That said, my hope is that everything we're doing has a clear purpose and will feel useful and connected for you. This steady rhythm of writing week by week and the revision process means that you won't ever need to start a big project from scratch close to the deadline. Making a lot of work can help us get less constrained and anxious about that work and help us break into something looser and more playful. That's the goal. And that's why 25% of your grade (the Sketches) will be assessed as Complete/Incomplete.

Likewise, a video introduction or course trailer might include a brief introduction to how we became interested in the topic or genre or preview questions students can look forward to exploring. In each of these modalities, we have the opportunity to connect to students on a human level. When we share our enthusiasm, our energy, perhaps our nerdy humor, or our own struggles and challenges as writers, we assure students that their individual interests and shared human struggles are welcome in our courses.

Keeping a teaching journal

Earlier in this chapter, we discussed three key considerations that shape course design: our institutional contexts, our students, and ourselves as instructors. Coming full circle, we recommend a favor to your future self: take 5–10 minutes to jot down notes on teaching *after every class session.* These reflections captured in the moment allow instructors to track how expectations meet practice.

A teaching journal offers us a way to think more deeply about our teaching practice. It's our own personal book about teaching where we reflect on what we tried, student engagement levels, muddy vs clear points, what went well, what needed more time, and so on. While many of us do this exercise in our heads, written notes can help us notice patterns over time and remember details we would otherwise forget. The reflective practice also helps us release any lingering tension after a challenging class or ground ourselves after an exhilarating one. In the short term, a teaching journal can help us notice interventions to align our teaching more fully with our purpose and values. Over the long term, these notes give us a chance to think through ways institutional context, students, and we ourselves change over time, and to refine and adapt our teaching to reflect these changes.

2

Assignment Design

Why assignments?

Looking back on our time as students, we recall creative writing courses where assignments or assignment sheets were seen as out of place. "You're here to write," these instructors likely told us, "Make some poems, write some stories, sign up for your workshop slots, and make the work you want to make."

When we had thoughtful peers engaging with our drafts, we got a lot out of these courses. But we also remember stressful conversations with classmates: "Where do I even start?" "What do you think he's expecting?" "Do you think it's okay if I … ?"

These questions, while present for graduate students, are especially pressing for undergraduates accustomed to receiving specific instructions. Without clear guidance, they start the assignment stressed, and although there can be a value to *productive stress*, we'd question whether a lack of clarity on an assignment is truly productive for meaningful learning.

In other courses, we experienced carefully crafted sequences of assignments that guided, challenged, and supported us. As we became teachers ourselves, we thought about how we had learned the strategies that serve us writers and tried to reverse-engineer them, to create structures in which students could discover their own tools, techniques, and approaches. We sought to design assignments that challenge and support students to build confidence in applying new techniques, but also learn to trust the process, *their* process, and develop a spirit of active experimentation.

Writing and learning: drawing on what we know

A no-assignments approach tends to treat writing as a "natural process" and assumes that the skills, craft knowledge, and cognitive habits required can be "picked up along the way." Writing Studies scholars, in contrast, have shown just how complex, contextual, and personal writing is.

We've seen plenty of writers (ourselves included) grapple with this hard truth: someone can spin off anecdotes and make their friends laugh without a second thought, but when they sit down to write, it's a whole different thing. This makes sense, however, when we recall how different writing is from speech, which relies on gesture, tone, expression, and so on. Writing is hard.

Students bring their own strategies from past writing contexts that might help them but might also get in their way. Students who have learned how to write five-paragraph essays or book reports or college admissions essays—or diaries or Tumblr posts or song lyrics—may find to their frustration that writing poems, stories, or plays asks something entirely different of them. Students are not only learning new skills but also figuring out which old skills and habits will serve them and which are more likely to impede their progress. This can be a confronting and emotionally challenging experience.

Students often bring intimate material to their writing and explore questions at the heart of who they are and what they care about. But even when they're not writing explicitly vulnerable material, a writer's sense of self is at play in what and how they write. Composition scholar Kevin Roozen explains, "The extent to which we align ourselves with a particular community, for example, can be gauged by the extent to which we are able and willing to use that community's language, make its rhetorical moves, act with its privileged texts, and participate in its writing processes and practices" (Roozen 2015a, 51). Creative writing courses are the first place many students start to ask: Who could I be as a member of a university community? Am I an academic writer? Do I want to be a literary writer? Can I write like *this* and still be me? Writing is not just about producing work and learning skills, but always also about identity and group belonging. If we accept that writing is *not* natural, that students are sorting through an array of past strategies that may or may not serve them in each new writing context, and that writing always involves identity work, how do we approach our teaching?

We create structures and assignments that treat these struggles as necessary and expected rather than aberrant and troubling. Rather than expecting students to absorb the complexities of craft, form, and genre "naturally," we invite them to read, consider, demystify, and discuss. While it's important for students to develop confidence in their abilities to choose what they'd like to write about and how they want to write, assignment sequences that gradually build capacity and increase self-direction offer more writers the tools they need to make meaningful choices.

Cecily Nicholson on teaching writing that engages the world

Creative writing courses include students with varying degrees of experience. How do you approach assignment design with this in mind?

I start with a discussion, like, what is poetry? What's this idea of verse? What is lineation? I introduce foundational concepts not as a test, but just to see where folks are at and start to get on the same page with the language we're using. This is also an opportunity to interrupt some stereotypes or firmly held beliefs about poetry that students bring from other contexts. My initial assignments invite people to step back and think about their senses and how they relate to the world, what language does, what they know, what they maybe would like to know. I start with a completion-based assignment. I read their work very closely and tell them what I think it's saying and doing. I point them to some things: "You might be interested in this" or "You're writing on this topic—how about that?" I see this as starting a conversation. It's me meeting them in a rough draft, not in a finished project.

How do you invite students to bring other disciplines into their creative writing studies?

It's key for students to bring other disciplines, methods, and ways of knowing into their creative studies. Sure, a writer writes, but a writer also needs to live their life and be an interesting and relevant person in the world. The specific practice of being a writer doesn't mean that we step away from all of the things that we're trained in and care about. Some of the most interesting work is being done in interdisciplinary modes and moving through multiple discourses. I think of Wayson Choy's work at the intersection of the sciences, for example. Personally, I do a lot of work in labor history and industry history, work that could be understood as historical research. The key is to find meaningful points of intersection. It's not just a generative thing, it's also a nurturing thing we can do for ourselves, choosing not to shut out other parts or silo them off, but instead exploring the ways they can integrate. I would even take that one step further and invite students to think and write about all the labor and knowledge that goes into being a parent or caregiver or good friend. These are also beautiful things that are worthy of poetry.

Do you assign collaborative/group assignments?

Yes! Often, I create a selection of readings, and I ask students to sign up in groups to engage and contextualize the material. They're marked on their capacity to work together to create a cohesive project and on evidence of having prepared in advance (as demonstrated by presenting in an organized way). I invite each person to think about what they have to contribute: Are they good at presenting? Are they confident with close reading and interpretation? Maybe they have tech skills to offer around making a recorded video in advance or maybe they're good at research. They're invited to divide and delegate tasks as a group based on different skills. It's important to be able to work with our colleagues and peers. In the world of writing, we are not isolated in anything that we do. We want to make publications and book objects and engage in events and conferences, and all of this requires us to communicate, share information, meet deadlines, identify goals as a group, work cohesively, have accountability, and so on.

CECILY NICHOLSON is an Assistant Professor in the UBC School of Creative Writing. She is the author of four books and recipient of the Dorothy Livesay Poetry Prize and the Governor General's Literary Award for poetry.
Image credit: Michaela Devine

Clarifying purpose, expanding possibilities

Just like the back-and-forth process of designing a course, designing an assignment requires repeatedly asking ourselves, "Why am I inviting students to do this? How does this align with the goals of the course and the motivations that led students to sign up for it?" When we push ourselves to clarify the purpose of what we're asking students to do, we're able to be transparent with them. A clear purpose doesn't mean an overdetermined outcome. The purpose of an assignment or activity might be:

- Develop an ability to sit with uncertainty and withhold judgment on the quality of work in progress.
- Put yourself in a position to be surprised and follow a new possibility.
- Test multiple divergent approaches to figure out which resonate and which don't.

Often, the experience in *doing*, in *puzzling it out* is where students find value. By modeling this philosophy, we can help students see that a good assignment is one where they feel sufficiently challenged, build confidence in applying newly learned concepts, and complete work that stretches them (even if the work itself feels messy or incomplete).

Assignments or assignment sequences in our courses might involve any of the following:

- Low-stakes generative exercises or exploratory freewriting (**Chapter 3**)
- Sustained multi-step writing projects (**Chapters 8 and 11**)
- Revision logs, revision plans (**Chapter 8**)
- Critical or analytic responses to reading (**Chapters 5 and 6**)
- Reflective writing on process (**Chapter 8**)
- Presentations or leading discussions (**Chapter 4**)
- Research portfolios (**Chapter 9**)
- Engagement in the work of others (**Chapter 7**)

Over time, we've learned to set aside any assumptions about what students arrive in our courses already know how to do, especially when it comes to practices like "respond effectively to peer writing," "have a generative conversation about a piece of writing," or "deliver a formal presentation." Like writing, these practices are best developed through scaffolded learning.

Scaffolded learning

Students bring widely different knowledges, backgrounds, and experiences to our courses. Cultural production is heterogenous, multiplicitous, and contextually informed. With this in mind, we aim to design scaffolded assignments that support students across degrees of experience and diversities of approach and aesthetic.

A scaffolded assignment or assignment sequence gradually moves from structured practice with high support and guidance to self-directed practice with increasingly lower support and guidance. Some benefits of this approach:

- Students who enter the course *without* much experience find the supports they need to commit to the course.
- Students who enter the course *with* considerable experience can let themselves play and experiment. They can also trust that the course will develop the capacity of peers and cultivate a peer group ready to challenge them.
- Students can build capacity quickly thanks to the lower cognitive load of focusing on one targeted skill or technique at a time.
- Students can experience early success, build confidence, and take pleasure in their work. These positive experiences carry them forward into more challenging assignments.
- Students get ideas from exploring and experimenting. The drafts they produce later in the term are not only more formally accomplished, thanks to their focused work on technique, but are also less clichéd, more idiosyncratic, and more fully their own.
- Students generate a wealth of material, putting them in a position of abundance and possibility as they select work to revise and refine.
- Students can receive coaching and guidance and try again.
- Students can connect with one another and build trust as a group (invaluable when the time comes for self-directed work or group critique).

Designing assignments that build incrementally

To design a scaffolded assignment or assignment sequence, we ask:

1. What's the purpose or goal of the assignment?
2. What skills do students need to complete the assignment successfully?
3. Which of these skills can we trust that students have developed before entering the course?
4. How can we build capacity in each necessary skill week-by-week?
5. How do we help students integrate their new skills and carry them forward as they leave the course?

Approaches like this give students an opportunity to practice discrete skills in low-stress ways and gradually build capacity as the assignment sequence invites them to claim increasing degrees of self-direction and choice. Even when working with advanced students, we tend to begin with multiple short low-stakes assignments that offer a high degree of structure or constraint and then invite students to identify an idea or direction to build on for longer assignments.

Table 2.1 Scaffolding Skill-Building in Asking Good Questions

A Goal for the Course	Students are able to give and receive constructive feedback on work in progress.
Related Assignments	Small group feedback sessions that build to sustained group critique.
Some Skills Needed for Success	• Writers can ask effective questions about their own work. • Writers can respond to questions from peers about their work with detail, depth, and willingness to reconsider their assumptions and choices. • Readers can respond to peer work with detail and insight, pointing to specific passages and craft choices. • Readers can respond to writers' questions about their own work and can make the mental leap to imagine and support the writer's vision. • Readers can ask questions that invite the writer to reflect and imagine new possibilities.
One Specific Skill	Students can ask effective questions about their own work.
Structured Practice	Students engage in small-group workshops to share and discuss new work. For each workshop, students ask peers a question provided by the instructor and keyed to the week's formal focus. Examples: *Point to a moment of specificity in this work that's lingering with you and talk about why. What do you see this specific detail doing for the work?* *What sounds stood out to you in this work? What effect does this use of sound have?*
Introducing a Self-Directed Element	Students continue small-group workshops. They are invited to choose, and if desired, modify one of the questions introduced previously.
Building Capacity for Self-Directed Practice	As they move toward coming up with their own questions, students engage in a "question workshop." They propose possible questions for peers about their work and take time to discuss them. Peers are invited to: (1) Ask questions about the proposed questions, or (2) Propose alternate phrasings of the questions. A live-edited doc or whiteboard works well. After receiving peer insights, students revise their questions if they wish. They also discuss what they've noticed about designing good questions. Example: *Original question: Are the actions concrete and clear enough to be followed without background knowledge?* *Alternate question: How did you interpret the actions in this work? Was this interpretation affected by prior background in the subject matter?* *Alternate question: What do you feel like you can guess about the background or context based on what you read in this work?* *Question about this question: Are you concerned about how readers with different experiences/backgrounds might respond?*

Coaching Self-Directed Practice	In preparation for an in-depth workshop, students prepare a guided memo that asks them to reflect on their goals for the workshop and propose possible questions to ask readers. The instructor offers coaching in an individual meeting.
Fully Self-Directed Practice	Students engage in a formal workshop process centerd around their own prepared questions.
Carrying Skills Forward	Students complete a reflection on their engagement in the workshop process and the work of others. Sample Instruction: *Discuss your growth as a writer in using the workshop process to get useful feedback on and develop your writing. (Among other things, you may wish to consider some of the following: how to ask good questions, decisions around what/how much work to submit per week, how to draw on the diversity of readers and their differences in perspective.)*

John Warner on writing as problem-solving and focusing on what makes us human

You've written about how students need a sense of who they're writing for and why they're writing. How might this show up in creative writing assignments?

We know we want our creative work to be emotionally affecting, and as a reader we definitely know when that's happened, but we may not be able to identify a clear statement of message or purpose. That doesn't mean it isn't present, though. There's a passage at the end of Andre Dubus' story "A Father's Story" in which the narrator, a devout Catholic, makes a choice to help his daughter out of trouble, a choice which he believes will consign him to Hell, but which he must do because he cannot bear the pain of his daughter on Earth. This passage makes me tear up every single time I read it, and I've read it dozens of times. I couldn't really tell you what the message is, but the purpose of the story—and I don't mean to sound hoity about it—is to move us through the unique capacity of storytelling.

I think it's important to get students thinking loftily in terms of those ambitions. The work we produce in class may fall short of those goals—I know mine did and does—but the intent matters because it's the first step toward achieving the goal.

You've described writing as "thinking and making choices inside an experience." How does this understanding of writing shape your approach to assignments?

I think of a writing occasion as a writing-related problem in which we have to work inside a rhetorical situation in order to deliver the goods for the benefit of our audience. Solving that problem is the experience, the challenge, and the challenge is satisfied (or not) by making choices. To that end, I want the assignments to be literally "challenging" in that they are simultaneously familiar—they require us to use our writing practices—and unfamiliar, we have to try to do something we've never done before as part of our practice. Each new poem or story is always both familiar and unfamiliar. We've written a story or poem before, but the specific contours of the new thing are unknown. This makes creative writing a particularly good way to inculcate some of the attitudes and habits-of-mind of the writer's practice around exploration and persistence, two things that I think are endemic to writing.

In your newsletter "The Biblioracle Recommends," you demonstrate how ChatGPT might respond to a creative writing story instructions with something "perfectly okay" for a beginning course. What advice might you give creative writing teachers in light of this?

I think there's a couple of frontline defenses we can adopt to deal with ChatGPT in this context. One is very natural to creative writing, and that's to value process and reflection over product and assessment. The whole point of trying to write a story or poem is to engage in the struggle of writing a story or poem. If we value that struggle over the artifact that can be assessed/graded, students will see that the experience is what's worth doing.

The other big recommendation from my point of view is to value the traits of a piece of writing that are essentially human, to go looking for the signs of humanity in a piece and then talk about those. In creative writing courses, over the years I moved away from talking about craft elements (character, point of view, plot, etc.) first, and instead asked students to be sensitive to where they feel a story's "life" or "energy." It could be a scene or a description or a single sentence, but what we're on the lookout for is the moment where the author seems to be tapped into something vital. It's that vitality, that life that is ultimately the springboard from which a story is going to become what it's going to become. The craft stuff is useful to know and can be a handy way of talking about where technique may help the life shine through, but ultimately, it's that life energy that's the fuel. Without that fuel we have nothing.

Given that ChatGPT cannot think or feel, has no sensory experience of the world and works entirely without intention, it cannot ever infuse a piece of writing with life, something that's apparent in reading the outputs of any large language model. We have to honor the unique things that humans can do.

John Warner has twenty-plus years of experience teaching college writing across institutions and is the author of nine books, including: *Why They Can't Write: Killing the Five-Paragraph Essay and Other Necessities*, *The Writer's Practice*, and *More Than Words: How to Think About Writing in the Age of AI*.

Balancing fixed and flexible parameters

Assignments have fixed and flexible parameters. In a beginning screenwriting course, the fixed parameters might be "a scene with three characters involved in a conflict presented using screenwriting formatting" and the flexible parameters might be who the characters are, the source of the conflict, the time and place of the setting. In an advanced poetry course, the fixed parameters might be "an 8–12 page chapbook of poems that enrich and complicate one another," and the flexible parameters might be the content and formal approach of the poems. Our challenges as instructors are:

1. Find the right balance between fixed and flexible parameters for the students we're teaching.
2. Communicate clearly what's fixed and what's flexible for each thing we ask students to do.
3. Help students claim agency and creativity within each assignment.

Instructors sometimes refrain from giving explicit assignments ("Just write whatever you want!") or give very minimal/flexible assignments ("A story due in week five") because they want to support students' creativity or feel reluctant to constrain students based on their own aesthetic inclinations. Especially when students are new to a genre or approach, however, this openness can feel daunting and overwhelming. As students rightly suspect, no instructions doesn't mean no expectations. An instructor who tells students to "write a story" undoubtedly has expectations of what a good story does or does not include, and, especially if they will be assigning a grade, would do better to acknowledge these expectations explicitly.

Perhaps most importantly, implied expectations in assignments land differently with students depending on cultural and linguistic background, neurodivergence, or previous experience with writing instruction. Priya Parker writes, "If implicit etiquette serves closed circles that assume commonality, explicit rules serve open circles that assume difference. The explicitness levels the playing field for outsiders" (121). If creative writing courses hope to serve a diverse group of students, they had better "assume difference" and make their rules explicit. Although an open-ended assignment might be presented with the hope of inspiring wild creativity and experimentation, it risks having the opposite effect: increased homogeneity as students try to figure out the unspoken etiquette of the situation, play it safe, and give the instructor (and their peers) what they *think* they want.

Of course, "the rules" (or fixed parameters) of an assignment, activity, or group engagement can be established in conversation with students if we take the time necessary to support this conversation. Opting for clear fixed parameters over vague assumed etiquette does *not* imply a top-down approach. When we speak openly with students about fixed and flexible parameters and what it means to negotiate between them, we also model a relationship to genre with crucial craft implications. Rather than assuming an implicit shared understanding of what constitutes a powerful poem, compelling essay, or effective screenplay, these conversations establish expectations while acknowledging that, for example, success for an experimental short film might look quite different from success for a TV comedy pilot episode.

In our conversation, John Warner discussed writing as problem solving and emphasized that "solving that problem is the experience of the challenge, and the challenge is satisfied by making choices." Similarly, in *Engaging Ideas,* John C. Bean and Dan Melzer discuss the value of engaging students in the meaningful problem-based work expert practitioners grapple with. When we require students to include a certain element (whether in terms of form or content) or to avoid a certain element (that might be a first or obvious choice), we invite them to step into this space of problems and choices. For example, an instructor might give this instruction: Write a 1000-word story that is told in third-person omniscient point of view (POV), includes at least two narrative turns and ends on an image. Rather than the pressure to "have a good idea," students experience the invitation to solve a flexible and appealing problem.

Each assignment comes with certain expectations (whether tacit or explicit) and some degree of openness where students can exercise choice. A good assignment sheet makes both clear for students and allows them to direct energy into making work (not reading our minds).

Some students may resist structure and need help understanding how it can support their practice. Others may fear claiming agency and need encouragement to explore the flexible parameters of an assignment. Still others might not initially identify the spaces for choice within constraints and may benefit from seeing examples of creativity driven by structures that initially appear restricting. To support each of these students, we must articulate the motivations and purposes behind our assignments.

An assignment sheet might include any of the following:

- Epigraphs/quotes/images.
- An introduction to the assignment (purpose, goals, how the assignment fits into the larger structure of the course).
- Guidelines/parameters that make clear what is fixed and what is flexible (length, genre conventions).
- Instructions for any process steps along the way (drafts, supporting work such as an introduction or artist's statement).
- Due dates/timeline for any process components.
- Assessment criteria (this could be a formal rubric or a description of how the work will be assessed. See **Chapter 10**).

Due dates and lateness policies

Exactly how fixed or flexible a due date is depends on the course context and type of assignment. A large class where TA grading hours are precisely mapped out has less wiggle room for late assignments than a smaller course. The due date for a portfolio of revised work at the end of the term might be more flexible than the due date for a workshop draft in a tightly scheduled sequence of workshops. In either case, students deserve fair, clear policies that allow them to make informed decisions.

We keep assignment due dates and times on the same days (i.e., Tuesday by midnight) as part of the predictable rhythm in the course. We avoid punitive language around late or missed assignments. Instead, we build in some slack with assignment groups that allow students to drop a missed (or lowest) assignment and invite students to reach out in advance if they encounter challenges that prevent them from completing an assignment on time.

For a large class, likely to have many late or missing assignments, we're honest with students about where we prefer to put our time (commenting on their writing, discussing their ideas during office hours) and where we'd rather not (answering endless due date emails and making constant adjustments in the LMS).

Here's a sample policy for a major assignment in a class of 200 students:

- The official deadline for this assignment is 5 pm on October 16th, with a grace period until 11:59 pm to accommodate uploading difficulties, internet failure, and so on.
- If you experience an emergency (such as an illness, injury, or family crisis), you may submit your work up to one week late without emailing to request an extension and without penalty. Because our TAs allocate certain hours for reading and responding to your writing, assignments submitted after 11:59 pm on 10/16 will be marked using the rubric but will not receive written comments. Late assignments will not be eligible for a regrade request.
- If you're dealing with a situation that affects your performance across multiple courses or will delay assignment completion by more than one week, you may instead choose to work with Advising. In this case, we will work with you and the Advising office to make arrangements for late or missing work.
- After graded assignments are returned, students with partial or missing work will have the option to submit or resubmit the assignment until the last week of term for a maximum possible grade of 60%.

Reflection and metacognition: making learning portable and transferable

We tend to think of our courses in terms of what students are producing: screenplays, stories, picture book text, songs, essays, and so on. But to truly serve our students, we need to think about what they're *learning* as well as what they're making. Composition scholar Howard Tinberg explains, "the objective is not just to have our students produce effective writing … We also want our students to demonstrate consciousness of process that will enable them to reproduce success" (Tinberg 2015, 75). We're not just trying to occasion better writing within the narrow context of the course at hand, but rather to support the ongoing growth and development of *writers*. But how do students acquire consciousness of process? How do they develop skills and awareness they can carry on with them?

For these things to happen, students must learn to reflect. They must become aware of the choices they've made at every level of the composition process—from writing late at night to adopting a three-act story structure to using a semicolon rather than a period—and come to see these choices as mutable rather than inevitable. They need to think about what worked and what didn't and speculate on what they might try differently next time. Without reflection, students may experience growth in their writing performance but find themselves unable to replicate or extend it.

To fully grasp the value of reflection, consider creative writing courses through the frame of experiential learning theory. Under David Kolb's model, for example, students move cyclically through **concrete experience, reflective observation, abstract conceptualization**, and **active experimentation** (Kolb 2014, 51). What might this theory look like applied to a specific creative writing context?

1 Students in a creative non-fiction course are asked to recall a memorable moment and describe it first in present tense and then in past time. This activity offers a **concrete experience** of writing.
2 To shift into **reflective observation**, the instructor invites students to discuss what they noticed about this writing experience: Which came more easily or felt more "natural," past tense or present tense? Students might also swap writing samples and reflect on what they noticed in the work of a peer.
3 To move into **abstract conceptualization**, the instructor invites the class to generate a collective list of principles of tense choice in personal essay writing. This list differentiates between experiences of writing and experiences of reading and identifies points of convergence and divergence within the group. Students draw on insights from past reading and writing, turning to shared course texts to consider the work of tense choice and recalling work in fiction or poetry courses.
4 Finally, students test these concepts through **active experimentation** in an assignment that asks them to make an informed choice about tense based on their goals for a personal essay.

Ultimately, this cycle becomes a spiral that writers both repeat and extend, returning to the same questions and challenges with greater insight and nuance.

Reflection is not a decorative frill or a busywork documentation of effort in a creative writing course; it's an essential locus for learning. Yet here, as elsewhere, we must consider when and how we're asking students to reflect and what framework we offer. We recall students who've said that reflecting on their highly intuitive writing process feels like being asked to analyze their gear shifting while biking up a hill: they'd rather just use whatever energy they have to pedal to the top. Others worry that the self-consciousness of reflection will detract from the magic and mystery of writing or see reflection as a performance for the instructor.

While it may be naive to imagine reflection as purely intrinsically motivated and self-driven, we can take steps to mitigate the reflection-as-performance that occurs when students feel unable to bring their genuine questions and struggles to the page or conversation. We might offer a model, design an assignment as "completion-based," or include instructions like "it's fine to use casual language, change your mind part-way through, or express frustration or uncertainty." As we design assignments, we can ask ourselves:

- How do students move between (1) doing and (2) reflecting on what they've done and why?
- Do our reflection instructions honor the intuition and mystery at the heart of writing and the diversity of student writing processes?
- When and how do students get the chance to apply and test what they're learned in one assignment or activity in a subsequent assignment?
- Do the assignment design and grading approach encourage students to grapple with real questions and struggles?

A.E. Osworth on GenAI, ethics, and assignment design

How have you worked with GenAI as a writer?

While GenAI like GPT is really bad at making art by itself, when you use it as a tool rather than thinking of it as an intelligence or as a threat to artists, it can be useful in a few ways: to induce failure, to reveal bias, to carve out space for something unspeakable. In my novel *Awakened,* the villain is an artificial intelligence. Originally, I was writing the villain myself, but it kept sounding too much like a person because I'm a person. So, you might use this kind of tool to induce a failure in language beyond your capacity. I'd also point to Lillian-Yvonne Bertram's work with revealing bias in their chapbook *A Black Story May Contain Sensitive Content* and other projects. Artificial intelligence (AI) programs are good at figuring out patterns and exposing the biases of a large population, processing more data than we could ever read ourselves, and Bertram digs into that. For carving out space for the unsayable, I'd point to Vauhini Vara's "Ghosts," published in *The Believer.* Vara begins by telling the AI one sentence about a topic that she could never write about: her sister's death. The AI makes up some highly generic crap. She steps in to correct that narrative. It iterates over and over and over again, with Vara writing more and more of the story. By the end, the AI only writes two sentences and the rest is hers. It's a highly assignable structure I've explored with students.

What about as a teacher? Can you talk about a specific course or assignment, what your goals were, and what you noticed?

When I teach "Introduction to New Media," I devote the final third of the course to artificial intelligence. Before this unit, we survey other kinds of new and digitized media. We start with assignments that are almost impossible to fake with AI because they have significant process elements. For instance, they do a cut up comic with photos they take using a film camera. In the AI unit, we look at large language models, Botnik keyboard, image generation, and generative poetry in a historical context. I ask them to attempt to copy their own cut-up comic using image-generating AI, and that lets them know what it's good for and what it's not. Throughout the unit, we dig into ethical questions, which are really sticky. Both image generation and language models are trained on a large corpus, and the people included in that corpus don't have any say as to whether their work gets pulled in or not. We keep asking: How do I personally believe this should be used? By the end of the term, many come down harder than I do on AI usage and art making because they see what's gained and what's lost.

What are the biggest misconceptions teachers seem to have about GenAI?

That it's entirely useless to them. But you can design assignments that involve GenAI in interesting ways. I might say, "Your assignment is to summarize today's discussion and ask GPT to come up with something that we missed." The point is that they have to summarize the day's discussion, but it feels transgressive to get information from GPT. GPT might be wrong. And then that gives us some room for conversation. I might ask them to find a source that confirms what GPT told them. And then we're talking about media literacy, as well. So that's a great way to use GPT in a manner that's not antagonistic.

There's also a misconception that this is a laziness thing, but I don't think that's true. Students turn to GPT for two main reasons. One is that they're overworked and stressed out, and they see it as a solution to get through less-meaningful parts of their degree. The other is that speakers of English as an additional language are often disadvantaged by assessments that prioritize correctness. So they turn to GPT because it's good at grammar. Students face active discrimination in classroom spaces for the way they speak and write. And discrimination in marks matters. So I'd ask: how can we address those underlying reasons?

What about student misconceptions?

Oh, students think it's better writing. But it's just grammatical writing. I see this especially with students who speak English as an additional language. I'm like, "No, no, no, your writing is charming as hell. It is imaginative. It is specific." You know, you can tell GPT, "Write about a food that you grew up eating." But GPT can't eat. It can't taste. It doesn't actually know anything. So, it'll pull statistically from a large corpus of writing, most of which is white and Western. Say you're not white and Western and the food that you grew up eating is from India. You'll likely get some exoticized description, some colonial bullshit. That's not better writing: it's less specific, it doesn't come from a cultural point of view, and it doesn't make any thematic argument. That's worse writing.

Do all creative writing teachers need to change how they teach in response to AI? What would you say to teachers who would prefer to ignore it entirely?

Well, you can ignore this stuff entirely, and people will still use it in your classroom. Nothing is going to stop it. It's like saying, I would prefer that computers didn't exist. These programs are free or cheap to use, and some students will turn to them. That said, I don't think it's your responsibility to try to catch them. I don't care to be a cop. That's not how I want to spend my life. If you don't want students to use AI in your course, have a clear policy and say why. I also assign process-based work that's harder to do using AI. Like, sure, you can try to have AI generate twenty-four film-looking photos for me. But at that point, you might as well just go out and take the photos. What process documentation can you ask students to show? For a fiction course, I might assign

Venn diagrams based on the characters they're coming up with that map the differences between them. At the end of the day, I find it so much more meaningful to ask students to actually grapple with the ethical questions of art and AI. Often, they wind up saying, "I don't want to use this in these particular ways because I disagree with it."

A.E. OSWORTH is a transgender novelist. They are a lecturer in the UBC School of Creative Writing where they teach fiction and new media. Their debut *We Are Watching Eliza Bright* was a finalist for the Oregon Book Award. Their novel *Awakened* (2025) is about a coven of trans witches fighting artificial intelligence with magic.

Image credit: A.J. Lowik

Assignment design and GenAI

As we're revising this chapter (Spring 2025), ChatGPT is making waves across teaching conversations. Although we're not sure what specific platforms or AI capabilities the future may hold, we expect AI to be part of the teaching landscape from now on. In keeping with James M. Lang's thoughts on the benefits of "slow-walking" rather than rushing into how to work with AI in the classroom (Lang 2024), we offer a few recommendations for teaching creative writing in the age of AI (based on conversations with A.E. Osworth, John Warner, and other thoughtful people).

1 **Emphasize process and purpose.** Craft assignments that foreground the act of making and invite students to reflect on why we make art. Use drafts, conferences, process notes, artist's statements, and other strategies to demonstrate your commitment to process.
2 **Foreground agency and intention.** Remind students that they have power as writers and why this power matters. Share published writing with high stakes. For each assignment, emphasize the choices available to students.
3 **Discuss positionality, perspective, specificity.** Remind students that the art they make comes from their unique perspective and the lifeworld they know intimately, unlike that of anyone else. Contrast their embodied perspective and its sensory and specific knowledge with the aggregative logic of AI. Create assignments that name and value a specific perspective.
4 **Demonstrate and talk directly about what AI can and can't do.** Consider running an assignment instruction through an AI generator and taking time to discuss the results with students. What's present and what's absent? Is this something they'd want to read for pleasure? What does it mean to experience and interpret writing generated without intention at the level of image, diction, and characterization?

5 **Contextualize AI within a broader ethical context.** Invite students to consider what GenAI is trained on: databases that include the work of many uncompensated working writers and artists. GenAI reiterates bias and is prone to discriminatory, non-inclusive language. Students sometimes think of computing as existing outside of material reality. Share details with them about the data centers needed to power AI and the vast amounts of water required to cool the servers they house.

6 **Be on the watch for reactive pedagogy.** In trying to avoid AI in the classroom, instructors sometimes respond reactively and introduce assignments (like timed handwritten exams) or policies (like intense surveillance and suspicious scrutiny) that don't truly align with their values. You may decide it's more important to foster an atmosphere of trust than to catch every policy violation.

7 **Expect nuance and diversity in student perspectives.** While some student writers might be tempted to use AI out of anxiety about their skills or pressure to rush through school work, others (or perhaps even the same students) might be anxious about AI and what it means for their futures as people who want to write.

The instructor's voice in assignment design

An instructor's voice shows up in the syllabus (**Chapter 1**), in class presentations and discussions, in assignment design, and in assignment feedback. These are all acts of communication. In each instance, we're making decisions about length (amount of detail to include in an assignment sheet or a written response), timing (when to distribute an assignment sheet or instruction), and tone. All of these decisions need to be made with the specific course and its particular students in mind. We need to ask questions like:

- Will a single long detailed assignment sheet give students a chance to plan ahead and pace themselves or will it leave them feeling overwhelmed?
- Which would be more effective: written feedback on a draft or a brief in-person meeting?
- What associations might students have with the term "apprenticeship" or the word "lab"?

As writers, we consider each act of naming carefully. What are the connotations of "revised draft" as compared to "final draft"? Instead of "short writing #1," why not try experiment, exploration, or sketch? These may seem like small interventions, but they can make a big difference.

Beyond specific word choice decisions for activities and assignments, we consider tone more broadly. We've seen assignment sheets that include prohibitions and warnings: "If you do X, you'll be marked down," or "Don't try to get away with Y." Tone matters. It is possible to convey clear expectations without sounding punitive and suspicious. An assignment should feel like an invitation from someone who wants to support your learning, not a contract from someone who thinks you're trying to cheat them.

It can be hard to gauge tone on our own, so we might text a passage to a friend or share a draft assignment sheet with a colleague and ask: "Does this sound supportive or condescending?" "Is the workflow clear?" "How would you feel if you were given these instructions?"

Calibrating feedback

As we design assignments, we need to remember what happens when they're finished: students turn them in and we respond to them.

Whether teaching a graduate workshop for eight or a large-enrollment introductory course of 250+ with TA support, we need to think about when, how, and in what form we (and perhaps our TAs) will respond to student work. While we take up these matters in **Chapter 8** and **Chapter 10**, for a course that supports students and is sustainable for the instructor, plans for process and feedback must be considered from the start. As we design assignments, we need to ask:

- Is this part of a larger draft or workshop process?
- If there's a workshop, will I as the instructor participate or not?
- How will I respond to students (at the end and/or along the way)?
- What is the relationship between grading (if appropriate) and responding?

Over years of responding to student writing from rough sketches to publication-ready polished thesis through conferences, marginal comments, rubrics, and letters, we think hard about what feedback best serves a student each time we design an assignment. Here are four guiding principles we've landed on:

One: Be clear on the goal of the feedback

Different types of feedback are appropriate for different stages of a project. **Formative** feedback considers the piece as a work in progress and responds to its potential with questions and ideas, whereas **summative** feedback assesses the extent to which a piece has achieved its goals. Both can be useful, but only if we're clear on which we're offering and why. In large courses, feedback sometimes needs to make clear why students received their grade and offer insights they might apply to future assignments. In smaller courses, we often decide that our energy is best spent on formative feedback, unaccompanied by a grade, early enough in the process for a student to build on that feedback in their revisions. In our conversation, Cecily Nicholson spoke to the value of offering students "an observation of their arc of learning," connecting their final work to where they started: "It's so exciting to be able to say 'In this moment you were working through something, and now we can see that you figured out point of view. You've streamlined your address and your pronouns. There's a coherence to the work.'"

Two: Consider how much feedback students can actually use

How much feedback a student can integrate depends on the level, the structure of the course, and the individual student. Often, students are better served by two clear examples of things that are working well and one question for further reflection than by a list of twenty suggestions. When possible, we like to give each student a chance to set the tone for the feedback they receive. This might look like:

1 Giving the bulk of our feedback as part of a Critical Response Process workshop driven by the student's questions.
2 Offering an optional debrief conversation for students who opt-in by completing a final reflection.
3 Keying final project comments to students' introductory statements, affirming the progress and accomplishments of students who talk about the project as complete and reserving in-depth responses for those who indicate an interest in continuing to develop the material.

Tone also makes a crucial difference in how much students are able to take in. As Cecily Nicholson put it in our conversation:

> I'll say "the narrator in the poem does Y" or "the poem is doing X." I'm trying to remove the accusatory language that makes us feel like we're on trial. After I write feedback, I'll go over it again and try to read it with sensitivity, paying attention to tone. I also invite students to meet and talk if they have questions. I want to convey that I'm invested in what I've offered, that I'm excited to see the work evolve.

Three: Do the math when it comes to time

Whether we're planning to schedule individual conferences on an early draft, participate in multiple simultaneous small-group asynchronous workshops, or offer rubric feedback and a substantive final comment on completed work, we pause and run the numbers. Mapping out our response plans in a way that acknowledges the reality of our schedules (committee meetings, project deadlines, daycare pick-ups, conference travel, etc.) gives us the best chance to offer generous focused attention.

Four: Make feedback part of an ongoing conversation

As previous mentions of "final reflections" and "writer's introductions" suggest, we prefer not to give feedback in a vacuum. Our responses are most useful as part of an ongoing conversation in which students maintain ownership of their work.

Assignment design inventory

Use the following questions to reflect on your assignments and revise them to be more intentional, inclusive, and inviting for students (and more sustainable for you).

1 Preparation and Scaffolding

- What do you hope students will get out of completing this assignment?
- Where does this assignment fall in your course and how does it build on or lead to other work students are doing?
- What do students need to **know** (knowledge) and need to **know how to do** (skills) to complete this assignment successfully?
- How will you help students build capacity for this assignment (for example, through smaller assignments that introduce each skill individually, in-class activities, readings)?

2 Genre and Audience Specifics

- What about this assignment is specific to the genre or genres you're teaching?
- What do you expect to see in **all** student work (fixed parameters)? What variety might you see **across** student work (flexible parameters)?
- How might you adjust the assignment by providing additional support for a less experienced student or opportunities for further exploration for a more advanced student?
- What do you anticipate being most challenging for students about this assignment?

3 Response and Assessment

- How will you respond to, and if appropriate, grade this assignment? (A letter, marginal comments, conference, rubric with boxes, rubric with comments, checklist?)
- Will you respond to any process components or only the final product? How are you approaching formative and/or summative feedback?
- How long do you anticipate it will take you to respond to (and possibly grade) this assignment?

Try on a student perspective

Finally, as with all other decisions in course design, we pause to place ourselves in the role of student—how would I approach this assignment myself? When John wrote support manuals as a technical writer for a software company, he would practice following the instructions repeatedly to see what problems might arise. This helped him write clearer instructions by identifying what was essential and what was not. Testing out our own assignments (or having a colleague test them) before students attempt them can confirm that what we're inviting them to do is clear, engaging, and aligned with the purpose of the course.

3

Structured Experiments and Generative Writing

Necessary inefficiencies

Students, especially in introductory courses, may approach writing with an expectation that it follows a straightforward linear process: have an idea, write it down, polish it, publish! But this is not how things work for most writers and artists.

Writers produce creative work in a variety of ways, but almost universally, we make a lot more than we end up using. Students may not realize that the published work they see from any writer is the tip of the iceberg. Supporting that visible published work is an immense amount of drafting, research, and revision that remains invisible to readers. Another common element is a process that's more circular and iterative than linear.

Even experienced writers struggle when attempting a new genre or writing for a different audience. And after years of practice, we still strain to shift from an efficiency-driven mindset of tasks and to-do lists to a mindset of creation, which involves exploration and play, but also risk and uncertainty. *What if nothing comes? What if it's bad? What if it's not worth it?*

If such questions continue to plague experienced writers, they're surely pressing for students, who juggle multiple courses, competing assignment deadlines, work and care commitments, and constant demands on their attention. How, then, do writing instructors design assignments and adopt classroom practices that help students accept—even enjoy—the inherent inefficiency of art-making?

To help students get as close as possible to experiencing the rich, messy, recursive process of an experienced writer, we support them in generating an abundance of material in a spirit of experimentation, curiosity, and play. The success of such an endeavor depends on:

1 How we structure this experimentation.
2 How we talk about it.
3 How we grade or assess it.

We use writing experiments to help students grapple with material, solve problems, and build toward larger self-directed projects. We also discuss intentional constraint-based work as integral to the work of expert writers. And we offer students low-risk completion-based grades for this work.

Why assign writing experiments?

Having broken down major assignments into discrete skills, instructors may find that these skills can be introduced effectively through low-stakes, generative exercises. Through concrete experimentation, students come to see how ideas and insights emerge from their engagement with material, rather than from waiting around for inspiration to tap them on the shoulder. Structured low-stakes writing experiments invite students to:

1 Practice specific targeted skills in a focused way.
2 Generate an abundance of "writing material" as part of an iterative process.
3 Experience how the act of writing itself leads to new ideas and possibilities.
4 Develop their own aesthetic sensibilities through active trial and reflection.

Over the years, we've spoken with instructors who dismiss prompt-based work as meaningless busywork or avoid it for fear of constraining students' freedom of expression. At their worst, prompts can be a sort of paint-by-numbers, teaching students to imitate gestures they don't comprehend or claim. Some see a place for prompt-based writing in introductory courses but view such structures as no longer helpful for advanced students. We've also met instructors who collect and assign writing prompts in a way that feels almost random: anything to get students writing.

We get where instructors on all sides are coming from. It is crucial to get students writing. It's also true that prompts can feel pointless, can be overly prescriptive, can be used to nudge students into a dominant mode and away from their own sensibilities and interests. Still, we see a place for thoughtfully designed and carefully integrated writing experiments in classrooms of any size or level. Here are a few common pitfalls to watch out for.

- **Mixed message: risk versus grade**. When we tell students that the purpose of a writing experiment is exploration and risk while assigning a letter or number grade to their work, we're putting students in a confusing rhetorical position. Do we really want them to experiment and try something new and uncertain (which might be a mess)? Or do we just want them to show us that they can perform? We recommend assessing structured experiments using a completion grade with an expectation that work is turned in on time, demonstrates understanding of the instructions, and engages in good faith with the invitation of the exercise. Along with the completion mark, we might offer light, encouraging feedback and questions.
- **Mixed message: importance versus worth.** Similarly, when we tell students that writing experiments are valuable and important, but all fifteen of them are worth a mere 5% of the total grade, we're giving another mixed message. If we believe this work is important, our assessment breakdown should reflect that importance.

- **Impression of busywork.** Equally off-putting is any perceived busywork, which students can detect from a long way off. Effective experiments are carefully chosen, thoroughly integrated into the structure of the course, and clearly introduced.

When these pitfalls are avoided, we've seen how structured low-stakes writing can foster an atmosphere of serious play that supports students to take creative risks and feel their way into their material, to learn through doing. By designing this work to be assessed using a completion grade, we've seen students get weird, get silly, get real, and take stylistic risks as they work without the pressure or judgment that a letter grade often asserts. We've seen them develop confidence in themselves and in their process.

Beyond the benefits for individual students, we've also witnessed the power of shared experiments for building community. When a room full of students write together—whether in a small workshop or a large lecture class—they participate in a common experience that takes away some of the fear and isolation that they might feel when they write alone. Ten minutes of active writing can spur rich classroom discussion that sparks a spirit of shared endeavor throughout the entire semester.

Discovering generative exercises

Writing experiments can take many forms, depending on the size, modality, genre, and level of the course. Let's consider a few possibilities.

The freewriting paradox

The technique central to many generative exercises and constraint-based experiments is, simply, freewriting: we present students with a question or context (or ask them to identify their own) and ask them to write for five, ten, or twenty minutes without stopping, deleting, or erasing. This approach draws on Peter Elbow, who tells writers, "Don't stop for anything. Go quickly without rushing. Never stop to look back, to cross something out, to wonder how to spell something, to wonder what word or thought to use, or to think about what you are doing" (1973, 3). For many, resisting inhibitions—learning to tune out the impulse to filter and edit—is the ultimate constraint.

In *Writing Without Teachers* (1973), Elbow talks about how writers pause to edit out awkwardness, wordiness, and errors and how pausing to correct may not serve our writing. In contrast, he invites us to remember times we have spoken articulately: "Seldom was it because you first got the beginning right. Usually it was a matter of a halting or even a garbled beginning, but you kept going and your speech finally became coherent and even powerful" (6). We get to "coherent and powerful" speech not by stopping and starting over but by continuing through the stumbling until our subject comes together and gains momentum. Likewise, students are more likely to write their way to what they mean by allowing themselves to keep going than by deleting and restarting over and over again. As Elbow notes, it's "not just 'mistakes' or 'bad writing' we edit as we write. We also edit unacceptable thoughts and feelings" (5). For writers who have experienced systemic oppression or who are writing about vulnerable or charged subjects, the risk of premature self-censorship is especially salient. By engaging in freewriting—uncollected and unread by others—as a starting point or building block, students can discover the power of working with their own unfiltered, yet externalized thoughts.

Writing together, writing alone

Writing in class

We might start each class with a short timed writing experiment (5–8 minutes). This structured exercise helps students:

1. Generate material for an upcoming assignment.
2. Apply a specific craft concept that was just taught.
3. Make the transition to the classroom, helping them relax into a low-stakes moment of creative play.

We let the students know ahead of time that they don't need to submit the work—or that this is a jump start for something they may choose to extend and turn in later—and that they should experiment. The richest part of in-class writing exercises can be the discussion afterward. Students make and share profound insights and discover a new sense of possibility for their work.

In-class writing can also invite students to think through concepts, venture opinions, and make connections. Readings, lectures, and craft essays introduce complex ideas that students might not give themselves time to reflect on. Confused or overwhelmed, they might not know what steps to take to forge connections that will allow them to remember and apply these ideas in their own writing. Small reflective exercises during class allow students to generate questions for further discussion or trace points of contact between course material and their own experiences and interests.

Tariq Hussain on generative experiments for lyric songwriting

What factors do you keep in mind when creating generative exercises in songwriting?

The idea is to have students develop a creative practice. When one is regularly writing, ideas start to flow more quickly and easily. I encourage students to complete the exercises quickly and keep that inner editor out of the room. I tell them, "Set yourself a timer and tell yourself: I will work on this for ten or twenty minutes, not more." I also indicate that they don't have to submit complete songs. A verse will do. Keeping each exercise manageable is important since they're doing so many of them.

As many of the lyric writing exercises involve making demo recordings, I remind students that the goal of making demos is not flawless singing or virtuosic guitar playing. In fact, imperfection is often better—we just want to hear your ideas! I also underscore that all work completed in my class is work in progress, drafts. There's a tendency for students to think of things they turn in as the "final versions." No, it's just a version, I suggest, and who knows how you might develop these after the class is over?

You do an exercise where students build a song from scratch in small groups and then perform it in front of the class. How do you help students feel onboard with going through a group process and sharing their work?

In my big intro course, students craft a rap song together and perform it. Rapping is much closer to speaking, so students are more comfortable sharing with the group. And since they don't have to think about melody and singing when rapping, it's also more reasonable to expect them to come up with something in 5 to 7 minutes. It also doesn't hurt that rap is a well-loved style for many students in this age group. Before I ask them to do the exercise, I show them a clip of Canadian rapper Shad doing some freestyling, that is, making up verses on the spot while a beat is playing (he's very good at it!). Seeing an example of freestyling by a professional is super helpful. Not only does it clarify for students what they're being asked to do, it also shows that the task is doable: hey, Shad pulled it off, so can we!

From day one, I reiterate the value of being vulnerable and trying stuff out, exploring, experimenting. I also continually remind students of the importance of supporting each other as a group. "Everyone in the room is a writer," I say. "Everyone is nervous, vulnerable, and if you're willing to share—and there's no pressure to do so—you can be sure that we're all going to support you."

TARIQ HUSSAIN teaches lyric forms in the UBC School of Creative Writing. He is a Juno-nominated songwriter and recording artist known for his solo work and his work with the band Brasstronaut.

Image credit: Brendan Meadows

Writing at home (or in the library, the coffee shop, and on the bus)

When students write in class, it's clear that they only have ten minutes and can't produce something brilliant and polished. For at-home writing experiments to be useful, students may need a reminder that the purpose is exploration, not perfection. We might tell them to set a timer for twenty minutes or give a modest maximum word count. We can also "prime" at-home experiments with a quick jump-start in class. If a writing experiment involves a sustained metaphor, for example, students might take three minutes in class to jot down a list of possible metaphorical connections. This way, when they open up their notebooks to complete the experiment, they're not starting from a daunting blank page.

It's also crucial to close the loop. Writing completed between classes needs to be brought back into the shared space of the class. As with in-class writing, a reflective debrief works well. Students might spend a few minutes jotting down notes in response to a question like "What surprised you in your writing for today?" or "Which of the two options did you choose and why?" and then discuss their responses in pairs or small groups. An asynchronous course might likewise dedicate a discussion forum to debriefing writing experiences.

In the right context, Bronwen has also seen great results from inviting students to share structured experiments by reading them out loud to the group. Sharing new exploratory work in this way requires some trust, but it can also build trust. When students read new work out loud, they test out embodying that work. And they feel the work received. Even if no one says a word, the writer hears the little hums and sighs, ripples of laughter, and subtle intakes of breath that speak eloquently. Equally valuable, when each writer shares writing from a common structure, students realize how different they are. Each person may have written what felt like "the obvious response," but they're never the same. Our own perceptions can start to seem obvious or banal to us. When we see our responses in community with others, we see them more truly.

Students have written copies of new experiments to follow along on the page as they listen. At the end of a reading/listening session, they write about their experience reading and writing, as well as what they've noticed about the work generated within the framework of this specific experiment. As weeks go by, students gain intimacy with one another's interests and aesthetic sensibilities. They also begin to see their own choices more clearly as *choices* among a plurality of possibilities, and, often, to experiment with a broader range of techniques and gestures.

Of course, there's also a risk to sharing early work. Some students may become self-conscious or feel a need to perform for the group, flattening their idiosyncrasies or tidying up risky work before it has a chance to reach its full potential. In our conversation about teaching songwriting, Tariq Hussain said:

> I encourage students to fight that tendency towards doing something purely for likes, to remember that the purpose isn't just to impress everyone. Because when we do this, we stop taking chances, we stop experimenting. We become addicted to the rush of applause and we start to edit our words and curb our spontaneity. But it's when we do the opposite, when we aren't afraid to show our quirks and unique qualities through our work that we grow into ourselves as writers.

In cases where one student feels like an outlier—in terms of identity or aesthetics—the pressure to conform may be particularly salient. In this, as in many things, effective teachers are guided by close attention to the specific students in the room.

Here are a few considerations to support success when inviting students to share work in progress with peers:

- **Have clear community agreements and content policies in place (Chapter 4).** This way, you'll have a shared understanding of the care necessary to bring vulnerable or charged work into the classroom space, and students will know what options are available to them if reading or listening prompts a strong response.
- **Give students multiple options of what to share and how to share it.** When students are able to choose one of several recent exercises, they can manage their exposure and vulnerability with new work. They might also have the option to share an excerpt (even a single sentence), share a recording rather than reading on the spot, or invite a classmate to vocalize in their place.
- **Review work before students share it in class.** If students submit work the night before, for example, you can complete a quick review and reach out to students if you have concerns.

Ways to experiment, invitations to play

As we discuss in **Chapter 2**, an assignment that offers an intriguing problem can help students shift from the panic of the blank page to the inviting space of creative problem-solving. While constraints may be most familiar in poetry—where students compose sonnets or experiment with a specific type of line break or metaphor—they can be equally effective in other genres. Constraints oblige students to make choices beyond the default and cultivate skills that might otherwise go undeveloped. Inventive instructors have found myriad ways to offer students an "intriguing problem" for their writing. The "problem" might be formal, intellectual, emotional, physical, or some combination of these. Table 3.1 lays out elastic and overlapping approaches we hope spark exploration.

Table 3.1 Approaches for Designing Constraints

Approach	What Students Do
Rhetorical situations	*Write to a specific audience or within the frame of a particular context.*
Thought experiments	*Create work that speculates or explores a counterfactual.*
Macro structures	*Explore narrative turns, move between exposition and scene, or shift between observation and reflection.*
Micro structures	*Explore at the level of the phoneme, word, line, or sentence.*
Somatic engagements	*Engage in observation walks or movement-based work, focusing on sensation.*
Material engagements	*Work with paint, fabric, clay, mud, leaves, spices, or other physical materials to engage the senses and return to writing from a different angle.*

Approach	What Students Do
Translations across language or medium	*Play with homophonic translation, deviant translation, or translating a concept or formal gesture across genre or medium.*
Textual engagements	*Work with source material, such as erasures, direct imitations, writing into, quoting.*
Process/protocol	*Work through steps for generating and then manipulating and transforming material.*
Tools/technologies	*Write by hand, use an anagram generator, or experiment with any tool that foregrounds writing as technology.*
Tropes	*Work with (and subvert) tropes drawn from fairy tales, myths, or genre expectations.*
Collaborative exercises	*Write together, design instructions for one another, pass writing back and forth.*
Supporting work	*Plot, outline, map, interview a character—all writing that supports a draft but isn't the draft.*

Sample Assignment

Let's get specific: a few generative exercises

Books like Lynda Barry's *What It Is,* Bret Anthony Johnston's *Naming the World: And Other Exercises for the Creative Writer*, and Anne Bernays and Pamela Painter's *What If?* and sites like Sheryda Warrener's *The Provocation Collection* and others offer a generous array of experiments, so we've just gathered a small handful of ideas from the instructors we interviewed and our own teaching.

Where I call home

Read Jamaica Kincaid's *A Small Place*. Write a short piece addressed to an imagined tourist visiting a place you have called or currently call home. Like Kincaid, tell the tourist what they might see or appreciate as well as what they might miss or misinterpret. You may adopt a similarly antagonistic tone or try out a different one, but be deliberate in your choice of tone.

Big and little me (from Claire Donato)

Holding *Alice's Adventures in Wonderland* in heart–mind, craft a gesture (a short story, a poem, a film, a song, a sculpture) in which you too are very tiny and perhaps also very big, wherein you decide what tiny and big means to you.

Developing your if (from Kate Schapira)

Questions:

- If the well-being of the place where you live was complete, what would it be like during the day? At night?

- What are some things you'd be doing, in the day or night?
- What are the relationships between global well-being and this specific place?

Practice: Write or tell the story of your life, starting tomorrow, if one of your "ifs" were true. ("If the water sprinklers were safe for kids ... ") Start by making the vision vivid and thorough: what it looks like, feels like, smells like. Address the how, the who, and the where as they come up: how your medication reaches you in this vision, where the food you eat is grown and who grows it. Describe where the things that used to make you anxious went, and how that was accomplished.

If you're doing this as part of a group, add to and riff on each other's stories. Make your additions reparative, not just critical—for example, if someone's vision of no-car cities would be great for everyone except people who use mobility devices, make a suggestion that will allow for wheelchair vans and adaptive trikes.

Form translations (from Diana Khoi Nugyen)

Take the structure of a known poetic form (like the haiku) and adapt it to another arena, like audio. Create an audio-only clip that has three "movements"—one at least 5 seconds, one at least 7 seconds, and then one at least 5 seconds. Add some constraints: these must be "found" sounds from in or around one's home with no human speech. Play an excerpt of Leighton Pierce's film "Fifty Feet of String" (1995) as an example (although it incorporates video, too). By tasking the brain with engaging in a poetic structure but with a different medium, we are given permission to play in an area we may not be versed in (but one likely is versed enough in the haiku concept), which might result in new creative possibilities.

Portals (from Nalo Hopkinson)

At the beginning of any class that includes spec-fic, we talk about portals, how much science fiction and fantasy use the idea of the portal to another place. I ask students to imagine they're sleeping and something wakes them. Could be a sound, could be a funny colored light under the door, any sensation. They open the door, and outside is a portal. What do they do next?

This gets some cool stuff happening and some really contrary stuff happening too. One student imagined throwing his cat through the portal. It also starts them learning about narrative, how narrative has to follow on naturally from things that are happening. You have to imagine actually moving through the portal, somehow. You have to imagine being on both sides of it and how they differ.

Pattern play (from Hoa Nguyen)

Repetition—the drawing from patterns—is an ancient technique in poetry, tracing poetry's origin to incantation and song. Something happens when you repeat a word, phrase or line; maybe this can be called shapeliness. When repeated, words or phrases can take on new dimensions, subtleties, and connotations. Repetition lets a reader recognize and experience words newly.

Begin by making a list of the following:

- Somewhere you went today
- An observation of the weather
- An article of clothing
- A meal
- And finally, 10 randomly selected nouns (avoiding abstract notions like loneliness or hope in favor of the more concrete person, place, or thing variety). For each word, generate a complimentary word that is slant or off rhymed. Some examples: line/time, window/finger, uterine/cinnamon, red juice/furious. Note that this introduces occasions for assonance and alliteration.

Write freely, using as many of the words/phrases from this list as possible. Whenever you encounter a phrase, word, or line that feels evocative, repeat it.

Once the raw writing is complete, craft to carve out shapeliness. Read the results aloud to cull any awkward-sounding phrases and eliminate large abstractions such as "forever," "peace," or "humility" (such words often lack immediacy when they appear in poems). Rewrite and rearrange the text to discover corresponding and compelling patterns.

Write my scene (from Zac Hug)

This is a multi-part exercise we do when students move from outline writing to completing a script draft.

Part One: Select two scenes from your outline: one you love and one you're unsure of. Isolate each scene outline in a PDF and send them to me. Write both scenes in script form.

Part Two: You have received two scene outlines from another student. Without context or questions, transform these outlines into script form and send them to me.

Part Three: Review the discussion board where you'll all see two versions of each scene: one written by the original writer and one written by a classmate without context. Let's see what we notice!

This exercise lets us enter into a conversation about formatting scripts, see how another writer might interpret the visual language the original writer used in the outline, and bond by fumbling together into a new phase of scriptwriting.

Birth stories

1. Spend 8 minutes writing the account of your birth from the perspective of your father, mother, grandparent, sibling, aunt, uncle, nurse, or doctor. Use as many of the five sensory details as possible (sight, touch, sound, taste, and smell) and include 3–5 lines of dialogue.
2. Now add a few lines of tension.
3. Then, add a humorous moment.
4. Now write 3–4 sentences that break from the time of that whole scene to an important or embarrassing moment in your adult life.
5. Take a moment to share one surprising thing that arose in the writing of this and one challenging thing.

Using constraint-based experiments to build toward larger projects

Structured writing experiments are not mere warm-ups or throwaways. Indeed, a well-chosen constraint can kick-start an entire project. When we break down complex craft and technique elements into inviting low-stakes exercises, students produce work they never would have thought possible. Bit by bit, students find themselves completing bold, ambitious work. Writing constraints help writers of all levels put parameters around their work, breaking it down into smaller, more manageable parts. As they generate material around a focusing agent or solve the problem that a constraint raises, they build momentum and develop confidence in the work they produce.

Often, moving forward is a matter of choosing and completing the right constraints. For example, writer Mona Awad read "Thirteen Ways of Looking at a Blackbird," a noted imagistic exercise in perspective by Wallace Stevens. Stevens' structuring principle offered Awad a constraint for her own work: to focus on discrete glimpses of a woman's struggle with body image and explore how that struggle played out in specific scenarios: dressing rooms, a tense lunch with a friend, a visit with a parent, sex, a cardio machine war at the gym. Her book, *13 Ways of Looking at a Fat Girl* (2016), focuses on tensions she wanted to explore, creating the multi-faceted portrait she was interested in. Examples like this remind us (and our students) that generative constraints are not just for beginners and can be designed to support work in any genre or style.

Not just for beginners: an invitation to reflect

Students sometimes see writing experiments or exercises as rudimentary work, an activity they might hope to outgrow as quickly as possible. As we've reflected on our own writing habits and spoken with friends and colleagues about theirs, we've become convinced that this is not the case.

In fact, many writers develop forms of structured practice for each new project, in a sense giving themselves "assignments." Likewise, many writers (us included) continue to seek out instruction—through reading craft books, attending conference panels, participating in short-term workshops, and so on—to keep adding to their toolkit of approaches for drafting, revising, and refining.

As we write this book together, we're also working on other projects: a collection of poems, an essay collection, a novel. Here are a couple of examples of generative constraints we've given ourselves:

For a narrative nonfiction book, Bronwen uses a Lynda Barry-inspired method of generating new material. Having copied down evocative words onto paper and put them into a teacup, Bronwen draws a word from the cup, writes (by hand in a notebook) the first five to ten concrete images that come to mind, and then picks the image with the most energy to extend across two or three handwritten pages. Some of this material will end up in her book, and some won't. The goal is to follow the sensory power of memory and surprise herself.

In his novel about a rodeo clown, John employs a series of strange comedic moments that the entertainer performs during the competition to entertain the audience, while distracting the animals and protecting the cowboys. Each comedic moment involves a different object that holds some historical meaning for the clown. John also generates new material by incorporating disparate colors to mimic the bright make-up that the clown wears on their face, each color representing a range of expressions from desire to delight to danger.

- As you design generative constraints for students, reflect on the role of structured practice in your own writing formation and, perhaps, your ongoing practice, and consider sharing an example with students.

A case study: writing experiments in a graduate fiction course

Here's one example, from John's graduate fiction course, of how generative writing experiments with built-in constraints can be scaffolded over the semester. The weekly experiments laid out in Table 3.2 are guided by the learning objectives for the course and connect to the readings and craft discussions for each week. The aim is to help students practice and execute craft concepts, generate material, try challenging and focused techniques in prose style, draft a story, and then draft it again through a different constraint, and once more from another constraint. Students submit a brief self-reflection each week that tracks their evolution of the pieces and deepens their skill acquisition.

In a generative writing course like this, students create new material, experiment with form and technique, and develop their individual aesthetics. Low-stakes writing experiments with built-in constraints nudge them to the edge of their competency where new material, insights, and breakthroughs can occur. Later in the course, after they've had a chance to see how constraints work, students create their own constraints to challenge their respective projects and skill sets.

When we encourage our students to create from a space in which they are hemmed in by a problem to solve (constraints), we invite them to consider the freedom they might experience responding to those boundaries. We teach them that they can write beyond their default modes and impulses, stretching into new possibilities and discovering new pleasures.

Table 3.2 A Generative Fiction Workshop Structure

Week 1: Genesis of character	Building on a set of questions to explore a character, students dramatize this character through a moment of "shame" that opens up a "wound" the character is not consciously aware of, nor is the wound stated in the work; it's implied.
Week 2: Character relationships at play	Students pair the character they developed in Week 1 with another character in an interaction where the power dynamic inherent between them prods at their respective wounds. Having finished this scene, they write a short slice of summary to connect the scene with a second scene that further advances the conflict and character from the first scene.
Week 3: Narrative strategies at play	Students work on different narrative strategies to build a 5–8-page piece incorporating the work done in weeks 1 and 2 and using the narrative strategies discussed in class (scene, half-scene, summary, flashforward; avoiding backstory, flashback, and use of memory or dreams).
Week 4: Prose style at play	Students focus on prose style by writing a 250–500-word sentence and insert it into the appropriate/strategic spot in their story. They include an analysis and rationale for the sentence, then rewrite the same sentence using only 25 words.
Week 5: Deep POV and narrative voice at play	Students focus on cracking open their manuscript by considering different points of view and narrative voices. They write from four different characters' POV and narrative voices.
Week 6: Compression at play	Students focus on compression. They are challenged to write their story several times using only ten sentences: (1) Ten sentences on their character before the story actually begins; (2) a ten-sentence story; (3) a ten-sentence story from their antagonist's POV.
Week 7: Beauty and joy at play	Students move away from tragedy and negative emotions to develop moments in the manuscript where beauty and joy might bloom. They write a new piece, using the same characters, in which what escalates is not trouble or conflict, but beauty, pleasure, hope, or kindness.
Week 8: Narrative turns	Students focus on narrative turns in their manuscript. They bring experiments 1–7 together into one coherent piece, and put the final touches on the working draft by: (1) working in at least two major narrative turns in the piece, and (2) working turns into at least 20% of their sentences.

A student perspective: Jasmine Sealy on resistance to generative writing

What makes a generative exercise feel like busywork versus feeling important if not essential to your development as a writer?

The term busywork can be a bit of a misnomer. The truth is that writing is work; I am a writer who resists that notion. I want to be in a constant state of generative flow. But that state of blissful, almost unconscious creativity is sustainable only for brief bursts, enough to write a short story perhaps, but nothing long-form. Generative exercises can help students strengthen the muscles required for the long and effortful work of novel-writing.

How have generative exercises helped you in writing your novel? Can you trace specific scenes, characters, or elements back to specific exercises?

In an advanced fiction writing workshop during my MFA, we were given a series of questions to consider about our characters. I was in the early stages of drafting what would later become my novel *The Island of Forgetting*. The question that most stood out to me was *"What are the false or dysfunctional narratives your character carries around all the time?"*

This question completely exploded my understanding of what the novel was going to be about. As I was writing in first person, I'd been struggling with how to withhold information from readers in order to create intrigue, when the narrators should ostensibly be able to reveal everything about themselves and their thoughts on the page. By thinking about false narratives, I was able to heighten the dramatic tension by leaning into the narrators' unreliability. The way each character grapples with false narratives, and the ways their own self-image compares with how they are seen by others, eventually became the lynchpin at the heart of the mechanics of the novel. In thinking about the characters' internality, I ended up unlocking the thesis of the book itself.

JASMINE SEALY is a Barbadian-Canadian writer. Her debut novel *The Island of Forgetting* was published in 2022.
Image credit: Marcy Media

Drawing on the work of others in ethical ways

New instructors often have questions about what from their experiences as students they can ethically incorporate into their teaching practice. A student who's so inspired that they want to spread teaching materials further is a great compliment. But developing effective teaching materials also takes time and creative thinking. So what kind of riffing and borrowing is appropriate and when does this cross a line? A few recommendations:

1 **When published, cite.** When you're drawing on published teaching materials, cite your sources. Giving credit through citation is a responsible thing to do. Beyond that, it's also an opportunity to show students how networked and interconnected we all are.
2 **When unpublished, ask (and attribute).** All teachers draw on insights and examples from their own teachers. Effective teachers are in dialogue with other teachers, passing materials back and forth and modifying them to suit their purposes. If you want to draw on materials designed by a friend, colleague, or former teacher, it's respectful to ask first. And it's usually a good idea to include some attribution, however informal: "Now we're going to try an experiment inspired by my friend Amy, who's a painter … " you might say.
3 **When an approach is general, adapt it.** Giving credit can be taken to a paranoid extreme. As long as you're working from a place of respect, trust your instinct on this. If you find three or four versions of something in different books/courses and you're doing a version that draws on others but also adds your own flavor, it's fine to work without citing. If every screenwriting book on the market includes a section on pitching, and you also have experience with pitching and want to do a pitching activity with students, go for it.
4 **Consider when to quote and when to riff.** Sometimes it makes best sense to incorporate a teaching activity whole (i.e., "This week we're going to try out Lynda Barry's daily diary review frame, and here's a video where she explains how it works"). Other times, it's better to synthesize and adapt a model activity or assignment to fit your specific context and take on your voice. Teaching, like writing, is a field of shared endeavor—we are all indebted to those who have come before us and all doing our part to imagine what else might exist.

Fostering an atmosphere of serious play

As we've discussed, terms and keywords matter. How students respond to a "writing exercise" might depend on how they feel about the word "exercise" in other contexts. Consider how generative writing fits within the broader course and choose a term that evokes that relationship. A few examples:

- A writing **experiment** suggests intentional work undertaken with curiosity toward results. The goal is not perfection, but rather *doing* via problem-solving.

An experiment suggests that the reward is the experiment itself, not necessarily the work produced. As in the sciences, an experiment may fail to produce expected results and still be worthwhile because of what it allows us to notice and experience.

- A **sketch** isn't polished, finished, or final. A sketch explores an idea and figures out its rough shape. A sketch might also be a chance to play with a new tool, technique, or material. We might lean into the visual art metaphor and say, "If the purpose is learning how to handle charcoal, which is famously smudgy, and you do a sketch in pen, it might be a great drawing, but it won't teach you what using charcoal will. Try this new thing!"
- An **exploration** suggests movement into terrain that holds potential surprises and discoveries, with an emphasis on what we notice and experience, rather than on what we achieve or accomplish.

As students cultivate curiosity about their work and ask questions like "What happens if I try … ?" they learn how to escape the trap of premature judgment. They generate new material, observe patterns developing, and respond with a feeling of play and openness, suspending critique. The language of experiments, sketches and explorations can help students embrace the conundrums constraints pose.

Diana Khoi Nguyen on hopeful risks, happy accidents, and play as experimentation

What does play mean to you in the context of writing?

Play is central to writing and any form of art-making. I define play as taking hopeful risks from a place of security or sense of safety—that if one falls, no real hurt will occur. When penicillin was discovered, it wasn't intentional but an accident; scientists noticed that no bacteria were growing in one area of the Petri dish and instantly recognized the usefulness of this! Play should involve creating optimal conditions in which happy accidents can occur.

I believe play and surprise are inextricably linked. What makes something an act of play or playful is that it surprises (and often also brings joy). To produce surprise, one must engage in forms of play—trying new things without knowing what the result(s) might be—being playful for playful's sake, without fear of failure.

So many students are also working, care-taking, commuting, and so on. What approaches have you found for helping students step out of a mind-set of to-do lists and efficiency and into one of experimentation and play?

As someone juggling many personal and professional responsibilities, I sympathize with others who occupy multiple roles. I recommend approaches from my own practice: to incorporate experimentation into my essential tasks and roles. I might try something unconventional or counterintuitive when loading the dishwasher, or preparing vegetables for dinner; I might take a playful path through the bathrooms while cleaning them; I might disrupt my commute by including a layered activity (mapping a recitation of a poem for each bus stop), or even choosing a different way of moving along the same path. Essentially, how can we bring a silly attitude to a rote activity, where one maybe feels a little uncomfortable (because it makes one feel self-conscious)? I'm thinking about how improv actors think on the spot—given a few constraints to work with. Experimentation and play aren't just for the page, or creative writing and making, but are an ethos, a way of being—a way of thinking and engaging with things in and around us. The mind is remarkable at pulling new possibilities from familiar situations. We just have to reorient ourselves and make ourselves available to these possibilities.

How might play and experimentation in a writing course be collaborative or relational?

Play is also inherently collaborative—either with an object (prop) or with another person (or several). Because multiple minds have access to possibilities that just one person can't drum up alone, it's often through conversation, brainstorming, and mutual excitement that new ideas arise.

How do you talk to students who might see play as a distraction from "the real work" of writing?

I think of this possible student all the time—like a devil's advocate in my classroom. When one emerges (and they will at some point), I will be as honest and as transparent as I can: I'll share examples of how my acts of "play" have resulted in x and y poems, which have been published or successful in other traditionally registered ways. In fact, I'll share many examples of how play has yielded "success" not only for myself, but for other poets and writers as well. And I'll emphasize that play is an evolutionary activity that exists across so many mammals—to build and prepare the mind and body for essential activities: bear cubs play to build muscle and hone their bodies for when they eventually need to hunt, and so on. What seems trivial on the surface (but does it?) is vital.

DIANA KHOI NGUYEN teaches in the Randolph College Low-Residency MFA and is an Associate Professor at the University of Pittsburgh. A poet and multimedia artist, she is the author of *Root Fractures* and *Ghost Of*, and her video work has been exhibited at the Miller ICA.

Image credit: Karen Lue

A few final suggestions

When designing writing experiments for students, consider the following tips:

- **Be transparent.** Explain what students are doing and why they're doing it.
- **Avoid creating experiments that feel disposable.** Although generative experiments involve making work that gets discarded, they should never feel like busywork. Experiments should be relevant to what the students are doing and should involve some challenge (which may be technical or emotional).
- **Invite students to write about how they used their constraints.** They might reflect on how they completed their work, what challenged them and why, and how they worked around those challenges. Reflective writing helps student writers learn to interrogate their own writing.
- **Consider how to close the loop.** It's important to incorporate writing experiments into the shared space of the class. By inviting students to discuss or share their work in progress with peers or with us, we foster dialogue that is part of the creative process rather than a postmortem after the fact. Here are a few possibilities:
    - Students turn in experiments to the instructor, who might offer light feedback, or schedule a meeting to discuss the work.
    - Students read the work out loud as a full class and also submit it in writing to the instructor. The class discusses writing experiences and observations as a group, without offering critique.
    - Students discuss their writing experiences (challenges, choices, insights) without sharing the work or with only sharing a brief snippet (i.e., a single sentence, image, moment of dialogue). This can happen in small groups or large groups, verbally or via online discussion boards.
    - Students share writing in small groups and peers respond to a single question (provided by the instructor) designed to offer insight into what comes across to the reader. Example: "Name a detail that's sticking with you. What broader context does this detail evoke?"
- **Offer students explicit opportunities to claim their experiment-generated writing.** When students work with generative experiments for the first time, some initially disavow the work they produce. They may think, "Sure, I made this, but you told me how to do it and it's not really mine." This sense of the writing as distinct from the self and capable of being observed and manipulated can be useful, especially for students who overidentify with their texts as fragile extensions of themselves. But students benefit from an explicit invitation to claim agency in what they continue to develop and what they leave behind.
- **Coach students to create their own constraints, for themselves or for one another.** Students might design constraints that draw on their deep reading of a self-selected writer. Or they might design a personalized constraint for a peer in the class that offers this peer the scope to deepen what they're already doing well while also challenging them to try something new.

Since working with students in a generative workshop guided by writing experiments, we've seen students work in different forms, try different points of view and voices, and experiment with verb tenses and narrative and poetic devices. Not only are they producing more exciting and accomplished work, but they clearly find the process both daunting and exciting. They approach their writing with openness and curiosity rather than defensively producing work they fear might be torn to shreds by a hypercritical workshop.

Students who work reflectively with generative experiments come to demonstrate a command of intent and process and are better able to work with revision as a result of their exploration of divergent possibilities. They are more receptive to following hunches and ultimately more in touch with their writerly instincts. Writing requires an iterative cycling between the uncertain, reaching for what has not yet been articulated, and the rigorous analysis of what is on the page. As students participate in generative experiments, they come to understand that making *is* thinking, that we don't come up with ideas and then turn to the page to execute them, but rather come to ideas through our material engagement with words. While students are learning important tools of craft and technique, they are also ultimately learning how to trust themselves and their process.

4 In-Class Activities and Active Learning

Designing for meaningful gatherings

Emerging from a socially distanced and isolated time, instructors and students alike have been pushed to interrogate and affirm the particular values of collaborative synchronous learning. What can we do in-person that we can't do remotely? What can we do together that we can't do alone?

As we've spent less time in Zoom rooms and more time gathered around a seminar table or mic'd up at the front of a lecture hall, our hallway chats with colleagues have circled the pleasures and challenges of sharing embodied presence. How can we ensure students see classroom time as valuable? How might we equip students to create and sustain writing communities after our courses end?

We've seen transformative learning happen when we gather. Yet, with the concern of declining attention spans, we can't assume that the attention, curiosity, and trust necessary for active learning will manifest on their own. "Students are busy, stressed, distracted—they have good reasons to check out of parts of their schooling—," John Warner said in our conversation, "but like any human being, they're also curious and eager to be engaged in something interesting." Like Warner, we've looked for ways to help students tune in when they may be tempted to check out. This chapter discusses approaches to cultivate a classroom climate that supports deep engagement and uses class time to practice, explore, and experiment.

What are the ideal conditions for meaningful gathering? Attentive presence, a sense of belonging, a feeling of trust that allows for real risk. We can cultivate presence, invite belonging, and attempt to earn trust. But we can't compel these states. As Claire Donato (**Chapter 1**) said: "Safety is something earned; it is not a given. Camaraderie and love are slow, and no classroom can be a 'safe space' from day one." Donato also emphasized that "for some students, a classroom will never feel like a safe space because of the imperialist white supremacist heteropatriarchal (to quote bell hooks) socio-historical weight the classroom bears, which is entwined with historic inequity."

Part of reaching toward greater safety and camaraderie, then, involves acknowledging the limits of institutional spaces and the legitimate reasons students have to be wary—the weight of hypervisibility a Black student experiences at a majority-white institution, for example, or the gap a first-generation college student feels between the experience they seek to portray and the expectations and assumptions of their peers.

As instructors, we can remain mindful of these limits while bringing intention to classroom choices that make presence, belonging, and trust as available as possible for students. Despite our best intentions, issues will undoubtedly arise. In **Chapter 12,** we review specific challenges in group dynamics that can occur and offer some strategies for responding to them. Here, we focus on proactive steps to design for meaningful gatherings.

Presence

We're in the room together, but are we present together? Instructors and students often rush to class from another class across campus or a part-time job, from an argument with a roommate over dirty dishes or a tearful daycare drop-off. We all arrive from other spaces where we have experienced an array of emotions and challenges. As they settle into their seats, students may be thinking about a bad grade on a mid-term, a friend who didn't text back, an unfinished scholarship application due in a few hours.

Presence requires attention. Before students can direct attention to course concepts or classmates, they need a chance to attend to their own body-minds and arrive fully. In our conversation, RJ McDaniel (**Chapter 12**) advocated for "encouraging students to be mindful of what they're experiencing mentally and physically and facilitating opportunities to take a breath and reset when necessary." We might invite mindful presence through guided freewriting, a round robin check-in, or just a few collective deep breaths. Kate Schapira shared an initial three-word check-in ritual from a recent course on medical narratives:

> The structure is: three ways that you're feeling, you don't have to explain, nobody's allowed to ask you questions, you just say the words. Today, before I asked students to share their words in class, we stood up together, and first we just took a couple of breaths, and then we hissed and then we hummed and then we groaned. Movement can be a reminder, like, "Hey, here we all are in the room. Don't worry about it." In a class that has to do with bodies and embodiment, that feels especially important.

In various courses, we've begun each session with a brief reading from Inger Christensen's book-length poem *alphabet* (1982), started with five minutes of freewriting in response to Bhanu Kapil's questions from *The Vertical Interrogation of Strangers* (2001), or simply played a song and invited students attend to their breath while they listen. "Many students have experienced environments where mindfulness is actively discouraged," RJ McDaniel explained, "and they may carry an inherent anxiety into the classroom space." Students may also have been taught to perform attention, which, for some, can take so much cognitive work they have little energy left for actually learning. When we acknowledge that doodling, looking out the window, or wearing headphones can in fact be strategies to support attention, the classroom becomes a more inclusive place. "When a classroom environment has established that it's okay to notice how you're feeling," McDaniel said, "it's easier for students to recognize when they're becoming overwhelmed, and to feel safe to take a break if they need to." From this sense of safety, deeper attention and fuller presence become possible.

Belonging

Students experience a sense of belonging when they feel connection with others in the room and with the questions and materials of the course. Students need to believe that they have something to learn from classmates and something to contribute based on their own perspective and insight. While a sense of community is never automatic, we've found that it can develop quite organically as students write alongside one another, sharing their attempts and discoveries.

The initial curiosity or engagement we hope to spark when we share a compelling passage or intriguing puzzle deepens when students can connect course questions and materials with their own experiences, interests, and goals. Some of these goals may be quite pragmatic: a required humanities or arts credit, or a good grade efficiently achieved. Without dismissing these concerns, we can invite students to ask more for themselves. We've discussed the importance of seeing each contact point—from course description to syllabus to assignment sheet—as a chance to welcome and connect with students on a human level. In class, we can show students we welcome their vulnerable stories and weird fascinations by responding with interest and enthusiasm whether they write about their current obsession with *90 Day Fiancé,* their shifts at White Spot restaurant, their speculative queer utopias, or their studies in wilderness medicine.

Another key aspect of belonging lies in fostering a culture of access. J. Logan Smilges (**Chapter 1**) discussed the importance of modeling for students how to articulate a need or request care from others. "This process requires a tremendous amount of trust on behalf of students," Smilges explained. "We have to streamline a building of rapport that in an ideal world would take place over a longer period of time. It takes so much courage. To recognize that courage, I work to celebrate it, to say, 'Thank you for sharing that with me. That's a really good point. I think other people would benefit from that as well.'"

Sarah Leavitt on how designing for beginners can help everyone

In teaching comics, you explicitly welcome students who say "I can't draw." How do you design in-class activities with these students in mind?

My thinking about that has evolved over the years. I used to just say, "It doesn't matter whether you can draw or not! Here are some comics with stick figures and dots." I still think that's a great approach. But I've shifted a bit. Usually when people say they can't draw, they mean they can't draw a representational realistic image. So, I'll say, "Comics have five basic elements, and drawing is one of them." As we get deeper into comics, we talk about composition or zooming in or repeating an image. These techniques don't rely on the technical quality of your drawing; they're more about how you arrange it.

On a practical level, I've noticed logistical things students do that interfere with their ability to draw. Designing with those students in mind, I assign a lot of timed exercises, usually three minutes or less so they just don't have the option of correcting. Other strategies: doing things over and over and discarding them, forcing students to take up the whole sheet of paper (otherwise the ones who don't draw start super tiny), having them use pens so they can't erase. Like so many things, if you design for the students who are having trouble, it ends up benefiting everybody.

SARAH LEAVITT is an Associate Professor in the UBC School of Creative Writing. Her graphic memoir *Tangles: A Story About Alzheimer's, My Mother, and Me* is currently in production as a feature-length animation. Her latest book, *Something Not Nothing*, is a collection of short comics about grief and loss.

Image credit: Bren Robbins

Trust

All of our work cultivating presence and belonging will fail, however, if we don't establish a foundation of trust. We've seen the transformative power of a classroom where everyone can speak up without fear, where we can hear criticism from others and admit our own mistakes, where students feel safe to take risks or disagree openly. For any of this to be possible, students need clarity. Clear roles, expectations, and boundaries allow students to relax their defenses and focus on learning. They need to trust that an instructor will intervene if someone says something offensive (clear roles), that they won't suddenly be asked to read what they thought was a private exercise out loud in class (clear expectations), that writing shared in class won't be discussed in the lounge or on social media (clear boundaries). Roles, expectations, and boundaries can never be assumed. They must be made explicit. While some expectations and policies are firm, many have considerable room for negotiation. Particularly in small classes, we've found it valuable to engage in a group process to arrive at a shared understanding through community agreements.

Community agreements

A community agreement is a set of guidelines around conduct, confidentiality, charged content, and whatever else is relevant to a specific course, co-authored by the class, revisited and renegotiated as needed throughout the term.

Many instructors simply lead a conversation in which they ask students, "What do we want to agree on as a group to support our work together?" to review key points open for negotiation, invite students to offer perspectives with a goal of reaching consensus, and draft a list of shared commitments to revisit as the term progresses. Others adopt a more structured process like the one Kate Schapira describes:

> For starting a group agreement, I ask everybody to write down three things, ways of being, norms, that have made a group they've been part of a good one. We lay these on the table and we walk around with stickers. If someone likes one, they put a dot on it. I type up all of the ones with dots, and we discuss them together.

When we co-author community agreements, we have a list of issues to be sure to raise if no one brings them up. What's available for negotiation depends on the size of the class: due dates are likely firm in a large class, but a small class might negotiate deadlines that offer flexibility for writers while giving their peers enough time to review submissions. We also make sure to leave space for students to raise concerns and priorities that have not occurred to us. Some common topics that come up in these conversations include:

- Communication norms
- Respecting names and pronouns
- Privacy and confidentiality
- Expectations around entering and leaving the classroom
- Eating in class/allergies
- Access needs
- Content policies

A community agreement, then, might include statements like:

- We agree to see ourselves as writing and speaking in draft, which includes the possibility of error, change, revision, and clarification.
- We are okay with praising people in the class to others outside the class (without revealing specific details of their work).
- We commit to assuming positive intent while acknowledging negative impact for any issues that may arise.
- We agree to attend to our embodied selves however we see fit and not question one another about it. This includes but isn't limited to eating in class, stepping outside to use the washroom/get water/or move around, stretching or changing body position to care for pain.

To keep a community agreement from becoming a superficial boilerplate document, it's important to unpack key terms and statements. Kate Schapira explained how she goes about this: "If someone says 'people are respectful,' I'd ask, 'What does that mean?

How do you show respect in this space? What is respect? How do we manifest it?'" One student might propose that eye contact shows respect as a sign of active listening, and another might raise a concern around what eye contact means or feels like for neurodiverse students. By airing differences of understanding, expectation, and priority, we're able to get into genuine negotiations that acknowledge real differences in the room and prepare the group to approach challenges that will inevitably arise with respect and care.

To truly serve the group, community agreements must be revisited as time goes by. This might be a simple check-in where we pass out a printed copy of the agreement and invite students to weigh in on how it's working for them and add anything new. Or it might, as Schapira discussed, involve confronting a gap: "Hey, we said this in the group agreement, but we're kind of not doing it. Does that mean that we should change the agreement or does it mean that we need to start doing it?" Schapira goes one step further and includes language in her syllabus inviting students to confer with peers and present her with proposed changes, such as reweighting assignments, revising due dates, or reallocating class time. She sees this as training in collective bargaining:

> It's a useful skill beyond the university to practice getting together to see where everyone is at: "Is this a situation where you're struggling and you need an extension? Or is it a situation where the structure of the course is not mapping onto the realities of people's educational lives and we need an extension for everybody?" I see it as preparing them to have conversations with other people about what is happening and what should happen.

While she's not always able to make the change, she's usually able to offer at least a compromise.

Content policies

We've spent a lot of time thinking and talking with colleagues about bringing charged material into the classroom (whether an assigned reading from Toni Morrison or a workshop submission dealing with childhood trauma) and about whether, why, when, and how to include content notes (sometimes called trigger warnings or content advisory). Content notes—statements on the work that name and flag potentially disturbing content—inevitably change the experience of reading. The note becomes the lens through which the class views the work, and, instead of getting an unbiased read, students might read with expectations, or even prejudices. We also know that triggers related to trauma can be far from straightforward: a seemingly innocent smell or song might evoke unavoidable visceral sensations. We understand why writers, teachers, and students might take issue with content notes as overdetermined, unclear, or inadequate. At the same time, we always discuss them as part of a conversation about the responsibilities of a writer, and typically use them to some degree.

In our conversation, Sarah Leavitt shared a catalyzing event that changed her perspective, "I spent a number of years not doing content notes and then I had this experience where somebody brought in a piece about suicide and it just messed up a couple of the other students. I was like 'What am I doing?'" Like Leavitt, we're most mindful of the potential for harm. Her current approach is to request content notes for material involving suicide, abuse and assault, and racist and homophobic violence, and then revise this list based on specific student feedback. Leavitt emphasized the importance of discussing not merely what to flag for a content warning but also what options are available to readers and writers alike:

> I also want to be clear about how the logistics will work, like "What if because of a content warning you don't want to read the work?" I make clear that I'm never going to force anybody to read the work, but my goal is to think together about anything we can do that will allow you to engage with it. In my grad course, there's a student writing about her own experience of child sexual abuse who has consulted with me a lot about how to present that. She's being really thoughtful, and other students have been fine to engage with it. I also want to set up a context where students writing about difficult material get craft feedback, not like "Oh you're talking about abuse, so it's all amazing." I've been really proud of students for saying, "I don't understand what happened. If you switch the panel order here, I think I would understand it better."

As part of a trauma-informed classroom built on trust, collaboration, and student empowerment, content notes are an extension of the conversation started in community agreements. We've seen how content warnings on assigned readings can help students take care of themselves by not reading the work in public or by consciously building in extra time to deal with strong emotions that might arise. And we've seen how content warnings on student work can give peers a chance to step forward or step back in a way that allows the writer to receive considered feedback. A discussion on content policies early in the semester signals respect and empathy. By discussing norms, expectations, and available options directly, we acknowledge that reasonable people can come to different conclusions and situate the class as a collaborative context of mutual care and shared decision-making.

Structure and pacing

By taking time to establish strong foundations, we set our classrooms up for success. In choosing how to structure our in-class time, we consider pacing at the level of the term, the module, and each individual session.

Mapping assignments, skills, activities

Plans begin with the big-picture mapping of learning goals, major assignments, and low-stakes assignments and activities aimed at building capacity (**Chapter 1**). We may identify distinct modules as in-class engagement shifts from discussion-based sessions to lab-style experiments to workshop-focused small groups. We map out possibilities by looking closely at what students will have done before coming to class (read X, written Y) and what they have on the horizon (a workshop, say, or a presentation). We return repeatedly to a central question: What can we do in-person that takes full advantage of our shared presence? Here are some further guiding questions we return to:

- **How does each activity connect to the learning goals of the course?** What are we hoping students learn from discussing texts or giving feedback to one another?
- **Have I articulated these connections to students?** Sometimes we foreground activities like giving feedback as a service to peers. While crafting thoughtful feedback is an act of generosity and care, it's also a chance to deepen skills. In giving feedback, students learn to read closely, identify patterns, and move from reaction to considered response, from vague impression to clear articulation. In sharing this deeper purpose with them, we give students a chance to recognize and practice these skills.
- **What skills are students practicing?** We might think about teaching students how to write feedback letters, but if discussion is a major component of in-class engagement, are we teaching students how to do it? We might look for ways to begin with more structured practice to build capacity before moving to self-directed practice. And we may come to the realization that if we don't have time to teach something, we're better off cutting it or not assessing it.
- **How does the class plan consider the full range of students?** Is there scope for strong students to find challenges? If some students need more support, what resources or options are available for them?

Pacing and variable attention

Beginnings and endings matter. The first sentence of a novel can draw a reader in and set the tone for the whole book. A final line can overturn a poem's meaning entirely. Beginnings and endings are equally significant when it comes to teaching, whether we're talking about the first day of a course or the final five minutes of a class midway through the semester. Consider the first day: students show up curious, maybe a bit apprehensive. In many courses, they read over the syllabus, have a chance to ask questions, and go their way without a real sense of what learning might *feel like* in the course.

In contrast, think of how most TV shows begin: with a cold open. They start mid-scene and quickly establish the stakes. Only when the audience is hooked do they pause to roll the credits.

Likewise, a class can begin with a poem read out loud, structured freewriting, or a discussion of a key question that will guide the course. There's still time to address policies and answer questions, and students leave with a tangible sense of what they can expect for the rest of the term. In our conversation, Sarah Leavitt shared her goal for the first day of class: "for students to form a group and begin to think of each other as allies, not competitors." Along with getting students to draw right away, she's also interested in "concretely opening up their idea of what comics are." She shares her own history with comics and brings in a big stack of comics with different styles and techniques for students to peruse and discuss. "My work is pretty personal, so I don't want to overshare but I do want them to realize that's work I'm open to," Leavitt explained. "I also talk about silly work—I don't want them to feel pressured to make intense personal work." Students leave the first class with a sense of possibility, as individuals and as a group.

A final session might just be a window to drop off final projects, but it could also involve a class reading and celebration of the semester's learning, a guided reflection on what students might want to carry with them, a chance to show appreciation to classmates and articulate their contributions, or an invitation to form peer writing groups that continue beyond the course. At the end of a ten-day intensive course where students had traveled to Vancouver from around the world, each of us asked students to address envelopes to their home addresses and invited classmates to write notes about what they'd valued about each peer's writing and/or presence in class. We stamped and mailed these envelopes a few weeks after the conclusion of the course when we knew students would be re-immersed in their everyday lives and struggling to hold onto the energy of the intensive and their sense of themselves as writers. Sometimes the end isn't the end.

On a day-to-day level, the start and end of a class are when student attention is likely at its highest. These moments are ripe for ritual, meaning, and intention. If we're not careful, though, we can find ourselves devoting this precious heightened attention to the necessary but lackluster "housekeeping" of teaching: homework reminders, due date clarifications, and so on. Instead, we might approach class pacing with variable attention in mind.

- **Arrival.** Students often need a moment to catch their breath and settle into the space. Freewriting, a quick round robin check-in, or even a few collective deep breaths allow space for full arrival and presence. We might also share a plan for the session, which helps students locate and pace themselves.
- **Start of class—high attentiveness.** Students are curious and engaged. Present new, rich information when their cognitive loads are able to synthesize new concepts with existing material.
- **Middle of class—lower attentiveness.** The middle of class is where student attention tends to flag. They may become cognitively overloaded and turn to daydreaming or worrying, perhaps giving in to the many clamorous distractions vying for their attention via phones and laptops. Varied practice through the middle of class helps students re-engage as they shift from a restorative activity like color-coding an assigned reading to an energizing activity like collaborative story-telling. Often, an effective class moves through a series of different types of engagement—solitary and collaborative, quiet and loud, reflective and playful.
- **End of class—revived attention.** Here, attentiveness, while not as high as at the start of class, is marginally higher than during the middle, largely because class is nearly over! These last few minutes can be fruitful for a reflective exercise and perhaps application of new information to set the stage for the week ahead.

A final crucial aspect of thoughtful pacing is flexibility. We may realize that an activity we've allotted fifteen minutes for actually takes thirty. Or only three of the thirty students completed the reading we planned to discuss. We may decide to let a particularly rich discussion continue rather than cut students off to keep with the plan. Or students may be extra drowsy and need something livelier than the scheduled revision exercise. For each class plan, consider: What can I cut (or shift to next session) if necessary? What back-pocket option can I fall on if the energy needs to shift or if we find ourselves with extra time? After each class, perform a quick debrief to capture how things went in your teaching journal (**Chapter 1**) to help you design your next class.

Taylor Brown-Evans on pacing and human connection in large classes

How do you approach pacing when teaching large classes?

When I first started teaching, I felt a lot of uncertainty around whether I would have enough to talk about. Because of that, I ended up relying a lot on engaging students, asking them questions, or giving them exercises, almost as a stalling tactic. Of course, I quickly realized that I did have more than enough content, that I did know this stuff and I did have something of value to share. But I also realized that I'd stumbled onto something that really galvanized students.

What started as a nervous lecture tactic ended up being a good tool to keep students engaged. If we focus on craft for too long, students eventually check out, and if we focus on discussion for too long, students get drained. When I was first crafting my lectures, I would build them in 10-minute intervals. I would say to myself, *I can talk about this for at least 10 minutes,* and then leave 10 minutes for discussion, and then do an exercise for 10 minutes. Eventually this developed into a framework. Knowing that framework was there freed me up to be looser in the actual moment and have an opportunity to play.

How do you design for connection in these courses?

By their nature, large classes can be impersonal, and despite being a room full of people, lecture halls can be lonely places. It is easy for students to feel reduced to their student number and grade, to revert to passive audience rather than actively engaged participants. I remember taking courses like that myself, and I remember those feelings of isolation and passivity. When designing the course, I try to create sessions that engage students not only on a level of craft, but also on a more human level. I'll pepper my slides with embarrassing puns and bad jokes, work in time for lively discussions, and openly acknowledge the stress and pressure students are under. I try to craft exercises that allow students to experiment and play without being judged or penalized for missteps. I build in group work with low-stakes fun or even funny exercises to encourage the social connections and playful collaboration that can be really beneficial for creative work.

TAYLOR BROWN-EVANS teaches Introduction to Creative Writing and Writing for Comics in the UBC School of Creative Writing. His writing and comics have appeared in *Geist, Poetry is Dead*, *The Feathertale Review*, and *Ricepaper Magazine*.
Image credit: Ingrid Forster Photography

Active learning possibilities

Seeking to deepen our pedagogy, we've found conversations with colleagues in other disciplines particularly useful for expanding our sense of what can happen in the classroom. A conversation with a theater colleague might inspire us to try out collaborative embodied warm-up activities to get students laughing and build trust. Likewise, a visit to a ceramics studio might help us think differently about what it means to make work alongside one another. Such conversations with painters, librarians, and biologists—along with thoughtful teaching and learning sessions held monthly in our School—have led us to books like *Making and Being: Embodiment, Collaboration, and Circulation in the Visual Arts* (Jahoda and Woolard 2020) and *Student Engagement Techniques* (Barkley and Major 2020) that have opened up new avenues and experiments in our classroom practice. Conversations with teaching friends have also offered us scope for invention, as we've pushed ourselves to clarify a problem or gap and encouraged one another to think capaciously about how we might address it.

Building on these encounters and experiments, we include active learning techniques throughout this book, whether discussing readings (**Chapter 6**), workshop (**Chapter 7**), revision (**Chapter 8**), or research (**Chapter 9**). In this section, we offer a handful of activities and notes that gesture toward the many possibilities for active learning in a creative writing context.

Writing together

We discuss low-stakes writing, including in-class writing, in **Chapter 3.** Still, we'd like to offer a few notes on in-class writing as a mode of active learning. We rely on in-class writing to give students a chance to gather their thoughts before speaking, to try out a new technique with an opportunity to receive immediate feedback through peer conversation, to generate material without pressure. In-class writing also offers opportunities for step-by-step pacing, obliging students who might tend to skip and skim in search of shortcuts to experience a guided multi-step process as intended. We've found that when students write together, many let go of the fear and isolation that they feel when writing alone.

A few key tips for in-class writing:

- **Give students a reason for doing the exercise so it doesn't feel disposable.** Does it link to a longer piece they're working on? Is it connected to something they've read for class? Does it aim to help them discover something new?
- **Clarify parameters and expectations.** Remind students that the exercise is for them and that they won't be asked to share it with others. Or, tell students that they'll have a chance to type up and revise their work before submitting a draft for a complete/incomplete grade. Or, inform them that they'll be discussing their writing experiences as a group and will have the option to share a brief passage if they wish.
- **Give instructions both verbally and in writing (on a slide, hand-out, or whiteboard).** As with many inclusive design principles, this is a necessity for some students and a benefit for all. Providing written instructions also gives latecomers a way to begin the exercise without interrupting peers.
- **Use a visible or audible timer.** This helps students pace themselves and transition into the next activity.

James M. Lang on classroom discussion and building rich networks

How do you approach classroom discussion?

I think expansively about what counts as discussion—it's any strategy that gives students opportunities to articulate their ideas and respond to the ideas of others. Discussion goes awry when teachers don't provide enough structure or support to ensure that every student receives the benefit of those activities. For example, a teacher might ask students to read a piece of writing, and then start a discussion by saying: "So what did you think?" That's a low-structure discussion prompt that will likely lead to a small number of students responding, while others sit silently and listen.

In *Small Teaching* (2016), you write, "The more we can help students develop rich networks in our content areas, the more we enable them to build meaning and comprehension" (98). What's a favorite classroom strategy for helping students develop rich networks?

At the start of every course, I hand out exam booklets and ask students to bring them to class every day—but not for daily exams, I add to their great relief. Once a week, I end our class activities ten minutes early and ask students to take out their exam booklets and respond to a thought question based on our discussions for that day. Those questions are designed specifically to help them build their networks, seeing how a poem by a nineteenth-century writer might connect to an environmental question we are concerned about in the twenty-first century; or even how that poem might give them a new perspective on something they have learned in an environmental science course. I vary these questions over the course of the semester, but each one invites the students to think beyond the boundaries of the classroom walls. I am delighted and amazed by the creative and unexpected connections students make between the course and their lives, their other courses, and cultures beyond the campus.

What advice do you have for teachers who feel worn down and struggle to connect to their own curiosity, wonder, and enthusiasm?

I had a professor in graduate school who gave me some counsel about teaching. I have followed her simplest piece of advice to this day: read the material you have assigned, *every time you assign it*. In other words, if you are teaching Zadie Smith's *White Teeth*—an almost 500-page novel—for the twentieth time, you should be reading it for at least the twentieth time. Because if you are teaching great works of literature and writing, as we should be doing, those works will always repay repeated readings. Not only will I find new ideas with each reading of a 500-page novel, so will I discover new ideas—if I bring my full attention to it—in a twelve-line Wordsworth sonnet. The discovery of those ideas excites me and energizes me as a reader, and I can then bring those emotions to the classroom. That matters because we have good research informing us that emotions are contagious in the classroom. If I want my student to feel curiosity, wonder, and enthusiasm, I first have to cultivate those feelings in myself.

JAMES M. LANG is a Professor of the Practice at the Kaneb Center for Teaching Excellence at the University of Notre Dame. He is the author of multiple books and essays of creative nonfiction and higher education pedagogy, including *Small Teaching: Everyday Lessons from the Science of Learning.*

Deepening discussion

Discussion allows students a chance to connect, respond, co-create knowledge, hear differences of opinion, and ask follow-up questions in real time. What better use of our time together? Yet, discussion facilitation requires delicate balance. In *Discussion as a Way of Teaching* (2005, 192–214), Brookfield and Preskill review reasons instructors might say too much or too little and analyze sample scenarios where they exhibit too much control or too little participation. We've certainly erred on both sides, doggedly returning to a question when students have raised other concerns they'd prefer to discuss, or opening with a half-baked query only to see the discussion meander aimlessly and never fully coalesce. We've also experienced rich conversations that moved an entire group forward in their understanding of an idea or technique.

After a symposium with Melanie Boyd and Jason Nisenson (**Chapter 9**), Bronwen followed up on their recommendation to check out *The Art of Focused Conversation* (Stanfield 2020), which advocates for a method of moving sequentially through objective questions, reflection questions, interpretive questions, and, finally decisional questions. Here's an example of sequential questions for a seminar discussion of Dionne Brand's *The Blue Clerk* (2019):

Objective questions

- How is this book constructed, including as a physical object? What do we notice about it before we even start reading?
- Let's read the stipule and Verso 1 together. What expectations do these sections establish? How are they teaching us to read this book?

Reflection questions

- Let's hear about some experiences people had with reading. Would anyone like to share a moment of getting a reference or connection, of looking something up (if you did that), or of feeling like something was out of your reach or withheld?
- How does it feel when the book eludes you?

Interpretive questions

- Who are the author and the clerk? What is their relationship?
- What does this book make of our desire to decode?

Decisional questions

- How do you understand your own consciousness as a writer? Do you have a clerk and an author?
- How (if at all) did this book invite you to understand your writing process differently?
- If you wanted to draw on this book, how might you design an exercise or assignment for yourself based on it? What rules or guidelines or processes might you lay out?

In this seminar, structured conversation allowed a group of students with different skill and experience levels to feel a sense of movement and arrival in their discussion of a complex book. Objective questions offered a low-stakes starting point in description and established a shared understanding of the book's key formal properties. Reflection questions gave students a chance to voice frustrations, discoveries, and differences in experience without embarrassment. Interpretive questions pushed them to connect details and propose arguments, while decisional questions invited them to reflect on ways to draw on the book (and the conversation) in their own practice as writers.

A few tips for navigating classroom discussions:

- **Watch out for the tendency to bounce the conversational ball back to the instructor between each volley.** If this keeps happening, consider taking a step back and asking students to call on the next person to speak.
- **Learn to be comfortable with silence.** Ten seconds can feel like sixty when you've asked a question and you're waiting for students to respond. It can be tempting to leap in with clarifications or start answering the question yourself. Often, if we wait just a bit past what feels comfortable, someone will step forward.
- **Prime the conversation with writing.** Especially if you ask a broad or open-ended question, give students a few moments to freewrite or make notes to gather their thoughts.
- **Give students a chance to warm up through low-stakes partner chats.** If students seem reluctant to speak as part of a full group, invite them to debrief with a partner or small group before bringing their thoughts to the larger group.
- **Questions are invitations—test them out on yourself (or a friend or colleague).** Questions like "Does anyone have any thoughts on sensory detail in comedy?" might leave people at a loss, whereas questions like "Think of a scene in a movie or TV show that made you laugh out loud. Describe it. How did it *get* you?" might have people eager to describe what would surely include a lot of sensory detail. As Lang suggests, when in doubt, increase structure.
- **Dedicate class time to practicing the craft of question construction.** In **Chapter 2**, we offer sample materials for helping students learn to ask good questions about their work in progress that might be adapted for other purposes.
- **When teaching online, make full use of online-specific features like break-out rooms and the chat.** Discussing experiences of online teaching, Taylor Brown-Evans described how the chat "democratized the conversation in the class" by allowing students to "contribute to the conversation with a quick note, an emoji, or reaction." He told us, "The chat allowed for a parallel conversation amongst students that did not disrupt the lecture. I could pick up on an idea that came up, answer a question, or riff on a joke, all without interrupting the lecture itself. It was like getting to see the notes students pass back and forth in class in real time."
- **In online and/or large group contexts, consider using programs that aggregate student responses.** Programs like Mentimeter and Pear Deck allow students to connect via phone or laptop and respond to questions, which are then projected as word clouds, pie charts, and scrolling images of individual answers. Anonymized or text-based responses offer students a less intimidating way to remain engaged and bring dialogue to what might otherwise feel one-sided.

A place for lecture

Although active learning is irreplaceable, we've come to appreciate what lectures have to offer (Nordman, Hutchinson, MacKay 2021), from the ten-minute craft micro lecture in a graduate course to a mic'd up auditorium lecture to 200 students. A few tips for effective lectures are:

- **Clarify lecture goals.** Use structures like "At the end of this lecture, students will be able to … " or "Students think A about X. At the end of the lecture, students will think B about X."
- **Shape a narrative.** It's incredibly easy to overpack a lecture and end up rushed. Offer 3–5 main points that build upon one another as a starting point.
- **Offer a road map at the start and transition clearly.** It might seem obvious (to us) how the pieces fit together, but we need to push ourselves to make transitions and connections explicit for students.
- **Review your key terms and reference points/examples.** Are they clear? Relevant? Accessible? Necessary? Connected? (See **Chapter 5** for more on selecting key terms.)
- **Be prepared (and prepare to pivot).** Thorough preparation will give you the confidence to go off script if and when called for.
- **Test your tech.** (And be prepared for tech failures anyway.)
- **Use slides for pacing and interaction, not information delivery.** Avoid giant blocks of text, with an exception for model text you plan to read out loud and unpack with students.
- **Find opportunities for interaction** that support different comfort levels.
    - Between students in pairs/small groups.
    - Between students and you.
- **Figure out how to calm your nervous system and center your body.**
    - Make a starting checklist (i.e., plug in computer, connect projector, test microphone) to reassure yourself that you're not forgetting any steps.
    - Pause to take deep breaths if you feel your pulse/voice racing.
    - Bring water and take sips to pause and pace yourself.

Creative collaborations

Building on the central practices of writing and discussion, instructors can introduce elements of movement, collaboration, performance, or place-based attention.

Here are a few things to try:

- **Group reassembly.** Cut up a published text (into paragraphs, sentences, or lines) and give groups of 3–5 students the task of reassembling the pieces. When reassembly is complete, students walk around the room to compare versions. This naturally leads to a discussion of choices made and reasons guiding these choices. As a final step, students review the published original and interpret choices.

- **Co-write a story word by word.** Consider working in increasingly larger (or increasingly smaller) groups.
- **In-character interviews.** Students take on the persona of a character in their current project and respond to peer questions while attempting to remain in character and invent on the spot as necessary.
- **Read out loud with movement.** Each writer gives the class instructions for ways to move or respond while the writer reads their work out loud. Sample instructions: echo back the word "you" each time you hear it, gradually move from standing to lying on the floor over the course of the reading, close your eyes until you hear the word "light."
- **Elaborative questions**. This is an effective partner exercise where students work together to discuss and deepen their understanding of a central concept. For example, an instructor might spend some time talking about point of view and then ask students pairs to discuss the following questions one at a time:
  - What is point of view?
  - How does it work?
  - Why is it necessary?
  - What are the different types of point of view?
  - What are each of their strengths? Weaknesses?

When students grapple with such questions in real-time, they make connections between new and old ways of knowing or understanding point of view. They also have the chance to follow up with the instructor or peers when they encounter confusion or bump up against concepts they understand differently.

- **Take students to a museum or gallery.** Ask them to choose an artwork or object to observe closely and write in response to. Or take them to a space on campus and ask them to observe how people interact with the built environment. Or take them outside and ask them to pay attention to plants, birds, insects, and other non-human presences.

Presentations

Presentations offer students a chance to bring solitary research and process into the shared space of the class. When students present in class, they practice taking on the role of expert or authority. Often, the experience builds confidence that carries forward into the rest of the course. As elsewhere, clear purpose and well-defined expectations (especially around time!) set the stage for effective presentations.

Sample Assignment

Translation project in context presentation

As a step along the way for your major translation project, you will deliver a formal presentation with a goal of helping the class contextualize your project and support its development and revision. This presentation invites you to practice the skill of speaking clearly to a receptive audience about a work in progress. Presentations will include five components:

1 **Introduce the work you're translating.** What do we need to know about this work (writer, publication environment) to support your workshop?
2 **Discuss your target audience.** What audience will you center in your translation? What does this target audience mean for your translation choices?
3 **Contextualize your project.** Who else is working on similar projects? What ongoing conversations does your project join?
4 **Situate genre and craft.** Introduce a craft keyword and demonstrate its significance in a specific passage.
5 **Preview language challenges.** Introduce one specific language challenge with concrete examples.

Presentations should:

- **Be 10–15 minutes in length.** Practice to make sure that you can fit what you want to say.
- **Include a visual aid (slides or a handout).** Your visual aid need not be elaborate but must include the full text of any passage you're discussing in detail.

Co-teaching, community partnerships, and other experiments

Over the years, we've co-taught with colleagues in our own unit, theater, linguistics, and computer science. Such collaborations involve considerable planning, and often run up against the barriers of disciplinary silos and institutional structures. Still, they can be deeply rewarding. Community partnerships that reach beyond the institution ask—and potentially offer—even more. In the interest of space, we've chosen to feature an interview with Kate Schapira, who has deep experience in this area.

Kate Schapira on getting community partnerships right

You teach courses that involve partnerships both within and beyond the university. Can you tell us about one?

I've been laying groundwork with a community partner for a new course called "Writing Climate, Writing Community." Brown University students will have the opportunity to support the outreach and communication work of a Health Equity Zone working group focused on sea-level-rise-related flooding. First, students will get familiar with the town.

At the same time, we'll have visits from community educators on things like interviewing, non-extractive relations, and research, building the skills students will need to do a good job. Students will then write up some possible things they might like to support and put themselves on offer to the working group. They might work together to make an outreach plan for neighbors, write a series of columns in the local paper, work with the historical society, organize an event, or support an oral history project ... The goal of the course is to ask: how do you write about a community in a way that's situated within the community and led by what's actually going on in town?

What advice would you have for a teacher who wants to start a new collaboration involving a special collections archive or college farm or community organization?

I would say go! If you don't already have a relationship with the organization, go to their volunteer days or their open hours. Become a presence and start a relationship. Before you even talk to your boss, go and keep going back. If you can't make the time to do that, then you do not have time to do this project. And a thousand percent, I guarantee you will learn more about what the project should be, who the people are, and whether the thing that you were thinking about is even necessary. Also, it won't just be "people in zip code 02905." It will be Aaron and Monica and Gina and Ellen. And that will make a real difference in how you set this thing up. As an institution with resources approaching a possible community partner, you always want to start by asking: what do you need and what have you tried?

It's also key to be transparent and communicative with any community partners. If you're going to write stuff and publish it, show it to people. Or consider co-writing. There's a jointly authored paper by Ron Reed and Kari Norgaard about climate and emotion in an Arctic Indigenous community. Ron Reed is a tribal official of that community, and Kari Norgaard is a scientist, and they wrote it together.

Throughout this work, you want to be careful that you're not just community-washing the program or the university. When the program I'm working in said, "We see this as work with a 10-year horizon," I thought, *okay, great, that makes me more willing to do it because it gives everybody time to try to do it right*. There needs to be a time investment, a willingness not to require instant products, or to have products take a different shape than what was originally intended. And a willingness to put up some cash. Another question to keep asking is: how does the project, the course, the conversation, leave value in the community that stays there? We have to keep asking and listening to the answers.

KATE SCHAPIRA teaches non-fiction writing at Brown University and supports local efforts toward environmental justice, climate justice and peer mental health support. Her first work of non-fiction *Lessons from the Climate Anxiety Counseling Booth* offers actionable steps for imagining a radically more livable future in order to bring it into being.

Image credit: Cat Laine

Guiding principles

When designing active learning activities for a class, we keep these guiding principles in mind:

1 **Consider what can be done together that can't be done alone.** Activities like small-group conversations and collaborations make full use of embodied presence.
2 **Time spent building trust and establishing community expectations is essential, not extra.** Instructors may be tempted to cut or bypass these admittedly time-consuming activities when the schedule looks tight, but doing so comes at a serious cost.
3 **As you construct a lesson, consider how one activity or module leads to another within the session (and within the term as a whole).** David Kolb's learning cycle (**Chapter 2**), for example, guides students along an iterative process that involves experience, reflection, conceptualization, and experimentation. How do students move between *doing* and reflecting on what they've done and why? Do they have opportunities to translate specific reflections into concepts they can carry forward?
4 **Remember, planning is essential but plans themselves often need to change.** Leading classes requires planning ahead, but we must also learn to read the room and respond in the moment (see **Chapter 12**).

5

Craft, Culture, Context

Reasons to situate craft terms within cultural and historical contexts

Recent work by Matthew Salesses, Felicia Rose Chavez, Paisley Rekdal, and others has highlighted how thoroughly craft is bound up with culture and underscored the harms of teaching craft as if it were culturally neutral. Having read this excellent work, instructors may find themselves asking, "How do I apply these concepts within my own classroom?" In this chapter, we offer tools for instructors working across levels, genres, and institutional contexts who seek to interrogate and expand their craft vocabularies in response to the diversity of literary practice and the needs and interests of their students.

A writing course may teach craft terms and concepts explicitly or may use them more implicitly within a largely workshop-based structure. In either instance, craft language can easily suggest false universals. In a Poetry Foundation blog post, poet and scholar Timothy Yu discusses his early experiences in writing workshops:

> Workshops followed the standard model: the only texts were the poems of my classmates, perhaps supplemented by a few poems by contemporary or classic poets. I was continually haunted by the sense that I didn't "get" what my instructors and peers were looking for in a poem, but there was really nothing to help me out, other than a vague sense that my tastes were not quite correct or refined enough to help me write at the level of sophistication expected of me. Meanwhile, my classes in literature and sociology were pushing me toward understanding aesthetics and poetics as not eternal absolutes but historical and social constructs, often deeply implicated in, and responsive to, politics. (Yu 2022)

We're struck by two things in this passage. The first is the dramatic contrast Yu lays out between creative writing courses and literature/sociology courses. In his creative writing courses, Yu is given decontextualized model poems and a vague universal vocabulary of craft. In his literature and sociology courses, in contrast, he's taught to see literary movements and their terms as historical, contextual, and political. Our second observation is how easy it was for Yu to assume that the fault lay with him: he felt incorrect, lacking in taste, unrefined, unsophisticated. Understandably, he saw the path to literary criticism as more open to him.

Like Yu, we studied both literature and creative writing. At times, we've felt resistance to the term "craft" and preferred terms like "form" or "technique" without being able to put a finger on why. Eventually, we came to realize that our real resistance was to treating craft terms and practices as: (1) universal, (2) ahistorical, and (3) assumed. Let's unpack this a bit.

1. When we treat a term as **universal**, we act as though it can be applied evenly to everyone everywhere.
2. When our craft language is **ahistorical**, we use the same terms for work composed hundreds of years apart without paying attention to the original context of each piece and how terms change over time and from community to community.
3. When our craft terms are **assumed**, we behave as if we have a shared understanding of what a word like "voice," "image," or "flow" means. But instructors and students come together from diverse communities and arrive with subtly—or even radically—different understandings of what these terms indicate.

Instead, we advocate for an inclusive approach to craft language that is:

- **Specific** to the writer and their individual context (whether the writer is a sixteenth-century Spanish poet or a classmate).
- **Historically engaged**, attentive to both the present and the past (and to how the past lives on in our language, literature, and lives).
- **Discussed and defined** as a group.

Across levels and contexts, we propose that craft terms be taught **critically** (with a spirit of questioning rather than accepting at face value) and **contingently** (with an awareness of plurality, contradictions, and cultural context at work in the terms we choose to talk about how texts make meaning).

Craft language offers a map

If we think of creative work (poems, stories, songs, TV shows, comics, and so on) as a landscape, we might think of the language of craft as a way of mapping that terrain.

Craft language can help us see things we wouldn't otherwise notice

Once we name something and map it across a text, we notice it differently. Learning that enjambment can happen with or against syntax changed Bronwen's relationship to poetry. In addition to seeing short lines and long lines, she suddenly saw lines that worked with grammar and lines that disrupted and pushed against it. The craft terms James Longenbach introduced in *The Art of the Poetic Line* (2007)—end-stopped lines, parsing lines, annotating lines—made her notice poems differently and make more intentional choices in her own poems.

Craft language can help us talk about what we perceive

The more elements we learn to name and recognize, the more prepared we are to discuss what we're perceiving. A shared lexicon lets a class speak with more specificity about one another's work. "Something changed here with who's talking" can be helpful, but "You started in close third-person POV, but this section is moving from mind to mind more like omniscient POV" might totally change a story's trajectory (as long as both people know the relevant POV terms or the class can pause to clarify).

Each craft vocabulary names things that also carry different names for different people

When a place has been occupied by different people over time, a river can have two or more names. Likewise, craft terms overlap and sometimes say more about who is talking than about what's described. We might use two different words to mean roughly the same thing. Do we refer to the third-person point of view as limited, objective, subjective, or free indirect? Or we might use the same word to mean two entirely different things. Unless we pause and talk about our terms, how they came to us, and how we intend them, we may easily find ourselves talking at cross purposes.

We use the word "occupied" intentionally here. How often have colonial names taken over and partly or fully erased the original names of lakes, mountains, cities? How often have English terms been slapped onto Indigenous poems or Japanese stories with no attention to the formal vocabularies of their makers?

A craft language names features that can also be known without naming

Someone who lives in a place may not be able to map that place, but may still have a deep knowledge of it. Likewise, someone might be able to use craft elements without explicitly naming them or even recognizing exactly what they're doing. All too often, a language of craft has been used as a bludgeon. Being able to define "free indirect discourse" might be useful, but not knowing the term won't prevent an attentive writer from being able to execute this style of narration beautifully.

Any craft language relies on reduction and distortion

No map can show everything at once. One might show topography, another political boundaries. But there's always more that could be shown, always more to be known, more to be discovered than any map can fully represent. Likewise, our interpretations and discussions can't pay attention to everything at once. When we talk about the structure of a novel, its syntax and sounds temporarily retreat to the background.

When we discuss texts, we draw maps based on our interests. We always direct attention to some things and let others fade. Classrooms must make space for multiple visions, multiple priorities, multiple maps.

Every craft language is cultural, political, and contested

Nothing on a map is neutral. Which way is "up"? What culture's place names are used? Where are the borders drawn? Likewise, craft terms and perceptions of craft are cultural, political, historical, and contested. When we talk about "the speaker of the poem," for example, we're assuming a version of poetry that foregrounds a dramatized persona, which applies to some poems but not all.

In fact, an ill-fitting term can be an obstacle to having a good conversation, whether we're looking at published work or a student draft. To contextualize a term like "speaker of the poem," we might bring in examples where the speaker of the poem feels close to the writer, examples where the speaker is clearly a persona separate from the writer, and examples that collage sound or visual elements and don't dramatize a unified speaking presence at all. Now we're having a conversation. Students can now make informed choices about whether the term "speaker" is useful for the work they want to make.

Considerations for assigning craft readings

In assigning craft readings, consider possible purposes, such as:

- Introduce key terms and provide examples.
- Offer close readings of specific examples that model for students how to notice formal details.
- Offer strong polemics that students can argue for and against productively.
- Offer contrasting points of emphasis and take positions that illustrate current debates in the field.

Especially when working with introductory courses, think carefully about how much of a craft reading students would benefit from and how the reading connects directly to the learning outcomes for the course and the class session. Although it might feel simplest to assign a fifteen-page craft essay as homework reading, students might derive more benefit from seeing a single paragraph projected on the board in class and spending time unpacking it sentence by sentence.

Across levels, take time to consider which voices you're prioritizing. When a course has a rich array of voices represented in primary texts but all craft or theoretical texts are by white writers (or male writers or straight writers), the course risks giving a false impression that only a certain kind of person is capable of theorizing and reflecting. Any craft text is always also sending messages about culture, who can be a writer, and who matters as a reader.

System building and system critique

In thinking of craft language as a map, we might consider all of the ways we use a map. Sometimes we follow a map carefully to reach a destination. Sometimes we scrawl a map on the back of an envelope to show a friend how to find the restaurant where we'll meet later—major roads and landmarks are all we need. Or perhaps we map out plans for a garden: carrots here and runner beans along the wall, a map of what will be. Sometimes we look at a map and question everything: Why does Oklahoma have a panhandle? Why are so many things around the world named Humboldt? The answers to these questions take us deep into history and politics.

Sometimes we follow a map, sometimes we make a map, and sometimes we question or critique a map. These can all be valuable approaches to craft as well.

Instructors need to support students in both **system building** and **system critique**. A system or structure helps us organize what we know and carry it forward with us. As we discuss with James M. Lang in **Chapter 4**, networks, structures, and systems allow students to categorize, contextualize, and integrate new learning. The key terms and modules that make up a course give students a structure to which they can attach emergent insights that might otherwise be lost in a floating soup of new concepts and details.

But any system emphasizes some things at the expense of others and is subject to question and critique. Any term has nuance and contradiction when we dig into it. Any approach sheds light on some questions while obscuring others.

In each class setting, we must pay attention to where students are in their learning and what will best serve them. We need to ask: "How can I present a useful structure without letting it become dogmatic or monolithic?" and "How do I support students in questioning and critiquing key terms and concepts without leaving them feeling confused, overwhelmed, or abandoned?"

To return to the map metaphor, it's misleading to pass out a map and say, "This is the only true map!" But it can be equally unhelpful to give a beginning student five different maps and say, "These are all possibilities—good luck on your journey!"

A good start lies in simply acknowledging that systems and structures are always partial and subject to critique. An instructor might tell a screenwriting class, "All characters must have a want, a desire, and a need." Or, they might say, "One way of thinking about character development that I've found useful is want–desire–need. Let's look at how this structure plays out in a few examples." Here are some ways to build fluency and capacity with an initial structure:

- **Work with a published text that offers a supportive example.** The instructor invites students to identify elements in a script they've all read. Students then share their observations. They might notice what elements they identify differently and perhaps pull up specific passages as supporting evidence.
- **Work with a published text that offers a challenging example.** Students analyze a script where one or more key elements from the structure seem to be "missing" and talk about why that might be the case and what the effect is.
- **Students use the structure to map their own drafts.** In mapping and analyzing their drafts, students might notice something "missing" or "unclear" and decide to make revisions or additions. Or they might push back against the structure as not apt for their purposes. Both can be valuable responses.

Once students grasp an initial structure, nuance and space for questioning can be introduced in several ways.

- **Ask students to draw on knowledge and experience from beyond the course.** An instructor might simply ask, "Does anyone else have another system we might use for thinking about character?" and be ready to talk about role-playing game alignment charts from Dungeons & Dragons or whatever else students bring to the table.
- **Historicize/contextualize the system or key term.** An instructor brings in documents (historical or contemporary) that define or introduce the structure they're using. For a conversation about poetic images, an instructor might present and contextualize Ezra Pound's "A Few Don'ts by an Imagiste" and invite students to read the manifesto carefully and critically.
- **Invite students to look for gaps or lack of fit.** Invite critique and questions by asking, "How might want–desire–need as a system to develop character miss something important or fail to explain characters we find compelling?"
- **Present an alternate structure.** The instructor presents an alternative approach and says, "Here's another structure for thinking about character. How does it place emphasis differently?"

All of these activities involve wrestling with knowledge construction that builds on an initial framework. This is the "big ideas" work we discuss in **Chapter 1**. Depending on students' background experience and comprehension, we decide when the group will benefit from an activity to reinforce their understanding of a system (system building) and when they're ready to question and complicate (system critique).

A beginning poetry course might introduce four key terms and spend the whole semester reinforcing them, whereas a graduate poetry course might begin with collectively mapping poetics terms on a white board and discussing how these terms overlap and where understandings differ. Advanced students might take system critique one step further with a **Craft Across Contexts Exercise** that explicitly asks them to compare and contrast multiple perspectives on a key term (also a useful exercise for instructors designing a new class).

As we reiterate in **Chapter 1**, a course can't do everything. A course focused on generative writing might not engage deeply with craft vocabulary, much less with critiquing and contextualizing a craft lexicon. Yet, every course can cultivate awareness that any craft vocabulary (whether derived from classical rhetoric or invented collectively as a class) is made by people to help name what we notice, organize our thinking, and make arguments about what matters to us.

Sample Assignment

Craft across contexts

This exercise invites you to interrogate and contextualize a specific craft concept relevant to your current project as part of your revision process.

Step One:

Select a specific craft element or technique central to your project. Go for something like metaphor, omniscient narration, conflict, or voice. It should be particular enough to be manageable (i.e., not creative non-fiction or prose) but meaty enough to have some complexity.

Step Two:

Identify and consult at least three different craft books (or essays or articles or interviews) that introduce (or define, discuss, illustrate, etc.) this term. At least one should come from a perspective that has historically been marginalized. You might also return to sources that have shaped your current understanding of this term.

Step Three:

Analyze each source. Contrast them with one another.

Possible questions to consider:

- How much range/consensus did you find across the various sources?
- Who is the intended audience of each text? How can you tell?
- When was the text published? Republished or revised? Does anything in it feel dated?
- What examples/models does each writer use to illustrate the concept?
- To what extent does each writer address differences in audience or culture?
- What other terms come up in the same conversations or map differently onto similar terrain? (For example, one piece might talk about point of view, while another might instead talk about perspective, or psychic distance. Or one writer might use voice and tone interchangeably, while another might make a point of distinguishing between them.)

- How does this element or technique emerge from or align with particular historical or contemporary literary contexts or movements?
- What social or political claims have been made involving this element? (i.e., "Free verse poems are liberatory, while fixed form poems are constraining" or "genre fiction does x, literary fiction does y.")

Use these questions as a guide to notice and question. You might make some messy notes, underline or make marginal comments, or come up with a big list.

Step Four:

Out of everything you've noticed, what's interesting and what matters? How might you apply what you've learned in asking for peer feedback or shaping your next revision? Write up a synthesis of roughly 250 words.

We can't talk about craft without talking about audience

Any conversation about craft is also an implicit (or, preferably, explicit) conversation about audience. Confusing *to whom*? Defamiliarizing *for whom*? Subverts *whose* expectations?

As beginning writers, students might think they're writing "for everyone" or maybe "for no one but themselves." But as writers mature in our craft, we come up against the fact that there is no universal "everyone" to receive our work, no universal work we might make that would speak with equal power to "everyone." We start to think not of "the reader," but of actual readers.

Often, however, writing classes don't discuss audience directly or acknowledge the plurality of possible audiences. Poet Chris Green writes, "we owe it to our students to examine how texts actually exist and are used in the world beyond the workshop. The workshop needs to address lived situations rather than assuming and perpetuating the presence of a falsely sublime (generally a white, educated, middle class) reader" (2001, 162). Green invites teachers to consider how poems are actually used by people who read and write them across different contexts and communities and how writing workshops and classes might respect and support this full range of practice.

Rather than invoking "the reader" as a vague presence, we might help students imagine a specific embodied audience by sharing examples like the following passage where Barbara Jane Reyes contextualizes her choices in *Letters to a Young Brown Girl*:

> This romantic notion we grew up with, of putting our work out there and being discovered by big heavies as the next hot thing, writing as if that is the goal—it's been a relief to reject this outright, in favor of addressing who I've been meaning to address: my younger self, a young woman of color who is so angry, looking for herself out there in books, films, and art, and finding minor characters afflicted by white love. It is not a

> new idea by any means, to stay ground-level in the community and create art centering the community, speaking in the languages of the community. My poetic forebears have done this for decades. (2020)

Reyes locates herself within a long tradition of community-focused writing, identifies her ideal reader as "a young woman of color," and positions her approach as an alternative to waiting to be "discovered by big heavies as the next hot thing." Her model invites students to claim similar agency. Or, as poet Harryette Mullen explores in her essay "Imagining the Unimagined Reader: Writing to the Unborn and Including the Excluded," students might take pleasure in "contemplating unknown readers who inhabit a future [they] will not live to see" (Mullen 1999, 199).

When pushed to think about audience, some students realize that they compose with an imagined judge (a dismissive former teacher or snobby critic) in mind and have to work to imagine a more hospitable audience, an ideal reader whose receptive ear will let them make the work they feel called to make. Other students think of audience as "everyone" and find it helpful to focus on a single reader, such that writing a story carries the intimacy and precision of writing a letter. Some students might begin to create a composite ideal reader that crystallizes over several drafts, rather than imagining their audience at the start of the project. If they can write effectively to a specific reader, they come to realize, it's likely that other readers will connect with the work.

Of course, while students work to envision ideal readers, they're also working with actual readers: the instructor, structurally positioned as an expert or judge, and classmates, a large group or a small one, homogeneous or diverse along any number of axes (race, class, age, ability, language background, etc.). Like John Warner (**Chapter 2**), we're mindful of the pitfall of writing "something that will do well in the workshop," a reason Warner "distrust[s] the workshop model as a pedagogical center for creative writing courses." He said, "I discourage any writer from thinking of the workshop as their audience. We're hunting bigger game than that." We've found that open conversations about the plurality of possible audiences and contexts and invitations to position their work as part of a broader conversation can help students see their instructor and peers as supporters of work that reaches for a horizon beyond the course.

Here are some revelations students arrive at when invited to think and talk explicitly about audience:

- I can choose who I'm writing for. I get to decide what to explain and what to assume, what style or voice to adopt.
- Not everyone has to understand or enjoy my writing (and in fact, it's not possible to make work that would be universally understood and enjoyed).
- When I'm reading peer work, I may not be the target audience and might need to do some extra work to be able to offer useful feedback.
- When I'm reading peer work, sometimes I am the perfect reader, and all of the things that have felt strange or isolating about me are what make me uniquely able to engage with their work.

In **Chapter 7**, we dig more deeply into the relationship between target audience and peer feedback and offer strategies for coaching students to be supportive readers capable of imagining an audience beyond themselves and agentic writers able to draw on the unique insights of each reader.

A few questions for exploring audience with students through reading

- How do audience choices manifest formally in this text? What can we point to on the page?
- Audience is rarely singular. Looking closely, can you detect an awareness of plural, split, or multiple audiences?
- How does this text handle culturally specific vocabulary?
    - What words (if any) did you look up? What about words or phrases that you guessed at based on context?
    - What kind of work does it ask readers to do, depending on their background/familiarity with its material?
- Do you find yourself responding differently to pop culture or Tagalog references than you do to Ancient Greek or Shakespearean ones?
- What does it mean to read a text as someone who does not belong to the community centered in the writing (whether because we're from the future or because we belong to a different cultural context)?

Writing what you know, writing what you don't know

Just as students benefit from considering a target audience for their work, they often need support in considering: (1) how the material they're writing connects with their own lived experiences, and (2) how the material they're writing reaches beyond them.

Some students may feel entitled to write about any and all material with little thought to how their lack of knowledge or familiarity might lead them to perpetuate harmful stereotypes. We've also encountered students who are so nervous about appropriating or causing offense that they attempt to write in a way that only touches or draws on their own experiences. But no individual is an island. As Jess Row shows in *White Flights: Race, Fiction, and the American Imagination* (2019), avoidance and isolation carry their own harms.

There's no pure position to write from in which our writing doesn't touch anyone else and we have no ethical mandate. Writing always draws on what we know and extends into what we don't (yet) know. Drawing on examples from Paisley Rekdal and others, we shift classroom conversations away from oversimplifications around what each person is "allowed" to write. Instead, we invite students to focus on: (1) why they feel drawn to this material, and (2) how to engage with the material responsibly (which can involve both practical and ethical concerns). In **Chapter 9** we offer a deeper consideration of the role research can play in creative writing as well as some concrete assignment strategies.

Billy-Ray Belcourt on teaching craft at the intersection of Indigenous Studies

You teach creative writing with an Indigenous focus across undergrad and grad levels. How do you approach key terms and craft vocabulary?

I introduce students to both literary craft concepts and key terms in Indigenous Studies, so I try as much as possible to illuminate how they intersect and modify one another. For example, I teach a unit on the processes of dispossession through which the University of British Columbia came into being. Students read institutional texts that articulate this history in ways that don't fully account for the violence of land seizure or give space to Musqueam knowledge. I pair this discussion with craft lessons on erasure poetry and introduce students to erasure as a method to intervene in official state and/or institutional language. People and histories are erased and so we can unearth and make visible their presence through literary acts, however humbly. In this way, students encounter a craft technique in a sociological context as well as a sociological context that can be engaged with in a literary way.

Can you tell us about an experience—as a student, writer, or teacher—in which the craft vocabulary at hand felt insufficient or inaccurate for the material?

When I was first trying to write a novel, it became obvious to me that the craft knowledge I had accrued about novels and fiction was limiting my creative horizons. That is, I had taken on a notion of the novel as an individualizing technology. I wanted to write a novel that felt communal, that didn't simply chart one protagonist's emotional journey. I hadn't taken creative writing courses, so this education in the novel was mostly improvised and unorganized. In order to write the novel I wanted to write, I had to trust my instinct that I didn't have to be allegiant to plot and limited perspective; I had to allow myself to be experimental and messy (and much to my relief, I later realized that there was a brilliant tradition of these kinds of novels with which I could align myself and from which I could learn a great deal).

Can you share an example of a specific keyword you've introduced that helped students make a leap in their writing or thinking?

I designed a poetry course primarily about methodology to guide emerging poets toward developing a writing practice into which certain methodological processes could be embedded. I stressed that by methodology I meant a system or procedure that makes specific kinds of writing and/or research possible. I broadened the term to also include forms that have pre-existing rules (like sonnets). At the end of the term, a student wrote in their evaluation that being asked to think about poems as having methodologies that can be sustained over time opened up new terrain for them. My hope was to encourage students to experiment with ways to generate poems that don't rely solely on spontaneous thought but also and alongside methodological traditions that they can make use of and adjust. They were also empowered to invent their own procedures and protocol, which many in fact did.

What are some approaches you might use to contextualize or historicize a formal mode with a deep and complex tradition?

I teach a unit on the sonnet, a form that has a long and well-documented history. I go over that history but don't limit it to the invention of the form and the key players—instead, I linger on the larger political landscape of Europe and the world in the sixteenth and seventeenth centuries, which is to say the landscape of imperialism. I ask students to open up an epistemic frame in which to hold the sonnet's tradition alongside the beginning of the Trans-Atlantic Slave Trade and the new humanism that accompanied it. I teach contemporary sonnets by Black poets that disrupt and reimagine the form as a space to insist on Black freedom and life. A form, I thus emphasize, can be remade in order to address social injustice.

BILLY-RAY BELCOURT is from the Driftpile Cree Nation. An Associate Professor and Canada Research Chair in the UBC School of Creative Writing, Belcourt is the author of five books, including *A Minor Chorus* and *Coexistence*. He has been awarded the Griffin Poetry Prize, the City of Edmonton Book Prize, and two BC and Yukon Book Prizes.

Image credit: Jaye Simpson

Teaching form and technique contextually

It's clear that the content of a poem, story, screenplay, or creative non-fiction piece is culturally inflected: What race are the characters? Where is the story set? What social registers does the work use and what are its reference points? It can surprise students, however, to be asked to think of craft, form, and technique as similarly culturally located.

Forms like the haiku, the sonnet, and the ghazal emerged in particular times and places and have traveled and transformed across long histories of translation and reinterpretation. Likewise, techniques like present-tense narration and close third-person point of view have held different meanings across time and place. What does this mean for instructors?

If we ask students to write a haiku, we might spend a moment talking about Japanese haiku tradition, the rise of anglophone interest in haiku following World War II, and debates over how best to render haiku in English given linguistic and cultural differences. While we may not always have time for a deep dive into the history of the sonnet or the role of oral traditions across cultures, we keep the following approaches and interventions in mind.

- **When presenting model texts from across time and place, avoid flattening them.**
    - A poetry course might offer a unit on the love poem that places poems by Sappho, Elizabeth Barret Browning, Frank O'Hara, and Danez Smith alongside one another. How amazing and thrilling that texts from the past can still speak to us! And how fascinating, perhaps, to observe a shared language of praise across these poems. An instructor might show multiple translations of Sappho, discuss the publication history of *Sonnets from the Portuguese*, look at images of painters O'Hara collaborated with, or play a video of Smith reading and discussing their work. (For more on contextualizing readings, see **Chapter 6**.)
- **Call into question any elitism and cultural snobbery in conversations of craft and technique.**
    - If students refer to sci-fi as trashy or describe performance poetry as a lesser form than written poems, invite them to dig more deeply into the norms and contexts that inform their reactions.
- **Design course structures that offer students opportunities to incorporate forms, techniques, and approaches from the contexts and discourse communities they find meaningful.**
    - As instructors, we may be asked to stretch beyond our own aesthetics and education. And we might need to practice being okay with not being the expert (as well as doing our own homework to support students in their chosen work).
- **Especially in upper-level courses, invite students to contextualize the formal gestures that show up in their writing. Students might consider questions like:**
    - Where does this (form, technique, approach) come from?
    - In what context was it initially meaningful?
    - How has it changed along the way?
    - What does it mean to include it in my work?
    - What ethical considerations should I keep in mind in using it?

Possibilities for collaborative knowledge creation

Across this chapter, we've advocated for a relationship to craft terms that is critical, curious, and attentive to cultural and historical context. As instructors, we often propose a structure or system to help students organize and retain new knowledge. Other times, we devote class time to an iterative process of co-constructing key terms. In both instances, we remain open to ways students might complicate, clarify, or question structures and systems based on their collective wealth of literary and lived experiences. Here are some guiding principles and key decisions that inform our teaching of craft, form, and technique across levels.

Introduce craft concepts as relative, not universal

Instructors can make a universal claim like "A protagonist needs to be a 'round character' who changes by the end of the story," or we can say something like "Many stories in this tradition hinge on a key choice that leaves a character changed." In the first instance, we're setting up a false impression of universality in a field characterized by radical and significant differences. In the second, we're offering students a structure, acknowledging that this structure is based on a specific context, and inviting developing writers to try out a technique and see how it serves them. It's impossible to teach all possible approaches and contexts in a single course, not to mention that students would quickly become overwhelmed. But we can always teach in a way that acknowledges the breadth of what we're *not* including as well as the richness and value of what we are. This acknowledgement can be as simple as introducing "SOME screenwriting or songwriting devices" rather than "THE screenwriting or songwriting devices."

Present possibilities and choices rather than rules

Writing instructors sometimes present a rule or aphorism like "Show, don't tell!" It's pithy, memorable, and easily repeated. But what does it really mean? And what are students likely to do with it, especially when discussing one another's work? To be sure, a beginning writer's story or poem would often benefit from more concrete, sensory detail. But an aphoristic rule like this can easily become a shortcut that avoids deeper interrogation. Show, don't tell, a student might think, cutting a line in a story where she risked a bold, risky, and effective emotional insight. "Show, don't tell," a student might tell a peer, pointing to an exquisitely crafted paragraph of exposition in a personal essay.

Instead of presenting a rule like "show, don't tell," an instructor can say "One way to make your writing rich and evocative is to use concrete sensory details, and we're going to try that today." Now the students have a goal (to make rich and evocative writing) and an approach to try out (using concrete sensory details). As they move forward in their writing, they can return to this combination of goal and approach as choice rather than orthodoxy.

Another aphorism that shows up in our classes is, "You have to know the rules in order to break them." To this, we say, "Whose rules?" With so many different traditions, norms, and expectations to draw on, what rules could possibly require universal adherence? A student focused on "breaking the rules" positions themself in an antagonistic counterrelationship to something they don't like (or don't understand or feel like engaging with) rather than paying attention to the (often significant and historical) body of work aligned with their aesthetic goals. Instead, we frame craft in terms of possibilities and choices, traditions and expectations. We encourage students to identify the broader conversations they see their writing participating in and to select their own models and key terms. As Alex Marzano-Lesnevich said in our conversation (**Chapter 9**), "Once you see it, you can sharpen it. You can amplify choices about it. And if a tool's not useful, you get to throw it away." Similar to Tessa McWatt, we "ask writers what they'd like the experience of the reader to be." In allying ourselves with a student's vision, we can offer practical methods to deepen their work.

Tessa McWatt on diversifying narrative craft

How do you approach discussions of narrative craft with students who write from a diversity of cultural, literary, and aesthetic traditions?

Craft is culturally determined. Not all cultures or writing traditions have concerns about narrative arcs and Aristotelian principles of rising tension and catharsis. Nor do they have the individual protagonist as the main driving force of the story. This focus on the individual is western (European based), capitalist, and is at the center of many contentious issues for Black and Brown people from cultures around the world. Many storytelling traditions outside of the European tradition involve collective rather than individual struggles in how stories are told. They also might engage in structural shapes that challenge the notion of the arc.

For this reason, it's important not to assume craft as universal in any way, and to allow students to write from their own traditions while also being aware of the market they might be trying to be published within. It can be a matter of offering them an understanding of the contradictions inherent in so-called "diversity" in publishing. It is crucial to the livelihood and growth of literature to do more than just welcome the diversity of positions, aesthetics, ontologies and world views into the consciousness of each and every writer. Not only do these positions and aesthetics foster a fair and inclusive workshop environment, but they are also a gift to all writers, who should be open and perpetually learning from new epistemologies and methods. How bereft literature would be if this were not the case.

What are some of the approaches you might suggest to mentor a student who writes from a tradition you don't have deep experience with?

My strategy is to LISTEN, to understand their traditions, to get them to tell me what I should be looking for in their writing. To trust that they are the experts in their cultural approaches and to work with them in a decolonized way to have them take center position and for me to respond to them and the needs they have of me. We usually find a way to understand each other, and I learn more than I could have imagined. The experience is humbling and important to me as a writer. Each time my craft ideas are challenged, I have incorporated new concepts into my practice and my teaching, allowing for many forms and structures to be a part of craft.

TESSA MCWATT is a Professor of Creative Writing at the University of East Anglia. She is the author of seven novels and two books for young people. She won the Eccles British Library Award for *Shame on Me: An Anatomy of Race and Belonging*, which also won the Bocas Prize for Non-Fiction.

Image credit: Bill Knight

Engage with craft across all course texts

In *Ordinary Notes* (2023), Christina Sharpe identifies "a certain mode of reading connected to a tradition of colonial practices in which every book by any Black writer appears as sociology" (147). In this mode, "all of that book's explorations, its meaning, and its ambitions lodge in a place called identity" (147). Sharpe describes two ways this happens: directly "as in, *in this book about identity*" (147) and indirectly "by way of excepting a particular Black writer from this dreaded trap by writing that they 'bravely' eschew identity" (147).

Unfortunately, we've observed both tendencies in creative writing teaching. An instructor might turn from a rich discussion of technique in Virginia Woolf to talk about how important Zora Neale Hurston is for Black identity (without digging into the myriad examples of skillful craft at work in *Their Eyes Were Watching God*). Or an instructor might assign work by an Asian American poet working in an avant-garde tradition and praise them for "getting beyond identity." In either case, instructors assign powerful work by racialized writers and yet, as Sharpe writes, "decant all complexity, all invention into that thing they name identity that they imagine is both not complex and not relevant to them" (147). What a loss.

More frequently, creative writing instructors seek to diversify their syllabi by adding writers working in traditions, languages, and contexts unfamiliar to them. But unless they take on the challenge of research—reading writer interviews, following up on scholarship, history, popular culture, and so on, thus expanding their own craft vocabularies and reference points—they may find it easier to follow students' impulse to talk about *what* rather than taking them one step further into *how* and *why*. We owe it to our students not only to engage with a diverse array of voices, but to immerse ourselves in their worlds sufficiently to speak to their formal gestures and meaning-making strategies.

Teach craft concepts in dialogue, not in isolation

Students (and instructors) can be tempted to isolate and oversimplify a specific craft element. "Present tense narration is more immediate," someone might say, or "Short lines make a poem feel breathless and speedy."

But like elements in a chemical reaction, no single craft element works alone. It's the combination, the reaction between elements, that makes meaning. Present-tense narration might function to varying effects depending on point of view. Short lines can be read in diametrically opposite ways depending on how line breaks align with syntax. Instructors need to help students hold this complexity as they grow in their craft.

We can model complexity by sharing concrete examples in which a common formal gesture combines with others to varying effects. A poetry instructor might bring in poems by e.e. cummings, Lucille Clifton, Rupi Kaur, and Jos Charles that all employ a lowercase "i". Through discussion, students realize that they interpret the formal gesture of declining to capitalize "i" in different ways based on their own literary and lived experiences. To one, it's a sign of intimacy evocative of a diary, to another, a gesture evoking the casualness and abbreviations of text conversations. A third finds it pretentious or associates it with Instagram poetry. Furthermore, they notice that cummings, Clifton, Kaur, and Charles all achieve different effects through lineation, diction, syntax, orthography, and other craft elements in play. The lowercase "i" has no single stable meaning; instead, it takes on meaning in dialogue with the collective formal gestures of each poem.

Consider when to lead with definitions and when to start with examples

We can teach craft deductively from definitions and we can teach craft inductively from examples. Often, we do some combination of both.

- In introductory courses when students are most in need of creating a system to organize and retain new knowledge, we typically begin with definitions (supported by clear examples).
- In upper-level undergraduate courses, we might give students a packet of poems or three short stories gathered around a shared craft keyword like "pattern" or "voice" and invite them to identify moments where they see this keyword exemplified.
    - Over time, we might take these examples one step further and ask students to derive craft principles or takeaways based on their cumulative observations.
- A course in which students have a shared depth of experience in the genre at hand might begin by inviting participants to speak to craft terms they've found meaningful for understanding their work.

In each instance, we avoid treating craft terms as assumed in any way that might leave participants at a loss or speaking at cross purposes.

A student perspective: Danny Ramadan on learning craft and when to question it

As a student in grad fiction, you were noted for both your enthusiasm for craft and your willingness to question or challenge specific terms. Can you talk about that experience?

During my time as a student, I came to realize that I had limited time. A short time to train, enhance, and upgrade my writing techniques. I came to the program knowing that I was talented—I had published a novel already, to moderate success. What I knew was that talent was not enough for a continuously growing career as an author. Think of it like a carpenter: someone can have the most beautiful vision of what a grand stylish chair looks like, but unless they know how to choose the right wood, use the right tools, match the right materials, and calculate the exact balance: that chair will never stand on its own four legs.

So, I came in greedy for knowledge. I had a specific image of what my future looked like and a path to reach it. I also specifically wanted to be a Brown, Queer, Refugee author. I had to question craft tools not only through the lens of my own talent, but also through my other identities. Any craft terms that were useful, I treated as tools to enhance my talent. Any craft tools that felt outdated, or did not answer to my intersectionality, I challenged. Otherwise, what's the point of spending two years out of my adult life doing this work at a university level? I would better spend my time writing the next book.

Can you talk about creating a narrative structure that reflects the context and culture you are writing from and towards?

The structure of my novel *The Foghorn Echoes* is the energy bouncing back and forth between my two main characters like echoes. The book follows two boys separated by distance and dismays; yet they feed off of one another while the book builds upon both of these narratives. If I hadn't had the structure in mind, I would not have been able to accomplish a balanced narrative between the two main characters.

As a new adjunct professor, how do you approach discussions of craft so that students from all cultural communities feel like they can speak meaningfully about their own aesthetics and contexts?

Firstly, I try to be as unapologetically myself as possible when I enter the classroom. I am an educator, but I am also a queer Brown man with a refugee background. These identities I cannot leave at the door. Academia is not always the most welcoming space for diverse experiences, but bringing an authentic representation of who I am to the creative writing room allows others the comfort to bring their own authentic selves.

This is reflected in the way I dress and speak, as well as in the material I choose for the students to read. I especially focus on offering work by other authors from marginalized communities whenever possible. I also do not shy away from conversations about racial expectations and stereotypes, cultural appropriation, pink washing, and other intricate discussions that concern the writing community in the room.

Secondly, I tend to play the improv game of "Yes-and?" with my students. When a student offers an idea that's reflective of their culture, heritage, background and/or contexts, I agree with it, affirm it, build upon it, and open the room for more discussion based on it. I especially focus on creating an environment where authors of marginalized communities feel like the experts on their own identities, while receiving an affirming education on how to enhance their talent with craft tools.

At the end of the day, I am not trying to create replicas of myself in the Canadian literature scene. If anything, I'm denying the world the pearls of these wonderful authors if I erase their identities and replace them with my standards and aesthetics. My job as an educator is to help these students become the best version of their creative selves they can be.

DANNY RAMADAN is a Syrian-Canadian author and LGBTQ-refugees advocate. His latest novel, *The Foghorn Echoes* won the Lambda Award. His memoir *Crooked Teeth* was released May 2024. Ramadan has raised over $300,000 for LGBTQ+ identifying refugees.

Image credit: Amanda Palmer

Choose terms with care

We can emphasize the technical ("This is iambic pentameter") or lead with connection ("Sounds make a difference in how we experience a poem"). When are specific craft terms useful and when are technical terms alienating? Repeatedly, in creating a syllabus, designing an assignment sheet, planning a lecture, or structuring a discussion, we consider our audience and what specific terms and touchstones will mean for them.

- Advanced students might benefit from digging into terms with a rich history behind them like elegy, catharsis, or the uncanny or take pleasure in being able to recognize and identify anapestic meter.
- Introductory students can quickly become overwhelmed or intimidated by technical terms. Knowing this, we might structure a course around more inviting lay terms.
    - For a course of students with varying degrees of familiarity with poetry and different aesthetics, we might introduce specificity, intimacy, sound, pattern, surprise, excess/restraint, and insight as "seven pleasures of poetry."
    - In a generative multi-genre course, we might adopt memory, observation, research, material, and invention as structuring terms.

Classrooms aren't the only context where writers make careful choices about how to map the craft landscape. In his introduction to *How We Do It: Black Writers on Craft, Practice, and Skill* (2023), editor Jericho Brown talks through the volume's structure:

> *How We Do It* is divided into eight sections, with a range of essays in each: "Who Your People?," "What You Got?," "Where You At?," "How You Living?," "What It Look Like?," "Who You With?," "How to Read," and "Going Back." The titles here are intended to communicate the fact that these sections could not be narrowed down to the kind of jargon with which writers are accustomed. We weren't going to name the sections "voice," "tone," "setting," "character," or "good advice" because every essay here gets at more than any single topic. "Who Your People?," for instance, includes meditations on characterization and speech (2).

Brown deliberately redraws a map here. Carefully chosen section titles evoke Black vernacular, gesture to the breadth of each contribution, and announce the book as making new and particular contributions to craft discourse.

As a book like *How We Do It* underscores, each genre has its own traditions, and writers can find it provocative and revelatory to carry craft terms across genre contexts. A conversation with a playwriting colleague might leave a poet meditating on the difference between "poetic turn" and "dramatic reversal." Teaching in a program that encourages genre cross-training has given us a deep appreciation for the cross-pollination and generative wrestling with craft that happens in a room that brings poets, essayists, novelists, song-writers, and TV-writers together.

Whether teaching beginners or accomplished writers, each time we invite our students to map the rich and unruly worlds of literary production, we pause and ask ourselves: What does this term evoke? What might it help us notice? What might it obscure?

6

Working with Models and Mentor Texts

The case for connecting writing and reading

Books are made out of books. Writing is always in dialogue both with the world and with other writing. We encourage students to consider these two main sources that might inspire their work: life and art. Some writers pull source material directly from their lives, whereas others approach their lived experiences indirectly: the pain they experienced in the loss of a loved one is transmuted into a character's similar but distinct loss. We invite students to embrace mining life experiences as fair game in writing.

So, too, art experiences. Stories, poems, and essays take on meaning in conversation with one another and in how they echo, extend, and subvert the expectations created by historical and contemporary examples. We ask students to bring their life- and text-landscapes into classroom conversations, whether the texts they're in dialogue with include song lyrics, sitcoms, or Sappho. Such engagement, Rhetoric and Composition professor Kevin Roozen suggests, is "a key first step toward teachers acknowledging, valuing, and fostering connections with the different kinds of texts that animate learners' lives beyond the classroom" (Roozen 2015b, 46). With this in mind, we begin by thinking of the classroom as a site of mutual discovery and exchange rather than a site of delivery and reception.

The **Exploration of Inspirations and Influences**, for example, invites students to identify sources of influence and inspiration and reflect on how these sources show up in their writing. The assignment highlights three important facts:

1 Influence can be complicated and can involve friction.
2 Both influence and inspiration cross lines of genre and medium.
3 Writers need to go in search of inspiration rather than waiting for it to find us.

Felicia Rose Chavez shared a similar assignment from her teaching practice, drawing on Austin Kleon's Family Tree exercise:

> Students identify an artistic mentor (the tree trunk), then research who influenced that mentor. Steven King? Coretta Scott King? Great. Now research who influenced those influences, on and on until they run out of time (these folks serve as the ever-expanding

branches). They design a tree sculpture that features the best, most interesting stuff. I then ask: How does your work in this course pay homage to your artistic mentor? How are you sampling from, extending, or enlivening your mentor's legacy?

Along with inviting students to draw on the full breadth of their artistic influences, we also encourage them to dig deeply into the particularities of the genre and context in which they're writing. A fiction student who's been exclusively influenced by examples from film and TV will benefit from a closer acquaintance with the particular affordances and challenges of the short story. They may find that a moment of interiority is more effective than a described "reaction shot." Likewise, a student with a passionate appreciation for Keats and Wordsworth will benefit from greater familiarity with poetry published within their own lifetime, with a focus, perhaps, on poets engaging with the legacy of British Romanticism.

When the writing classroom is not enriched with a range of voices beyond the class, it risks becoming a vacuum cut off from the contexts in which students' writing makes its meaning or an echo chamber reinforcing the dominant preoccupations and aesthetics of the group. And, as any woman in a workshop of men, or students of color in a workshop of white students, can attest, this echo chamber can quickly become a lonely and constrictive space. In contrast, a classroom that considers a range of model texts and engages with craft and style, politics and ethics, invites students to weigh possibilities and make informed choices. As we discussed in **Chapter 4**, having a clear policy on content notes helps students feel emotionally safe and empowered to make decisions in how they interact with readings.

Sample Assignment

Exploration of inspirations and influences

As writers, our work is shaped by a range of influences and inspirations. Some are conscious, whereas others remain invisible to us until someone points them out. Some are chosen, while others derive from our origins or subject position. This assignment invites you to:

- Pursue new models and possibilities
- Meditate on current and enduring inspirations
- Grapple with influences—generative and constraining

Requirements

Identify 10–15 sources of influence and/or inspiration. Aim for at least one in each of the following categories:

- A book of poems by a living poet
- A specific poem published before 1945
- A song, painting, film, or other non-written artwork
- A source encountered before the age of 12
- A source you have conflicted or antagonistic feelings toward

For each item, write a roughly 250-word entry that includes the following:

- An introduction to/description of the source written for someone unfamiliar with it.
- A reflection that discusses how the source shows up in your work or thinking, what *specifically* about it influences or inspires you, and how it helps or hinders your writing. Use direct quotes (from the source and/or your own work) when appropriate.

Assessment

This assignment will be evaluated based on the degree to which it:

- Satisfies required parameters (number of entries, types of sources).
- Describes sources of inspiration and influence in clear engaging language.
- Demonstrates self-reflection and engaged thought.

Why instructors hesitate to make reading part of their courses

An active reading practice is essential for developing as a writer. Yet, reading can be the first thing cut from a crowded syllabus. Over the years, we've heard three main reasons instructors are reluctant to make deep and engaged reading a core part of their creative writing courses:

1. **Ability**. Concern that students don't know how to read the way they need to derive benefit or won't complete the reading in the first place.
2. **Time**. Struggle to make time to engage with mentor texts alongside everything else that's important for the course.
3. **Authority**. Reluctance to exert authority as an instructor by elevating certain model texts over others.

Let's look more closely at each source of hesitation and consider possible solutions.

Reading and ability

Students are often pressed for time with many responsibilities, and changing technologies have undeniably shifted our own and our students' relationships to monotasking and focus.

In *Engaging Ideas,* John C. Bean and Dan Melzer detail sources of students' reading difficulties, including a few that feel particularly relevant for creative writing instruction: a school culture that rewards skimming and "surface reading," difficulty in adjusting reading strategies to different genres, difficulty seeing themselves in conversation with the author, and resistance to the time-on-task required for deep reading (Bean and Melzer 2021, 136–8). Many writing instructors have been practicing reading habits and skills for so long that the strategies they use to situate, analyze, and interpret texts have become naturalized to a point of invisibility. But learning to read with the inquisitive reverse-engineering focus of a writer takes time and intentional practice.

Students often underestimate the length of time it takes to read, and especially to read something complex like a poem or novel. Drawing on Roberts and Roberts (2008), Bean and Melzer point out that students "may believe that experts are speed readers who don't need to struggle" (138) and can see their own difficulties as signs of failure or inadequacy rather than as indications that they need to allot more "time-on-task."

We need to ask if we've actually taken the time to teach the skill we're asking students to demonstrate rather than assuming that they don't care or are prioritizing other things. By breaking a skill down into its parts, we give students an opportunity to practice these parts individually in a situation of decreased cognitive load before layering them together. We invite students to bring a gentle curiosity to their reading and experiment with different strategies to find what works for them. By creating assignments that walk students through the steps of active and engaged reading, we help them develop skills rather than leaving them behind if they enter class without these skills already in place.

Hoa Nguyen on reading and writing relationally

How can writers learn from close reading?

Poems written by others inform the spectrum of one's study. It seems to me that poetry is about opposites and complements, sound designs and sense correspondences. I find it useful and important to bring attention to the poems of other poets, to live inside their patterns. These patterns require attention, to see how, in language, previous poets addressed states of experience, both interior and external, and how these speak to their audiences across time.

Creative imitation can be prescriptive and alienating for students. Under what circumstances is this not the case?

Poet Robert Creeley once said, "Imitation is a way of gaining articulation." When teaching with imitation, I instruct with cover songs and speak of stealing, after the god of poetry, Hermes, who was also the god of thieves and pickpockets. This form of stealing is akin to an act of translation, an alchemy of a previous form that, even though it resembles the old form, is transformed; it is in fact a new term, one transfigured into something new even as it remains somehow in relationship with the previous. Another way of saying this is that imitation is a means to personal innovation. As with "cover songs," we seek to be an innovator and not a wedding cover band. In class, I introduce this concept with music: cover songs played next to the original songs, ones that innovate on the original so much that it is a new song that also belongs to the innovator. A few examples:

- There's Bob Dylan's song "All Along the Watchtower," which I invite students to listen to next to Jimi Hendrix's version to hear how Hendrix recreated it wholly. Hendrix adds the sound of a vibraslap, an instrument that descended from the

African "jawbone," the lower jawbone of a donkey or a zebra, which has loose teeth that rattle when the instrument is struck. He introduces guitar wails with wah pedal riffs and a new kind of force or energy.

- In Aretha Franklin's hands, Otis Redding's song "Respect" is upended, turning it a feminist anthem as it spells out the word R-E-S-P-E-C-T and adds the girlfriend chorus of "sock it to me" to the backing vocals.

Imitation can become a mode of availability to arrive at articulation. With this lens, I refer to Charles Olson's suggestion that poems are a "field of action" in which the poet takes the original energy of an experience or perception and transfers that energy to the page.

What happens when a group of writers with different backgrounds, aesthetics, and composition approaches converge around a shared reading?

As Trinh T. Minh-ha writes, "A creative event does not grasp, it does not take possession, it is an excursion" (26). Our deep dive excursions can be attentive to the works' relationships—with other writers, with its situatedness in time and influences, with its voice signatures and aims. What happens is openness, connectedness, and creative action.

HOA NGUYEN teaches poetry, creative writing, and poetics at Toronto Metropolitan University. She is a member of the She Who Has No Masters collective. Her books include *Red Juice*, *Violet Energy Ingots*, and *A Thousand Times You Lose Your Treasure*, finalist for the National Book Award and the Governor General's Literary Award.

Image credit: Dale Smith

Assignments that focus on the reading process

We read in many different ways: on the page, on the screen, via audio recording, in long marathons, in short choppy bursts, with deep focus, amidst constant interruptions, immersively, analytically, distractedly, enthusiastically … Bronwen remembers falling asleep in her university dorm room trying to read Derrida despite her best efforts to focus. John listens to short story collections on his phone while commuting to campus and skips to the next story if the current one isn't holding his interest. When we share stories like these, our students take a deep breath and settle differently into their seats.

Sharing our own experiences in reading challenging texts, we normalize the struggle, and frame reading as an ensemble of learnable skills rather than a "you get it or you don't" experience. Often, the best way to help people feel capable of doing a difficult thing is simply acknowledging the difficulty. Rather than espousing a single narrow practice of "real reading," we introduce a plurality of modes and invite conversation on what students find valuable or frustrating about each mode. A student loves listening to Toni Morrison read her own novels out loud to appreciate the music of the language but also notices a struggle to remember names and plot details. Another likes being able to highlight passages on an e-reader and return to them easily. A third loves reading immersively but hasn't been able to focus since they started a job on top of school. When students can share insights and experiences openly, they feel able to approach reading with a spirit of experimentation. Here are a few strategies we recommend:

Reading experiments/reading logs

Build a course structure where students undertake "experiments" in their reading. An experiment invites curiosity rather than performance anxiety. We might ask students to try reading with and without background music, morning and evening, for a short time or a longer one, on a screen or on paper. We might simply ask them to share their insights in class. Or we might formalize this process with a reading log where they observe and reflect without judgment. Reading logs can serve as a starting point for class discussions. Or an instructor might draw on reading logs to notice trends across a class and identify interventions for targeted support in areas where students are experiencing difficulty.

Commonplace books

Commonplace books are notebooks dedicated to gathering, organizing, and reflecting on quotes, examples, and ideas from others. Bronwen knew all about commonplace books from her friend Jillian Hess' dissertation research, but she encountered them as a learning tool from colleagues Meg and Amer. Students use a commonplace book to:

1. Select what they find relevant and meaningful in what they're reading.
2. Slow down enough to recopy passages word for word by hand.
3. Reflect on and talk back to these passages however they see fit.

As Hess clarified in our conversation (**Chapter 9**), "Teachers since the Renaissance have known that merely copying down quotations does not amount to learning. It is merely a step in the process. True learning happens when we reflect on the sentences we've copied. The solution to this problem has always been to require original writing alongside transcriptions of quotations."

Sample Assignment

Writer's commonplace book

A Commonplace Book practice can help us:

- Develop a deep reading practice.
- Accept contingency and imperfections (messy handwriting, distracted mind, indecision about what to select).

- Pay sustained attention to form (the *how* of writing on the page).
- Clarify and extend our thinking by engaging with specific passages and reflecting on why they inspire, puzzle, delight, or infuriate us.
- Make connections between what we read and our own preoccupations and questions.

Reading with a focus on how a text makes meaning is an essential part of growing as a writer. We learn what is possible—and what might be possible—from noticing what moves, frustrates, or surprises us, and then taking the time to figure out how exactly each effect is achieved on the level of the transition sentence, poetic turn, metaphor, rhyme, or semicolon. In selecting quotations to collect, we make choices about what matters to us and what we want to sit with. In our reflections, we practice thinking on the page without a particular destination or outcome in mind. In this way, we open ourselves up for discovery. For each entry, include the following elements:

Left-Hand Page

1. A full bibliographic **citation** at the bottom
2. **Quotations** from the text. These can be full paragraphs, single phrases, even a list of interesting verbs. Include page numbers so you can find these again when you want them.

Right-Hand Page

1. **Date**
2. **Noticings, reflections, responses.** What caught your attention and why? You might respond to an idea or concentrate on form. Push yourself to make connections between form—at any level—and meaning-making.
3. **Questions** for yourself/questions to discuss with others. What are you left wondering about? What do you want to get someone else's thoughts on?

Optional: **Things to try.** What could you take from this text and incorporate into your own writing? This could be as specific as "Try writing sentences with semicolons that place concepts in a relationship the way James Baldwin does" or as broad as "Write a coming-of-age narrative and, after a few pages, use Baldwin's phrase 'But I cannot leave it at that; there is more to it than that' (34) as an impetus to dig deeper and wrestle with what you're leaving out."

Marginal notes and annotations

Bronwen remembers laughing when she came to the section of *Engaging Ideas* that described the practices of expert readers: "they 'nutshell' passages as they proceed, often writing gist statements in the margins. They read a difficult text a second and a third time, considering first readings as approximations or rough drafts. They interact with the text by asking questions, expressing disagreements, linking the text with other readings or with personal experience" (163). Sure enough, her pages were thick with tiny diagrams, synthesis statements, ideas for how to implement specific strategies in her own classes, and notes like "connect to Hayot," "but why?," or even "oh no!!" John often pulls books from the shelves in his office and invites students to scan his marginalia to illustrate how reading is a two-way conversation.

Writing on texts, especially printed books, can feel like transgressive desecration. To attempt it, students need both explicit permission and models. Instructors might show examples from former students or published authors, or even point to a site like *Genius.com* where students may already have encountered intensive annotation without realizing it. Platforms like Perusall allow students to engage in collaborative digital annotation of a shared text, asking and answering one another's questions, linking to contextual information, and making the collective work of reading fully visible.

Annotating the work of published authors can seamlessly transition to annotating the work of peers in preparation for group critique or annotating their own work as part of a revision process. Annotation can also be a step along the way to a **Close Reading Exercise**.

Sample Assignment

Close reading exercise

One of the best ways to learn the craft of writing is to study the work you admire. To really understand how a piece of writing works, or even how one small part of it works, it's helpful to articulate your observations and share them with others. A close reading is a brief analysis of a piece of writing intended to help you learn about some aspect of craft. Start with a craft topic suggested by the work, such as an element, technique, device, or choice that is:

- **a** Obviously essential to the piece.
- **b** Unusual in some way.
- **c** Puzzling or for some other reason interesting to you.

Ideally, try to read the piece at least three times.

1. Read for pleasure: content and first impressions.
2. Read narrowly, looking for specific language that illustrates your topic: words, phrases, sentences, paragraphs, scenes. Demonstrate either progression or variety by selecting a few passages to discuss in detail.
3. Analyze—attempt to understand and explain—those passages. A close reading records the act of exploration or the process of moving toward understanding. You don't need to assert knowledge you don't have; feel free to pose questions and try to answer them.

Text-mapping/graphic representations of readings

Whether working individually in a notebook, in small groups on poster paper, or as a class on a white board, students benefit from visualizing their reading dynamically. Relationship diagrams of characters in a novel offer a classic example of this, but others might include

Venn diagrams showing how different writers approach a common trope or graphs that plot the "emotional temperature" of a poem line by line.

All of these methods slow down the reading process, make it a central focus of the attention, and invite students to take an active role as readers. Each offers explicit instructions in one or more of the skills that will allow students to read broadly, learn from what they read, and bring their insights and observations into their own writing practice.

Selecting model and mentor texts: six guiding principles

1. **Select with purpose.** Select from a stack of exciting possibilities by attending to purpose: "I need a poem that illustrates sustained metaphor" or "I need a story with clear examples of both scene and exposition." This push to consider purpose helps cut through our many enthusiasms to arrive at a list.
2. **Clarify goals.** To select with purpose, revisit course goals and reflect on who is taking the course and why (**Chapter 1**). In an introductory course, we might decide to prioritize breadth and assign brief selections from a wide array of writers. In a graduate course with thesis projects on the horizon, we might opt for full-length collections.
3. **Prioritize depth of engagement.** Assign fewer texts and invite students to engage in greater depth. Students who become overwhelmed are likely to stop reading altogether, while students given the opportunity to spend sustained time with a single text often make major leaps in their ability to recognize and interpret formal choices.
4. **Include context.** Students benefit from seeing literary texts situated within a broader context. For a contemporary writer, this context might take the form of podcast interviews or videos of public readings. For a historical writer, letters, early reviews, aesthetic manifestos, or newspaper coverage of relevant events all offer valuable context.
5. **Consider accountability.** Students might neglect reading if they can safely assume that the instructor will go over it in class. Encourage students to develop their own relationships with reading by designing assignments and in-class activities that hold them accountable for wrestling with a text and coming to their own conclusions.
6. **Approach with equanimity.** In selecting texts with attention to our students' goals and interests and inviting students to contribute to the reading list, we end up reading some texts we feel a deep aesthetic connection to and others that we might not. Approach both with equanimity. An instructor who scoffs at Instagram Poetry or Fan Fiction risks alienating students who see not only their aesthetic preferences but also their identities dismissed. Likewise, an instructor who champions a favorite story or gets defensive when students complain that an essay is dated, too theoretical, or too personal risks setting up an antagonistic class dynamic that serves no one. When we approach texts with consistent attention, curiosity, and openness to the delight, frustration, or critique our students bring, students have space to explore, grow, and change their minds (and we do too).

Reading and time

We've certainly experienced the squeeze of time. We've mapped out an initial course plan only to realize that we have two or three courses worth of material. With practice, we've gotten better at using a course's purpose to narrow and select assignments, activities, and materials. We've also found that students have a richer, more valuable engagement with their writing (and with one another) when we devote serious time to reading. Engagement with models and mentor texts gives students time to build trust, establish shared touchstones and vocabulary, practice analytic skills, and ultimately enjoy a better workshop experience. We've experimented with several ways to make space for reading:

- We gain time by deferring workshop and devoting the first part of the course to generative exercises in close conversation with model texts. (See **Chapter 3**.)
- We experiment with the size of the group or unit of work up for discussion.
    - Small groups allow us to run multiple workshops simultaneously. To work well, groups need a clear structure (and might ask us to understand our role as leader or facilitator differently).
    - Offering multiple mini-workshops (perhaps focused on a small part of a larger piece or a specific aspect of craft) can free up space without compromising students' access to individual attention and engagement on their writing. (See **Chapter 7**.)

Nancy Lee on craft labs and diverse reading lists

What's a struggle or challenge around reading or models/mentor texts you've faced and how have you dealt with it?

Early in my teaching career I noticed that learners found it difficult to apply craft concepts if there was little similarity between the mentor texts and the creative work they were interested in generating. I now opt for "brief but many" model texts, excerpting paragraphs or pages from a mix of styles, voices, and crucially, genres, so that learners can see how concepts might apply as the work changes. I'll also include excerpts that contradict or subvert the concept we're discussing, so that we can examine the choices the author has made instead. My motto is "tools, not rules"—the goal isn't for students to mimic the execution of a craft element but rather to experiment and consider the relevance of the craft element when it comes to the work they want to create.

What are some guiding principles you use for selecting readings?

As a woman of color teaching a diverse student body, I want the readings to reflect the concerns, life experiences, interests, and voices of my students—representation matters, and I'm constantly assessing and curating for that. At the same time, I see the readings as an inspiring assortment of what fiction can be and do stylistically. In a large lecture course of first and second years, you're somewhat of an evangelist for how fiction is relevant to our everyday lives, so my baseline is contemporary fiction, with a classic here and there, and I update each term to include recently published stories/novels.

Can you tell us about your use of the "craft lab" and how you've refined it over time?

Because we're a multi-genre program, every fiction workshop includes learners at all levels of fiction writing experience, from published fiction writers to students trying fiction for the first time. The craft lab was initially conceived as a series of self-paced, online modules—videos, audio, readings, exercises—to run alongside our weekly workshops. Each lab module explored a different element of craft and offered the opportunity for the learner to do their own "experiments." Learners moved in and out of the modules, focused on the elements they most wanted to work on, and brought questions that arose to our weekly online hangout. Because the craft lab was self-directed, I was never quite sure how much students were getting out of it, so I did a survey. I was surprised to discover students wanted less workshopping and more engagement with the craft lab material.

So, I rearranged the course. We now spend the first half of the course in what I think of as a "facilitated craft lab." Students post their weekly experiments, but not for critique or feedback. Instead, the posting is an opportunity for them to self-reflect—What did they notice? What did they struggle with? What would they like to try next? Again, the goal of the craft lab modules is not for learners to produce a replication of the craft concept under discussion, it's for learners to thoughtfully consider how a craft concept might or might not intersect with their own aesthetics and goals for creative expression. Because students can see one another's experiments and reflections, each with its own distinct style and approach, we move away from ideas of "right or wrong" or "good or bad" and into the realm of "What else might be possible?"

NANCY LEE is an Associate Professor in the UBC School of Creative Writing. She is the award-winning author of two works of fiction, *Dead Girls* and *The Age*, and a poetry collection, *What Hurts Going Down*. Her books have been published in the UK, France, Germany, Italy, Spain, and the Netherlands.
Image credit: Kyrani Kanavaros

Reading and authority

In selecting readings, instructors might feel uneasy with the aesthetic and positional authority they exert over their students. The anxiety of asserting biases around craft, form, and technique can pose enough of a challenge for instructors to shy away from creating reading lists. These doubts are not unfounded. It's necessary to continually challenge our power and authority in the classroom and reflect on how we're using it.

For highly self-directed students or as part of a thesis process, we might simply offer personalized reading suggestions along the way. But even highly motivated students have to make crucial triage decisions about their time when taking multiple courses. Students tell us that they'd love to read more, but when readings or craft-based exercises are a recommended sidecar rather than a fully integrated part of the course, these activities get pushed to the bottom of the list when things get busy.

So, how do we create opportunities for deep engagement with reading without setting up a dynamic of mastery or aesthetic narrowing? Felicia Rose Chavez writes, "The imperialist dichotomy of novice/master (and its swift subliminal substitution, slave/master) translates to one who is dependent on, and controlled by, the other, one who is forced into a pretense of obedience in order to maintain self-preservation" (2021, 29). It's all too easy for a reading list to come across as "here's the approved style and what you're doing over there is *not it*." Reading should *expand* students' sense of what is possible in writing; it should never narrow. Like Chavez, we invite student agency in co-curating a class reading list. We also design independent reading assignments that combine choice and structure. And we pay close attention to how we discuss the readings we and our students share with the class, taking time to situate these texts in a meaningful context, demystify publication, and invite students to reflect on how they might wish to share their work beyond the course.

Creating space for multilingualism

All classes benefit from acknowledging literary production as transnational and multilingual. These suggestions, crucial for classes with a plurality of languages and language learners, are also valuable for others and can be applied across genres and levels.

1. **Assign works in translation.** Offer examples and discuss ways that literary influence and inspiration travel across language and geography.
    - Example: Pair odes to ordinary things by Pablo Neruda and Ross Gay.
2. **Assign multilingual texts.** Discuss craft choices such as using or not using italics, providing a gloss in English, blending or separating languages, relationships to audience(s), and so on.
    - Example: Students discuss translanguaging choices after watching a video of Eduardo Corral reading "In Colorado My Father Scoured and Stacked Dishes" (2013) and reading Kaveh Akbar's "Do You Speak Persian" (2017) [texts available for free online].
3. **Offer assignments that invite students to experiment with their own multilingual texts.**
    - Example: Bring words or phrases from a language other than English into your work. Draw on examples from multilingual texts and consider what the presence of non-English words does (1) for readers who understand them, (2) for readers

who understand some of them, (3) for readers who don't understand them at all. In your reflection, talk about which words/phrases you chose, your relationship to the language, and how you imagine the poem might land with different readers.

4 **Contextualize English as a language of colonialism and empire.**
   - Example: Give students a word history scavenger hunt using the Oxford English Dictionary and invite them to reflect on the points of contact (largely imperial/colonial) through which new words have entered English.

5 **Emphasize the plurality of Englishes and how our individual sociolects are regional, plural, and migratory.**
   - Example: Students read "A Skiff of Snow" (2014) by Melissa Range and look at what the poem has to say about accent, migration, and language, especially around the key word "skiff." Students read Safia Elhillo's "Ode to Sudanese Americans" (2021), and look at the words Elhillo introduces that are tied to the specific community she's addressing. When does she use multiple terms (i.e., "gamar boba" and "hoop earrings")? When does she offer or withhold context or gloss? [Texts available for free online.]

Things we can convey through these approaches:

- Creative writing is not reserved for "native speakers."
- Influence and inspiration travel (and transform) across cultures and languages.
- It's okay to be understood differently by different audiences and choose an audience to center in your work.
- English carries its imperial history within its words, and all writers working in English need to grapple with this history, although it hits us differently depending on our positionality.
- What we might see as strangeness or flaws as language users are often our strengths.
- We can write from the full range of our sociolects and vernaculars, which keep expanding and shifting through our lives.

Students co-curating the reading list

We've experimented with several approaches that invite students to co-create a course reading list. John emails grad students ahead of the term encouraging them to submit 2–3 fiction selections along with a brief rationale why they've selected these pieces. He then reviews suggestions and rationales, seeks points of contrast, and incorporates at least 1–2 readings from each student into the course reading list. From the first day of class, students see how their readings join with their peers' readings to generate a broad range of stories and aesthetic approaches, and their agency in co-authoring the reading list helps them feel seen and respected, inviting them to invest more deeply in the course.

To extend this further, each student leads a discussion of the stories they added to the reading list. The discussion begins with a 15–20-minute talk (building on a **Close Reading Exercise**) on one or two aspects of the story the student found illuminating or challenging (imagery, character, subtext, etc.) and their own connections and struggles with these topics. The class grapples with the work together, led by the student, rather than having the instructor lead the discussion and shape it through their identity or a prescribed topic of craft and technique.

Likewise, Bronwen developed a course in which each student chooses a poet and a poetic element for a sustained apprenticeship experience. Students read the work of their chosen poet deeply and repeatedly, often constellating out to explore interviews, reviews, literary criticism, peers, and influences (including music, art, theory, and so on). Over the term, students take turns inviting peers into their process by selecting a twenty-page reading sample and a context piece (such as a craft essay, performance video, or podcast interview) and designing an introduction, writing experiment, and questions for conversation emerging out of their apprenticeship. Each week, students complete two writing experiments: one emerging from their own apprenticeship work and one following that week's peer-designed experiment. Students also maintain a **Writer's Commonplace Book** to document and reflect on their reading practice. At the end of the term, students complete a documentation of their apprenticeship process, which includes close readings of specific passages, poems written in imitation and conversation with their chosen poet, and a reflection on their experience.

When asking students to engage in formal imitation, we remind them that the goal is not to transform into someone else, but to experiment with and deepen their own sensibilities. We initiate process discussions by sharing reflections like the following from Carl Phillips' *My Trade is Mystery*:

> Reading Woolf 's sentences won't make me write like Woolf—I can't do that, and I don't want to—but it allows me to engage with sentence strategies that aren't mine and to add those strategies to the many I've acquired all my life by reading. Again, figuring out and imitating a writing strategy from another writer doesn't mean you'll write like that author. Individual sensibility is what makes Woolf who she is. When we adopt another's strategy, we still end up deploying it via our own unique sensibility, which means the sentence we make as a result will remain our own. (Phillips 2022, 36)

The idea of a community sharing and creating knowledge together is central to a classroom where the instructor's authority can be dismantled. When students are involved in co-creating course reading lists and craft structures, they are positioned at the front of all pedagogical decisions, making for an experiential, relevant course.

A student perspective: Wanda John-Kehewin on learning through apprenticeship

In graduate poetry, you did an apprenticeship on the work of Layli Long Soldier. Can you describe this experience?

It taught me to look outside of myself at what other people were doing to be able to find my way. Studying her work made me think about the experiences of different Indigenous people from Canada and the US and go, "Okay, we're doing the same thing. We have a common goal of writing about injustices. But how?" Her work helped me break that mold of punctuation and grammar. I saw how you could even make your own words and just have this freedom instead of being constrained by the rules of old English poets. It was such a good experience, and the best part was she actually allowed me to interview her.

After our Zoom conversation, what stuck with me is that we are all human beings. I always thought poets who published a ton of books and got awards were so self-actualized. She's this amazing writer creating change through poetry, but she let me see the human part of her as well, how she was also going through some personal stuff. It was pretty amazing. We also talked about line breaks and what a short line can do, and she talked about learning from Fred Moten. It was beautiful to think of her learning from him and me learning from her.

Are there specific approaches from this engagement that you can point to in your thesis, published as *Spells, Wishes, and the Talking Dead*?

This thesis brought together everything I'd learned about poetry. It was such a thrill to learn these tools, like "You can use sound this way," or "Oh, okay, that's what tone is." Or like Jericho Brown's duplex, how a writer could just invent a form. In *Whereas*, Layli breaks punctuation rules. This got me thinking: I'm a Cree person, but I'm writing in English. So, does that make me an English poet? Seeing her break those rules got me thinking how breaking rules could be a way to take power back through words. Another way might be talking about things that aren't broadly discussed, like in the poem about the thirty-eight men who were hanged. Just saying: this is what happened, this is how I feel. I used to be afraid I'd come off as angry, but now I don't care. It was a beautiful journey of exploration, reading Layli, reading Natalie Diaz, discovering Indigenous poets outside my scope of knowing.

What else have you taken from your apprenticeship work?

Looking at other people's work helped me break free from constraints I grew up with about what poetry is and what language is and how we should conduct ourselves following the rules of language. You know, "proper English." I saw how you can break the rules and just express yourself using line breaks or white space. And you don't need to explain yourself either. You can just write it and people will get it or they won't. I always used to think I had to explain myself, but when I read Layli, I saw how she didn't explain herself, she just wrote.

I saw how poetry comes out of anywhere, from critical thinking, from experience. I serve as an Indigenous patient navigator at the hospitals part-time. I went to support an end of life yesterday, and the family were slowly trickling in and doing ceremony. This nurse came by with her file cart, trying to get through. I said, "Excuse me, can you go that way instead, please?" We're mourning here. We're the ones who know how to die. We've come from all this trauma. We spend a whole lifetime trying to survive and in survival mode, but we know how to let someone go. And then I thought, *wow, okay, there's a poem there. I've got to write that little tidbit down*.

WANDA JOHN-KEHEWIN is a Cree writer who came to Vancouver, BC, on the Greyhound when she was nineteen, pregnant, carrying a bag of chips, a bottle of pop, thirty dollars, and hope. Wanda writes about the near decimation of Indigenous culture, language, and tradition in many different genres in hopes of reaching others.

Image credit: Gary Alteza

Assignments that offer students both agency and structure

When students choose their own mentor/model texts, they benefit from assignments that offer structure for these engagements. The close reading talk and apprenticeship described earlier:

1 Give students a well-defined process for engagement and clear parameters for documenting and reflecting on their work.
2 Invite them to identify ways to apply their learning to their own writing.

Sometimes these assignments become the structure for an entire course with a fully student-curated reading list. In other contexts, we integrate student-selected reading alongside instructor-curated readings.

When we're asking students to follow a structure, as in the **Ecosystem of a Book** assignment, we need to communicate: How will it help them grow? How does it serve not just our goals but also their own?

If students can embrace the purpose of an assignment and align it with their own motivations, they'll be able to see a thoughtfully designed step-by-step process as supportive rather than constraining. Structured independent reading assignments also offer students a chance to return to the class as experts and share their "findings" in casual or formal presentations. Naturally, instructors benefit as well: expanding our knowledge of the writers and questions that matter to our students.

Table 6.1 Skills Students Develop Through Structured Reading Engagements

Writer as Beginning Reader	Writer as Experienced Reader
Reads in a vacuum.	Contextualizes what they're reading and situates writers and texts within a broader literary, cultural, and historical landscape.
Reads passively without a particular agenda or focus.	Reads with specific lens or question in mind. Is aware that this lens or question is one of many possibilities.
Reacts to what they read.	Is able to move from reaction to response by interrogating and contextualizing their reactions.
Experiences pleasure in reading.	Experiences pleasure in reading AND can figure out at a craft level how the text moved them and what they might integrate into their own work.
Sees craft terms as universal, fixed, and definition-based.	Understands craft terms to be culturally relative, contested, and politically inflected. Can read contrasting perspectives in craft or critical essays and take what they find useful from them.
Is afraid of sounding derivative or "losing their individual voice."	Is able to learn through deliberate imitation and understands the ethical stakes of intertextuality. Realizes that "voice" can be both found and crafted, both experienced and performed.
Has fan-like devotion to sources of inspiration and little attention/patience for other texts.	Has nuanced relationship to sources of inspiration and influence and understands that friction and critical awareness can co-exist with them. Is able to learn from texts whether they "like" them or not.

In making a reading plan for a specific course, we consider these questions:

- What are the advantages of everyone reading the same thing (whether selected by students or by the instructor)?
- What are the advantages of students reading different things? How might students "report back" on independent reading (whether orally or in writing)?
- When are full texts useful (i.e., to look at story structure) and when are short excerpts sufficient (i.e., to think about voice, dialogue, or description)?
- What logistical challenges may arise for sharing readings (time or funds to acquire books, changing online availability, etc.)? What accessibility concerns must be considered (i.e., in a course with a visually impaired student, PDFs would need to be machine-readable)?

Sample Assignment

Ecosystem of a book

For this assignment, you will select a single-author collection of poems, stories, or essays and undertake a series of steps to explore the book and the context it emerges from. Paying attention to this book alongside related interviews, reviews, and periodicals will help you develop a sense of the intersecting communities of writers, reviewers, publishers, and readers that books inhabit. As you read and situate this book, you will document observations and insights.

Step One: Select a single-author collection of poems, stories, or essays published within the past five years.

Write: Introduction

- Why you picked this book/previous contact with the writer.
- A brief introduction to the writer and the collection.

Step Two: Pick one or more craft elements to track through the book. For example, you might pay attention to time and track how the collection moves between past, present, and future within individual pieces and between pieces. Consider picking an element that you want to focus on in your own writing as well.

Write: Craft Elements at Work

- Talk about what you've observed about the craft element you picked and its work across the collection. Discuss contrasts and consistencies across different pieces within the book.
- Select at least two specific passages where something interesting is happening. Quote and analyze these passages in depth.

Step Three: Look into the publication history of individual pieces included in this collection. Check the acknowledgments page for the book and see where individual pieces were published previously. Look up these publications and see what they're like: Online? In print? Specializing in a single genre? Associated with an institution? Contrast periodical versions and book versions: How much time passed between initial publication and book publication? Has the piece been revised? Does it read differently when you encounter it in the periodical as compared to when you encounter it within the context of the final collection?

Write: Publication History

- Describe the publication history of this collection and discuss anything interesting that you've noticed.

Step Four: Locate and take in one or more interviews with the writer. Interviews can be in print, audio, or video. If possible, find an interview in which the writer discusses the collection you're focusing on.

Write: Interview Insights

- What struck you from the interview(s)? Did anything surprise you?

Step Five: Track down and read some reviews of the collection. Find at least two professional reviews (in venues like *Kirkus Reviews*, *Publishers Weekly*, *Los Angeles Review of Books*, or the *League of Canadian Poets*). Also, take a look at two or more reader reviews on a site like Goodreads.

Write: Reviews

- What themes, issues, and questions show up in the reviews? What do people praise about this collection? What do they critique about it? How consistent are the reviews in their "take" on the book? How do the reader reviews compare to the professional reviews? To what extent do reviewers'/readers' impressions align with your own?

Step Six: Reflect on how you can use what you've learned in your own practice as a writer.

Write: Reading as a Writer

- What have you learned through examining the ecosystem in which this book came to be? How can you use these insights to inform your own writing? Insights may relate to form, writing process and work habits, audience response, publication practices, or anything else that you find valuable.

Using mentor texts to demystify publication and professionalization

Instructors can be reluctant to encourage students to think about publication early in their journey as writers. "Let them have time to play and create," we might say, "they have plenty of time to worry about publication down the road." Not all students pursue creative writing with a goal of publication, and a narrow focus on specific publication venues as a barometer for success can suck all of the air and joy out of a course.

Yet, there can be a place for talking about publication in creative writing classrooms. If part of our job as instructors is to demystify how writing happens, we might see this as extending from first sparks of idea to the moment when a poem or novel or picture book meets a reader for the first time. How do we demystify publication and professionalization without presenting a narrow version of publication or literary success as the only worthwhile reason to pursue writing?

We might invite students to think about how they encounter writing they value (book, online magazine, Norton anthology, chapbook, YouTube, Instagram, etc.) and how each context shapes that encounter. When we select model texts for students to read, we can bring in interviews and conversations with writers about audience, publication, and context.

When students locate and reflect on author interviews, reviews, and publication history, they notice connections and crossings in the overlapping institutional ecosystems of libraries, universities, periodical publications, book publications, social media, and so on. In comparing their findings, students encounter indie zines, micro-presses, and writers who got their start on TikTok alongside big five presses and *Publishers Weekly* book deals. Reflecting on writers finding their audiences (**Chapter 5**) can help students interrogate the idea that they necessarily need to submit their work to literary journals or query agents. Through reading in context, they also begin to see themselves as potential editors, publishers, and curators of work they value.

7
Workshop Approaches and Alternatives

Rethinking writing workshops

For years, a particular version of group critique was understood as the signature—and at times sole—pedagogy in creative writing. Variously referred to by supporters and critics as "the Iowa model," "traditional workshop," "the silent-writer model," or "gag-rule workshop," this model is characterized by a largely unstructured discussion of a piece of student writing, offered without context, during which the writer does not speak. The driving force of the conversation is critique (Myers 1996, 125), in which the instructor may sit back quietly through the conversation, only to deliver an oracle-like pronouncement at the end. The ideal result is that the writer leaves the critique with insights about the strengths and weaknesses of their work, and that the class as a whole derives some insight, whether general or specific, that they can respectively apply to their own writing.

While this model went unchallenged within the field as a whole, as creative writing programs proliferated (146–7), individual teachers questioned the ethics and efficacy of this method and experimented with other approaches. For example, Chris Green's 2001 "Materializing the Sublime Reader" calls for classroom awareness of "multiple interpretive communities with differing rhetorics" (162) and proposes that "students compile a list of terms that they feel are appropriate to evaluating their poetry" (163). Bronwen's teaching practices still draw on examples she encountered in classes in the early 2000s with teachers like Catherine Imbriglio, who emphasized collective reading out loud and partner-based critique, and Thalia Field, who prioritized writing experiments and process discussions.

More recently, books by Matthew Salesses and Felicia Rose Chavez and Substacks by George Saunders and Rebecca Makkai show a sea change in how teachers approach the workshop. In particular, instructors increasingly recognize that the gag rule, in which a silent writer takes notes while peers potentially misunderstand or misinterpret their work, can be not only ineffective but actively harmful, especially for students who find themselves in the minority—in terms of race, class, gender, disability, aesthetic, or content choices—within a largely homogenous group.

Drawing on models from studio arts like painting and performing arts like dance, as well as Composition Studies, STEM, and Education, creative writing instructors today are more open to experimenting with a broader range of pedagogies and with alternate approaches to group critique. In particular, many creative writing instructors, ourselves included, have found Liz Lerman's *Critical Response Process* (2003) to offer an effective blend of structure and agency. First developed in the context of dance, Critical Response Process (CRP) has been used across a range of fields and disciplines, many of which are represented in Lerman and John Borstel's recent *Critique is Creative* (2022). Lerman encourages teachers to rethink how to approach critique but also to make full use of other teaching methods.

"People use critique not only to fix someone else's work but to teach," Liz Lerman said in a podcast interview (Lerman 2022, Commonplace Podcast Interview). "They teach by critiquing. And what I'm trying to understand is when do I want to just teach? And when do I critique and how does that work?"

Lerman describes an example of a student choreographing a dance where someone speaks too far upstage for the audience to hear them. She explains that this could be a deliberate choice or could be an oversight or could simply be something the student hasn't studied yet. As a teacher, she has several choices: to teach through critique, to pause and offer a mini-lesson on upstage and downstage, or to devote time in the next class to teaching these concepts and see what the student does with this information. Lerman concludes, "Sometimes, I think, we overteach with critique when we could just be teaching" (Lerman, Commonplace Podcast Interview). When workshop—or what Lerman calls "critique" or "group critique"—is the only pedagogical tool available for creative writing, all of our teaching has to happen through the critique. A student's work may become an object lesson for the class in a way that doesn't serve the student.

Faculty can be reluctant to open up the workshop to a more question-driven approach because they fear losing the ability to teach what they need to through critique. But when critique isn't the only mode of teaching, other possibilities become available. We can ask ourselves: Do I want to teach this concept through critique? Or do I want to teach this concept through a craft lecture or group close-reading exercise?

In this chapter, we walk through five key workshop frame shifts, give a brief snapshot of how we've adapted Lerman's CRP for writers, lay out some tips for coaching readers and writers alike, offer strategies for fully asynchronous and large-enrollment workshop contexts, and provide an inventory of the many decisions a teacher makes in crafting a successful workshop experience to fit their teaching context.

Five key frame shifts

Whether students have participated in a writing workshop or not, they tend to show up to class with some preconceived notions of what a workshop is. Over time, we've found that students bring fears and misconceptions we need to dispel for group critique to be effective. Here are some of the most common ones:

- Only bring a piece of writing to workshop when you feel completely finished with it.

- The point of a workshop is to tell a writer what's working and what they should fix.
- If a piece of writing is good, everyone will agree about it.
- In order to be rigorous, feedback shouldn't waste time trying to be nice.
- If the writer tries to talk, they're just being defensive.

Here are five key frame shifts we propose instead.

One: Group critique can be useful at any point in the writing process (as long as it's approached thoughtfully)

Students sometimes think it's only appropriate to bring their most polished work to group critique. Instructors sometimes take this approach as well: "Get it as far as you can on your own before asking for help," they might say, or "Don't waste the group's time by bringing a messy draft to workshop." While we understand why an instructor might make this request (perhaps after seeing hundreds of hastily dashed-off stories or half-baked poems), we propose that group critique can be useful at any stage of the writing process provided both writer and readers are clear about the state of the draft and the goals of the session. In discussing early drafts, we can hold a shared awareness of the work as in-progress and enter a collective space of helping a writer explore possibilities. Whether they're bringing in rough notes or polished prose, we encourage an approach of "This is in-progress. Help me figure out next steps" rather than "This is finished. Now you can praise it or judge it."

Two: The workshop is a space of collaborative discovery

Students often come to group critique in search of affirmation and/or solutions. To be sure, a critique session can offer both of these things. Without structural intervention, however, a session can easily default to a conversation along the lines of "This is what's working and this is what you should fix" or "I like this … I don't like this." We see several issues with this paradigm:

- Without taking time to establish a shared understanding of the work, readers and writers can easily talk at cross purposes.
- By jumping to praise and advice, especially with early work, we risk short-circuiting the full potential of a project.
- Without a writer having a chance to articulate their goals, readers might offer solutions that aim to revise the work against the writer's aesthetic aims.

What participants have to offer, we propose, is their *experience* of the work. Instead of "fix this for me," a writer might approach the workshop asking something like "help me see this more fully." In this encounter, everyone involved can travel somewhere together—readers learn more about what's on the page as well as about the writer's intentions and aims, while the writer discovers new possibilities and clarifies their desires for the work. Ultimately, workshop should energize the writer, rather than drain them of the optimism and energy they originally brought to creating the piece. It should also honor their responsibility for their work by not providing easy fix-it-like-this answers, but rather encouraging deeper reflection and experimentation.

Three: Lack of consensus is not only inevitable, it's desirable and worth pursuing

Students sometimes leave a workshop conversation confused and overwhelmed by the range of different opinions. "If something is good," they might say, "shouldn't people agree about it?" But different readers respond to different things, and if disagreement and difference of opinion aren't coming up in group critique, we're probably not digging deep enough (or students are suppressing differences out of discomfort or anxiety).

Bronwen remembers workshops where Thalia Field would say, "Great, so you feel like this could have been shorter. Is there anyone who'd like to make a case for why it should actually be longer?" Field didn't just make space for divergent opinions, she actively solicited them. In an atmosphere that encourages divergent perspectives, several things become clear:

- Readers are individuals with personal taste and preferences.
- There's no way to satisfy everyone's desires for our work (and attempting to do so would be ruinous).
- Reader feedback offers a wealth of information that writers actively need to synthesize, consider, act on, and, frequently, discard.

Four: Tone matters, and it's false to frame rigor in opposition to kindness

How many times have we heard a student declare, "I just want the truth, don't worry about my feelings," or "I can handle anything, just give it to me straight," or "I'm not interested in what's working, tell me how to fix the problems." Despite this bravado, rarely, if ever, have we seen this approach work in practice. Somewhere along the way, some students internalize a sense that kindness is sugar-coating and praise is not to be trusted. As Liz Lerman said in our conversation, "When people say, 'I can take it,' they are basically armoring themselves because they think it's going to hurt. For those people, it's not feedback unless it hurts." Like Lerman, we see the "Punch me! I can take it!" response as driven by fear and self-protection. All discussion of student work, no matter how brave or nonchalant the writer might appear, is a potentially highly charged emotional situation.

Like Lerman, we respond, "I hear you saying that. I'd still like to continue this process with you because I think there's another way."

We explicitly invite students to push back against any lurking rhetoric that "kindness" and "rigor" are somehow opposed to one another. When students seem skeptical, we might share a moment when minor critiques delivered dismissively left us demoralized and contrast this with the many occasions a warm supportive message that we needed to rethink a whole project left us confident and eager to get to work. We also emphasize the rigor to be found in moving from a gut reaction to a considered response appropriate to the writer's vision and the project's state of development. We want writers to feel the class is working on their behalf as a community, that we're "on their side" trying to help them achieve their vision rather than "against them" telling them what's wrong with the work. When we convey respect for one another and belief in one another's abilities, even a response that tells us that something isn't working (yet!) can feel like a generous gift.

Five: Only when the writer has agency to ask questions and guide the conversation can group critique reach its full potential

Why assume that there's a shared understanding of what the ideal finished thing should be when we might aspire to so many different possible goals? When a writer shares intentions, we can talk about where the work is relative to those intentions, what's already there, what's still potential, or where a writer might swerve with a happy accident.

Critical Response Process: core values and endless adaptations

CRP emphasizes the value of growth over perfection. In doing so, it offers writers agency and support in moving toward their vision. CRP consists of four core steps that present a clearly defined path for discussing work in progress, a "kind of ritual" to "hold you in relationship to values that would be otherwise hard to keep in the rush of daily living" (Lerman and Borstel 2022, xi). Each step provides an experience for everyone involved to be more "conscious, thoughtful, and aware of managing our impulses" (29). Four simple steps, a lifetime of practice. CRP deepens with time and experience, and benefits from coaching specific skills (like scaffolded practice in question-asking, **Chapter 2**). The **Critical Response Process Refresher** illustrates one way we've introduced the four steps of CRP to creative writing students. We warmly encourage instructors interested in implementing CRP to explore Lerman's work and her many collaborations with artists across disciplines.

Sample Assignment

Critical Response Process refresher

Step One: Statements of Meaning

At the center of a writer's work, there is meaning. By starting with statements that reflect on the meaning of the work, we acknowledge the work's presence and invite the variety of perspectives—aesthetic, intellectual, social, and so on—that readers bring to the work. Statements of meaning offer an early but important baseline of how readers see and interpret the work and the diverse value systems that inflect their perspectives.

We might call this step "observations" or "noticings." Readers answer the questions "What did you notice? What was stimulating, surprising, evocative, memorable, touching, or meaningful for you in what you just read?" Examples: "I noticed that these poems don't use punctuation/include very short lines/involve a lot of sensory language." Talk about what you as a reader (you, specifically, not some kind of abstract general reader) found moving, surprising, or meaningful about the work. Examples: "I was moved by the tenderness of these descriptions. They create a feeling of intimacy."

- *Tip for Readers: Nothing is too small to notice. Avoid critiques and suggested fixes. Respond to what the writing is* already doing *that is exciting, surprising, or stimulating.*
- *Tip for Writer: Spend time with the statements of meaning and take them in. Ask clarifying questions if you wish.*

Step Two: The Writer Asks Questions

The writer asks the readers questions about the work and their reading experiences. In answering, readers stay on topic with the question and may express opinions in direct response to the writer's questions.

- *Tip for Writer: Spend some time in advance articulating good questions. Think about how specific/general you want to be in your questions. If you feel like people misinterpret your questions, rephrase or clarify them.*
- *Tip for Readers: Respond to questions from the writer with honesty, kindness, and specificity. Point to concrete examples in the writing whenever possible. Remember to stick to the question and not offer opinions on other aspects of the writing.*

Step Three: Readers Ask Neutral Questions

Readers ask the writer neutral questions about the work, which serve a dual purpose: they allow readers to deepen their understanding of the work and the writer's goals while also giving the writer a chance to reflect on their work in fresh ways. Questions are neutral when they don't have an opinion buried in them.

- *Tip for Readers: Take time to make sure your questions are truly neutral (i.e., not "Why did you make the mom so mean?" but "How are you hoping readers might respond to the character of the mom?"). Ask questions you're genuinely curious about. Also, ask questions that might invite the writer to think expansively and imaginatively about their project.*
- *Tip for Writer: Respond to neutral questions from readers with openness and thoughtfulness. Be willing to question yourself and change your mind.*

Step Four: Readers Offer Opinions (But Only if the Writer Wants Them)
Readers name opinions by topic, and the writer has the option of assenting or declining to hear them. The writer may say "yes" or "no/not now." For example, we might say, "I have an opinion about your titles. Would you like to hear it?" And the writer might say, "Definitely, please share!" or "You know what? These are just place-holder titles, so let's not spend time on that now." Although the repeated formality of requesting permission can feel forced, this structure helps readers learn to identify and state an opinion with clarity, and gives the writer the context and agency to hear new ideas about their work without becoming overwhelmed. The structure of this step, of all the steps, offers safety for all involved to enter a challenging and respectful discussion.

- *Tip for Writer: Unless you have a reason not to, receive opinions with curiosity and consider them.*
- *Tip for Readers: Offer the writer opinions that support their vision of the project.*

Liz Lerman on developing Critical Response Process

What becomes possible when creators have agency over how their work is discussed?

You can dignify your doubts, your worries, your obsessions, your insomnia by recognizing that underlying all that are some real questions. Using CRP, you begin to understand how to turn feelings into inquiry. This signals to the curious and interested responder that you've already thought about a lot of things—maybe you've already considered and discarded something they'd recommend. That doesn't mean that they can't later ask you things it might be good for you to think about, but it addresses the fact that you've already been at this for a while.

When I was first figuring CRP out and my work was reviewed, I observed that I'd be in dialogue with myself for days, muttering over things, especially where I felt misunderstood. Giving the artist agency can help direct the conversation to the places that matter and get beyond the impasse of just feeling misunderstood. People would tell me, "Liz, you're a professional artist now. If you can't take the heat, get out of the kitchen," and I would always say, "Yeah, but I'm the cook. I have something to say about the heat."

As CRP has spread across different artforms and contexts, you've seen it refracted back in various interpretations. What do you see misunderstood or misapplied?

I was just in Sweden, and I said, "It's a little bit like landing on one of Darwin's islands because you're seeing this thing evolve on its own terms." Which, of course, I love. I don't want to police the evolution of the process. Still, there are a couple things I would speak to: one frequently confused thing is that it's all mushy. No! CRP is so rigorous! You can split hairs, which is really fun to do. One of my favorite sessions was teaching CRP to a bunch of Orthodox rabbis. They split hairs all the time. When people say CRP is mushy-mushy, it's because they don't want to get into the rigor of it because it's demanding. That's a misunderstanding that bothers me. It also bothers me when people think they're not supposed to have an opinion or not supposed to share their opinion. No, it's all opinion. All of the steps include opinion. In the first step, you're filtering: "It's my opinion that this is a memorable opening." You're just not talking about the stuff you think isn't working right now.

Sometimes people don't want to use the word "like." It's fine to say "I like"! The key is what are they saying after "I like"? I was a guest in a university course once where the students kept saying, "I like, I like, I like," and the teacher was frustrated. So, I asked them all, "What do you like about food?" And students said "I like to separate my food on the plate" or "I like putting different colors in" or "I like the social ritual." I said, "Do you hear how many ways you enjoy this? 'Like' isn't the portal. The portal is what comes after 'I like.'" But if a teacher says "You can't say 'I like,'" then students start feeling they're in a straightjacket and they hate it.

CRP has evolved and shifted over the years—from redefining statements of meaning to interrogating how "neutral" a question can truly be. What are you or others exploring or questioning these days?

There's tremendous interest, particularly coming from communities of color, in two parts of the process. One is the word *neutral*. For some, that feels like a way to shut down cultural traditions. There's work on revising the language to foreground how Step Three is about gathering research. It's being curious. Also, the process develops a relationship as it goes, but there's some feeling that you need to do more warm-ups before you start, that more can happen within a sense of community. We've been developing warm-ups and skill-builders for contexts where that would be helpful.

I've also been thinking about flexibility and when to intervene as a facilitator. I don't want to police the steps; I want people to get feedback. I've been in sessions where a facilitator constantly says "No, you didn't ask it right" to a degree that folks shut down. So, if someone doesn't follow a step exactly, and the artist is doing fine, not fidgeting and not getting defensive, fine, I might let it go. But I watch what happens right after. One person not following might be fine, but three might not be fine. There may be a point where you have to intervene. Being present is the most important. When I'm facilitating, I do a lot of timeouts and just say, "Hey, what just happened here? Let's take a look at this." If you understand the values that are embedded in the steps, then you can explore and experiment a lot. It isn't about maintaining the steps; it's about maintaining the values.

LIZ LERMAN is an Institute Professor at Arizona State University and a fellow at the Center for the Study of Race and Democracy. She is a choreographer, writer, educator, and the recipient of a 2023 Guggenheim Fellowship and 2002 MacArthur "Genius Grant" Award. She founded and led Dance Exchange from 1976 until 2011.

Image credit: Christine Johnson

Coaching curious agentic writers

Curiosity

What does it mean to be curious about our writing and the experiences others have with it?

Students naturally seek approval, support, and encouragement from peers; they want to hear that their work is well received, to feel like they belong and are doing well. All too often, however, developing writers approach peer feedback from a defensive stance, holding tight to their work as if braced for attack. Comments are parsed either as praise (reassuring but also suspicious) or criticism (a failure, maybe even a sign that they don't belong). Without support in developing curiosity, openness to uncertainty, and tolerance for messy progress, the workshop risks becoming a brittle space of self-protective posturing.

When our curiosity is activated, in contrast, we can enter a workshop centered and open to exploring the new possibilities readers open up in our work. We offer strategies to cultivate this habit of mind across this book, particularly in **Chapter 3**. To truly embrace this value, writers must learn to be comfortable with uncertainty. Lynda Barry refers to this state as being, "able to stand not knowing long enough to let something alive take shape" (Barry 2008, 135). When we discuss Carol Dweck's work on mindset (2006) or introduce experiments in non-linear revision (**Chapter 8**), we can help students release their grip on a fixed mindset (where the only way to feel good is to have talent—understood as innate and unchangeable—validated) and move toward a flexible or growth mindset (in which any skill can be improved with practice).

Agency

The frequent companion of defensiveness is passivity. An unempowered student might see the workshop as an ordeal to survive rather than a gathering of capable people eager to assist. Along with coaching students to move from anxiety to curiosity, we also support them in claiming agency across all aspects of a workshop, such as:

- **When to bring writing to workshop.** We talk explicitly with students about points along a continuum from completely personal to completely public. A writer might be ready to write something but not yet share it, or share it but not yet engage with it critically, or engage critically but not publish. The more students can recognize and claim agency over these steps, the better.
- **How to care for peers by including content or introductory notes.** (See **Chapter 4** for a discussion of community agreements and content notes.)
- **Which workshop approach to adopt** (in cases where they have options).
- **What questions to ask readers.** One writer might be interested in hearing how different readers experienced a piece in an open-ended way, whereas another might aim for targeted responses to measure the effectiveness of specific intentions.

Thoughtfully prepared questions will set either writer up for success. Students can also learn to ask questions that get at their own oversights or open them up for surprise, like, "What's happening here that I haven't addressed in my questions and maybe haven't even noticed?" or "What am I not asking that I should be asking?"

- **When to move the group forward if a discussion no longer feels fruitful.**
- **What to do with the feedback they receive (Chapter 8).**

Assigning an artist's statement to accompany a draft can be a great way to guide students toward claiming greater agency in their workshops. Here's a version Felicia Rose Chavez shared with us:

> This statement serves as a cover page and hits on the points below in an informal, conversational exchange.
>
> - Summarize your project in one to two sentences.
> - What surprised you while you were crafting the project?
> - What aspect(s) of the project posed the greatest challenge for you?
> - What successes resulted from the project?
> - What is your vision for a future draft?
> - Enumerate three craft-based questions about your project to guide feedback. What do you need help sorting out?

Ultimately, the end goal of the workshop should never be that a student survived or received only praise confirming their ability as a writer. Instead, the writer should leave energized with possibilities to approach their next draft. When we encourage student agency, we make space for students to assume ownership and responsibility over their work and process. They learn to articulate intentions, recognize craft choices, and ask questions that will yield useful feedback, supported by a steady assurance that their vision is valuable and worth pursuing. These are all useful and lasting skills whether students continue into a writing career or pursue other professions.

Zac Hug on the TV writers' room

Writing for TV is highly collaborative, with a writers' room working together to draft and refine parts of a larger narrative. How do you talk to students about this?

The shared ownership of a writers' room can be pretty different from what students expect in a workshop. Writers' rooms are so different from academia that I find myself explaining a lot, "In a writers' room, it would work this way, but in this room, because I want you to learn this skill, here's how we're doing this."

Rather than workshopping one or two scripts each week, I set up three or four mini-workshops that I rotate people through over the course of the term. So, three people read the pitch, and then three other people read the outline, and then three different people read the draft. By the end of the course, everyone's read something from everyone else. It's very common in a writers' room for a writer to be off writing and then come back to find the room has moved on. Those who read the initial pitch are very excited at the end to read the script and see how it's grown.

What have students picked up as a result of their hours of TV watching? And what are they surprised to discover in class?

When you watch good TV, it feels almost effortless. But when you're writing it, you realize that underneath every line of dialogue is an enormous amount of work. Not a single line of dialogue gets filmed that doesn't relate to another line of dialogue or a central idea or move the structure forward, though you don't consciously register this when you're just watching the show. Students discover the structure underneath not just the whole episode, but each scene, each exchange. They can get overwhelmed when they realize how granular it is. But my job here is also to say, "Okay, you know it, now forget it. Draft the story and then return to structure as a diagnostic."

TV structure can seem strict, even formulaic. How do you help students find space for creativity within constraints?

TV relies on old storytelling tropes that are constant: if you watch a show about teenagers, it's going to have a love triangle. You have to speak in the language of what television is to find what's unique about it. We talk very specifically about the trope that you expect. How can you embrace it first, double down on it, and then change one thing? So, a love triangle. I'll say, "Okay, what's one thing you can change?" And usually, they'll change the drive of one character that will change the dynamic of the triangle. And then I'll say, "If the character gets what they want, how does that cause a problem?" When you tell someone to subvert a trope, they might say, "Oh, the opposite of the pain of family that I'm writing about is the joy of family. I'm going to explore that for a minute." And it allows them to break out of the molds they're in or the ruts that we all fall into.

ZAC HUG teaches television writing at UCLA Extension, DePaul University, and the UBC School of Creative Writing. His TV writing credits include *Drop Dead Diva* (Lifetime), *Shadowhunters* (Freeform), and a wild amount of Movies of the Week for Hallmark.

Image credit: Devon Wycoff

Coaching attentive generous readers

The gift of specificity

Over time, we've moved away from thinking about feedback as "positive" and "negative" and toward thinking of feedback as descriptive and responsive. As readers, we can describe a writer's work back to them and tell them how we experienced it. And they can use this information to make decisions about how to proceed. What we have to offer is our attention. Often a student's first impulse in workshop is to begin with praise and judgment. "I liked your imagery," someone might say, "but the pacing wasn't working." In an interview with Aimee Nezhukumatathil (2022), Ross Gay describes this scenario as "babies with hatchets":

> I'm no longer interested in someone submitting their poem or whatever to be scrutinized, which often really means shaving off all the weird edges, the stuff we don't yet know how to understand. I'm glad to ask good, provocative questions of what we write, but I can't really stand how we used to submit our poems to the scalpels and hatchets of our classmates, many of whom, first of all, don't have a long relationship with the work they're hatcheting, and many of whom, secondly, are very new at this. They're like babies with hatchets, which is cute but very dangerous.

Gay points out that early judgment—especially from novices new to the writer and the work—risks "shaving off all the weird edges" of work in progress. To avoid "babies with hatchets," we propose two key interventions: (1) moving toward approaches like CRP that offer clear structure and foreground questions, and (2) coaching students toward closer attention to what's on the page and greater specificity in their responses to peers.

In our interview conversation (**Chapter 2**), A. E. Osworth talked about how to coach students on getting more specific: "Not just, 'it was funny.' Why is it funny? I'll say, 'Describe why this is funny and what knowledge base it's relying on.' Maybe it's funny because of juxtaposition. Or expectations. Likewise, why is this gross?"

When a reader points to the page and describes in detail what they notice, the writer learns precisely where a line of dialogue was hilarious or poignant, how a piece of description was unclear, why an image was resonant. In establishing an expectation of specificity, we eliminate much of the lazier and potentially harmful opinion-based feedback a student who has merely skimmed the piece might offer. From the start, we build the capacity for close attentive reading through engagement with published texts. Simultaneously, we work to build a shared vocabulary of craft that serves the particular students in the room. We've found students ultimately experience relief as they learn to translate gut reactions into nuanced responses and release themselves from the expectation of giving a verdict or judgment. Instead, they can offer their deep detailed noticing.

Strategies for when workshop vibes are off

Workshop groups are responsive to feedback loops, both positive and negative. Early trust and appreciation for peers can lead to more trust, more support, more encouragement, even lasting writing groups beyond the course. But, if harsh critique or bad faith shows up early, the resulting bad feelings can lead to suspicion, guardedness, and anxiety that similarly build and reinforce. Here are a few interventions to consider when things get off track:

- Reach out to students individually to see if they're experiencing any barriers to participation/engagement.
- Pause for a meta-conversation about workshopping, why we do it, and what we hope to get out of it.
- Pause for an exercise or activity that focuses on appreciating one another and building good feelings.
- Establish more structured expectations and accountability for engagement (i.e., x number of posts or bring notes to class).
- Experiment with scale. Shift peer feedback into smaller or larger groups, or into pairs.
- Reduce the amount of the course dedicated to discussing work in favor of other activities.

Reading generously

Student writers sometimes balk at the dedication and time needed to engage deeply with peer work. "It's not my genre," "I'm too busy this week," "I'm not a fan of the writer," "That writer doesn't give as much feedback as I give them," or similar refrains might be heard. As instructors, we need to think carefully about the balance of time dedicated to drafting, revising, reading published work, engaging with peer work, and so on. In courses where we choose to prioritize peer feedback, we need to help students understand why reading generously matters and how to go about it. Reading generously means:

- Spending time with peer work when rested and focused enough to take it in.
- Responding with honesty (and taking the time to identify where we might need to sit with a question or reaction to be able to ask a question or offer an opinion that is both honest and kind).
- Keeping in mind that our perspective is not universal and that we may not be the centered reader for the work (of particular importance for discussing work coming from a marginalized position). As Matthew Salesses writes in *Craft in the Real World* (2021), "When the workshop critiques a manuscript from the position of an unspecified, and therefore normative, reader—or when it similarly claims 'universal' values as if the values are not cultural—it makes fiction's greatest strength its greatest weakness. It demands from the imagination either conformity or exoticism" (120).

- Making the leap to support another writer's vision (which may include learning more about the aesthetic and/or cultural context they're working in).
- Coming full circle to recognize that generosity to others is ultimately generosity to ourselves as well, given the growth we experience as writers by engaging with work that challenges us or stretches us into new subjects, subjectivities, or styles.

Erika Meitner on helping students develop their own center

Your menu of workshop options includes so many exciting possibilities! Still, students can take a while to settle into a critique approach. How do you find a balance here?

For introductory classes, I use a structured approach. For advanced classes, before we use the workshop menu, I have everybody bring in their best poem so they can show it off to the class, and then I have them bring their most broken draft. They talk to us about where they're stuck with it, and we take it home, read it, and generate ideas for things they might try with it. When we meet, we start with the question, "What if?" In doing those two things, we eliminate people's need to show off as we go through the semester, and we become a community of practice. We also do an intensive draft week where they draft five poems in seven days, and just post them without commenting. If you see each other's terrible drafts, or sometimes great drafts, you start to understand their working process. So, before we get to the menu, we've done a lot to build trust.

Before each session, we go through what kind of workshop each person wants, and reaffirm what that workshop is. Writers learn as much by asking for the "wrong" workshop as they do by picking the "right" workshop. At the end, there's a moment for them to reflect. They can bring the poem back and we can do another kind of workshop if they want. That's up to them.

You've mentioned that your goal is for students "not to need the workshop"—can you say more about this?

To be super frank, I've worked before with colleagues who encouraged students' dependence on them in unhealthy ways. It became an almost guru-esque relationship where the student was looking for approval from the professor. I wanted students to develop their own center, and I became so uninterested in whether or not I thought a poem was good, so much more interested in questions like "How is this poem working? What does it seem to be doing?"

When I give written feedback, from intro poets to graduate students, I tell students to ask me two to three questions about their poem. I do a close read of the work and then answer the questions and ask them one back. And their question can't be "Is this poem good?" because I won't answer it. It can be "Is the ending working in conjunction with the poem?" It can be something about my interpretation or whether something is working in the context of something else. But it can't just be a value judgment. This is also a way to take a pulse of the class. If everybody keeps asking "Does this title work with the poem?" I know I need to do a craft lecture on poem titling.

If students develop their own center, they can ask people for focused feedback. I never want them to be in a position where they're depending on whether or not an editor takes poems in a journal to determine whether or not the poems are good. Anything I can do to move them farther along that path drives all of my pedagogy.

How do you set up a workshop so that students can wade into challenging issues or intense feelings without harming themselves or others?

I insist that we talk about the speaker in the poem, and I always correct students if they slip and say *you*: "No, we say *the speaker*." Maintaining that distance is so important for talking about really sticky issues because it allows some distance between the speaker in the poem's views and the person sitting in workshop even if it's clearly the same person. We talk about text-to-self connection, text-to-text connection and text-to-world connection. Whenever we're writing about another human, I raise questions like, "What is the text-to-self connection here? How is the self implicated in the poem? What is the speaker's connection to the material? How do you make that clear?"

ERIKA MEITNER is a Professor of English at the University of Wisconsin-Madison. A 2023 Mandel Institute Cultural Leadership Fellow, she is the author of six books of poems, including *Holy Moly Carry Me*, winner of the 2018 National Jewish Book Award and a finalist for the National Book Critics Circle Award, and *Useful Junk*.

Strategies for asynchronous and large-enrollment courses

Although "workshop" likely calls to mind a small group of writers gathered around a shared table, we've experienced dynamic critique sessions in both fully asynchronous and large-enrollment courses. In fact, we've discovered some secret advantages these contexts offer. Let's look at a couple of case studies.

A fully asynchronous workshop

Students in UBC's optional-residency MFA stream enroll in semester-long workshop courses with a twenty-seven hour active window. This means that students from rural Ontario to Boston to Hong Kong with different work and care commitments read and write on their own for six days and then come together to pop in and out of the course site as fits their individual schedules during the active window. In one workshop model we've used, students connect in groups of 4–6 for an adapted form of CRP. Each student has a dedicated discussion board set up with a comment for each step of CRP. Although CRP is typically a time-bound series of steps, in this example of an asynchronous environment, each step becomes a site for a particular form of engagement, and students engage in a lively back-and-forth simultaneously on multiple questions.

Some Challenges: It can be hard to read tone in the absence of voice and body language, so we encourage students to keep this in mind (and draw on emojis, memes, or GIFs as they see fit). It's also tougher to offer a gentle reframe or convey active listening, and we sometimes miss that magical co-creation of meaning that can happen in a synchronous workshop.

Some Advantages: Students who aren't verbal processors have the chance to think and respond at their own pace. There's less opportunity for a single student to dominate the discussion. Without the fixed time container of a 2–3 hour class, students can go deep with clarifying questions and follow-ups, getting to the heart of their inquiry. The writer can look back at feedback at their leisure without having to take notes.

Written critique swaps in an introductory course of 200+

Six key choices to support a rich group critique experience in, for example, a large TA-supported introductory class:

1. **Written feedback** (with an optional verbal debrief). Written feedback allows students, including those who were sick or traveling for sports, to engage fully on their own schedules (and creates a clear artifact TAs can read and respond to).
2. **A structured feedback process based on CRP.** Students use a detailed editable Response Sheet template that guides them through the first three steps of CRP.
3. **Swaps rather than groups.** Rather than working in small groups, each student selects three readers (one of whom could be from outside the class) and serves as a reader for two peers.
4. **Discussion Board as Community Notice Board.** Students use a discussion board to find peers to trade drafts with. Students note material in their work and name what they're looking for in a reader (which may include being ready to engage with challenging content). Students also note material for which their positionality and experiences make them an especially apt reader (such as "work from an Asian diaspora perspective" or "work engaging with climate change") and share their "special powers" as readers, which may include anything from asking brave questions to reading a draft multiple times. By identifying what they're looking for in a reader and what they have to offer as a reader, students cultivate awareness of their positionality and learn to name their growing skills.
5. **Coach preparation.** Before engaging with peers, students have coaching opportunities focused on how to shape effective questions.
6. **Assess engagement.** Students turn in packets that compile responses to their work and their feedback to others and are assessed on their engagement both as writers and as readers (and not, at this point, on their writing).

Some Challenges: Even with the added flexibility of written feedback, if a student misses the train on arranging swaps, they may struggle to catch up. We mitigate this by giving students ample time for the assignment and creating an extra discussion board for last-minute swaps. Google Docs allow both the reader and the writer access to the latest update and can be easily downloaded and compiled. A checklist cover sheet helps reduce the cognitive load of remembering all the pieces.

Some Advantages: Committed students can find each other and go deep with this approach. Because the class is so large, students—who might be the only Indigenous student or the only trans student in a workshop of twelve or twenty—have a good chance of finding readers who can approach their work as insiders and/or who align with their target audience.

A student perspective: Micah Favel on different workshop approaches

You've participated in different group critique models in your creative writing courses. Can you tell us about one you've found useful?

I found the asynchronous written swaps to be incredibly helpful because we had the opportunity to describe the different themes of our work and what we were looking for in both insider and outsider readers and then match with other students based on that. I had the opportunity to have my work read by those who had similar lived experiences to me, and as such, had a greater degree of insight into my work. I was matched with an inside reader who was also Indigenous, and I received feedback that felt especially relevant and meaningful.

Sharing work in progress with peers can be vulnerable. What can a teacher do to make this risk feel worthwhile?

In my last poetry workshop, we didn't share any of our work until the fourth week, which initially left me wondering when it would happen, considering it was a workshop course. However, this approach allowed my group to become more comfortable with one another and get to know each other a lot better. When the time finally came to share our work, the idea of being vulnerable and open with my group felt much less daunting. During those initial weeks, we engaged in activities that allowed us to explore our writing topics and present our findings to the group. This early engagement helped us to better understand the interests of each member writing, and as a result, we became much more invested in each other's pieces.

MICAH FAVEL is a poet. Much of her writing focuses on queerness, loss, and their mixed Plains Cree and settler Scottish identity. Her work has appeared in *Querencia Press*, *Queer Toronto Literary Magazine*, and the *Ex-Puritan*.
Image credit: Katie Tissington-Turner

Designing your workshop approach

The role of group critique in the course

In **Chapter 3**, we discuss activities like sharing part of a piece (even just a sentence), debriefing writing experiences, reading new drafts out loud, and small-group workshops with defined parameters for response. As these approaches demonstrate, group critique doesn't have to be all or nothing. Students can be both nervous and hungry to share their work, and strategies like these invite students to bring new, tentative, or experimental writing into a group conversation without having to treat it as fully claimed and intentional.

Designing a successful group critique experience depends on making thoughtful decisions that keep the goals of the specific course and needs of particular students in mind. Here's an inventory of key starting questions to consider:

- **How much of the course do you want to devote to group critique?** 10%? 50%? 80%? Any of these could make sense and work well, depending on course focus and goals.
- **When in the term will group critique sessions take place?** Once in Week 10, from Week 8 until the end, every three weeks interspersed with other activities?
- **What work will students bring for critique?** New work? Revised work? Partial drafts? Complete drafts? If students have the option to bring in work at different stages of development, what workshop approach(es) can accommodate this range?
- **What group size makes sense?** Pairs? Small groups of 3–5 students? A full class of 12? Small group critique can offer more students a chance to receive feedback on their work within the same class period. Without the instructor present for each workshop, however, students may need a clearly laid out structure and explicit practice in workshop skills. Other decisions arise: will the groups be self-selected or assigned? Will groups remain consistent throughout the term or change from session to session?
- **What workshop approach(es) will be adopted and who decides?** Sometimes, a single workshop approach gives students a valuable chance to hone skills. In other contexts, you might prefer to explore several possibilities, invite students to choose from a few options, or offer an à-la-carte list of activities/engagements.
- **What is assessed and how?** We typically defer assessing work submitted for group critique until students have had a chance to revise it, as we find that receiving formative feedback (comments aimed at future development of the work) at the same time as summative feedback (a grade that treats the work as complete) gets in the way of developing the work. Still, we assess group critique process through a series of complete/incomplete steps or through attention to developing skills (like asking good questions) under a heading such as "Engagement in Workshop Process."

Preparation and engagement

We've talked about the value of preparing students for group critique and how that preparation might take the form of developing shared vocabulary and touchstones by reading and discussing published work, taking time to build trust by sharing writing experiences, or practicing skills like asking good questions. As we discuss in **Chapter 8**, individual conferences can also help students integrate group critique into a larger iterative process.

Each group critique session involves preparation and decisions. These include:

- **Pre-reading or cold reading?** Students might share their work several days or a week before the session so that peers have time to reread it and take notes. Sometimes, however, reading a poem or a paragraph on the spot with a defined structure for response can be efficient and useful, especially when peers have the text in front of them.
- **What does the writer share with readers?** Along with their work in progress, writers might share a "context piece" (an essay, image, or other artifact to help peers contextualize the work, whether by introducing theoretical concerns, establishing an aesthetic example, or offering relevant information), an artist's statement, or prepared questions.
- **Synchronous or asynchronous?** Although this decision may seem to be made by the modality of the course, we suggest staying open to possibilities. An in-person course might use written feedback, and an asynchronous long-distance course might pair students up to connect via phone or videoconference.
- **Modes of engagement and response?** Do students prepare private written notes for a verbal workshop? Do they write feedback letters to give to the writer? Who decides? What guidance or structure do they have? In making these decisions, we consider the amount of time written feedback requires and the possibility of feedback letters being overwhelming or actively harmful to the writer, and tend to opt for quality over quantity and structure over open-endedness.
- **Who takes on what role?** Depending on size, level, and modality, we might ask students to take on defined roles. These roles include facilitator (who keeps track of time and moves the session through different stages of engagement), scribe (who takes notes so that the writer can listen), or support person (who meets with the writer before/after the workshop to help refine questions or debrief feedback). As instructors, we also have to decide on our own role: Facilitator? Participant? Observer? Coach?

As we make decisions about how to structure workshop engagements, we're always thinking on two levels: (1) What will serve the course? and (2) What will students take from this experience beyond the course? Students who learn to give supportive detail-oriented feedback will never lack for collaborators. And students who learn to articulate their goals and ask for the feedback they need will benefit from these skills in any future work with editors, mentors, beta-readers, or publishers.

Ultimately, group critique is not a destination, but a step along a larger process. For workshop to be useful, students must learn to synthesize feedback, identify "actionable" items in that feedback, weigh these actions against their own vision for their work, revise, reflect, repeat. We get into all of this in **Chapter 8**.

8

Revision and Iterative Practice

Why teach revision?

Revision might be the most powerful tool we can offer students, as writers and as humans. When students return to a piece of writing and change it based on experimentation, reader feedback, and their own growing clarity until it lives up to their inner vision, they develop an experience-informed sense of their capacity for transformation.

In **Chapter 3**, we looked at strategies to invite students to approach their work with a spirit of curiosity, play, and experimentation. Here, we build on that generative work and explore macro versus micro revision, revising in response to feedback, and developing an individual iterative process. Drawing on our conversations with writers and teachers, we contemplate ways to bring a revision mindset to our courses that begins on day one and is interwoven throughout the semester.

Revision means bringing keen and curious attention to writing with a goal of helping it reach its full potential. Here's the tricky part, though: we don't always know what that full potential might be. We have to mess around and test different possibilities. In fact, an experienced writer's process often involves doubling back to start over or undo something, rather than moving along a straight line. A lightbulb moment starts as a puzzle or even a mistake; a tertiary character in a scene suddenly becomes the protagonist of a story. Beginning writers can be tempted to rush toward a finish, uncomfortable in the limbo space of work in progress. Yet, to write seriously, they must learn how to live in that space.

So much in our lives and those of our students pushes us toward efficiency: deadlines, jobs, caretaking responsibilities, laundry, dinner, bills. But making art is inherently inefficient. How do we respect the real-time struggles students confront while gently inviting them to join us in building some small space in our lives ungoverned by the tyranny of efficiency?

When we teach deep revision, we invite students to participate in a culture of curiosity that replaces a culture of superficial polish. In this spirit of curiosity, we can tinker delicately or blow up our writing; we can move phrases, paragraphs, or entire sections around; delete entire scenes, chapters, perhaps even entire drafts.

Yet, students also find revision difficult because revising our work goes hand-in-hand with revising ourselves. In our conversation, Alex Marzano-Lesnevich said, "Revision might not just be a revision of writing on the page, but more crucially, a revision of how students think about what they're exploring." The further students go in developing a project, the more they're pushed to learn about themselves in step with the work. As they confront challenges in the writing, they also confront challenges within themselves: What's my process? Am I working efficiently enough? Do I still believe what I thought I had to say about anger? Am I smart enough to write this piece? How do I cope with feelings of frustration or stuckness?

The single most valuable skill in revision is the ability to manage our emotions. It's challenging enough to revise on the page, but when revision also means looking at our own tendencies, habits, moral and aesthetic blind spots, and ways of seeing the world, it's no wonder students find themselves overwhelmed or full of doubts. How can we cultivate the courage to keep going, the self-compassion to rest and return, the perspective to recognize doubt as a familiar step along the way rather than a sign of failure?

In this chapter, we tackle these important cognitive and emotional aspects of revision alongside concrete techniques and strategies appropriate to each stage of development.

Why is revision challenging to teach?

We've talked about how a single course can't do everything. From conversations with colleagues and students, we've found that revision is frequently the first thing to fall by the wayside. We tend to hear three main reasons:

1 Semesters are short.
2 Concrete examples of revision can be hard to come by.
3 Revision approaches and techniques vary widely from writer to writer.

Everyone agrees that revision is important. Often, instructors hope someone else is teaching it.

Tight on time: fitting revision into a busy term

Instructors teaching beginners can easily find their time filled up with introducing essential craft concepts. "Students need to know the basics and write a draft before they can revise," these instructors might say. Classes with an emphasis on group critique can quickly fill up with workshop slots. Genres like screenwriting might include plenty of iterative processes as students move from pitch to treatment to outline to draft but never quite make time for a second draft.

For instructors with heavy teaching loads, grading and written feedback also pose significant challenges. If an instructor gives detailed feedback on a stack of drafts, they might not have time to turn around and grade an equally large stack of revised drafts. They might reasonably decide to give the drafts a grade and allow students to submit revisions for a regrade. But students risk receiving a tacit message: revision is for people who don't get it right the first time. (We offer some suggestions in **Chapter 10** for these thorny assessment time crunch challenges.) In this chapter, we propose a range of strategies to develop revision techniques and habits in a busy term.

The challenge of making revision visible

While it's easy to find a wealth of examples of well-executed craft and technique across genres, revision can be more difficult to demonstrate. Students reading a published novel generally have no sense of the drafts, revisions, reimaginings, feedback sessions, editorial comments, and reworkings that led to the version they hold in their hands. Even experienced writers are tempted to compare other people's "ends" with our own messy "middles" and despair.

Fortunately, an attitude of secrecy and supposed instant mastery is giving way to a growing body of publications and resources aimed at demystifying revision. Journals like *Underbelly* and the *Guernica* "back draft" series feature drafts and radical revision alongside writer statements or interviews on the revision process. Likewise, books like *The Art of Revising Poetry: 21 US Poets on Their Drafts, Craft, and Process*; *Wonderbook*; *The Art of Revision: The Last Word*; and John McPhee's *Draft No. 4: On the Writing Process* pull back the curtain on how a napkin scribble or meandering freewrite can transform into a deeply intentional and fully claimed work of art.

How to teach revision when writers revise differently?

Even with this growing body of revision examples and resources, instructors may struggle to know where and how to begin. In "That Crafty Feeling," Zadie Smith contrasts what she calls "Macro Planners" and "Micro Managers." A self-avowed member of the latter group, Smith describes obsessively reworking the first twenty pages of *On Beauty* for almost two years. She writes:

> When I finally settled on a tone, the rest of the book was finished in five months. Worrying over the first 20 pages is a way of working on the whole novel, a way of finding its structure, its plot, its characters—all of which, for a Micro Manager, are contained in the sensibility of a sentence. Once the tone is there, all else follows. (Smith 2010, 101)

In contrast, Lauren Groff variously horrified and delighted writers in a *New York Times* profile where she described completing rapid longhand drafts in large spiral notebooks that she never reads again, relying on memory to carry forward the "most vital bits" from draft to draft. Groff also discusses working on several projects simultaneously: "I'm trying to Jedi-mind trick myself into not putting so much pressure on any particular project by having them be really loose for the first really long span of time," she said. "I'm writing toward—who knows? Letting it be exploration and joy, centered around either questions or a central thesis or an image" (Groff 2023).

In a world where one brilliant novelist obsessively tinkers with the first twenty pages for two years, while another races longhand through a draft she'll never reread, what common useful approach can a writing instructor offer? In addition, instructors sometimes see their own revision approaches as idiosyncratic and may struggle to identify a coherent transmittable method to guide students. As with matters of craft, we propose introducing students to a range of revision experiences and approaches, encouraging them to experiment and develop their own iterative process (which will continue to shift as they encounter new genres and projects and adapt to changing life circumstances).

Jillian Hess on revision lessons from the archives

You've consulted hundreds of writers' notes both for your book and for your Substack *Noted*. Can you describe a few specific items you've encountered that have stuck with you?

So many things! In order to learn how to write satirical essays, Benjamin Franklin would translate an essay he admired into poetry. Then, when he'd forgotten the original essay, he'd attempt to turn the poem back into an essay. This helped him improve his vocabulary. He'd also reverse-outline a favorite essay, then jumble the outline. Once he had forgotten the essay, he'd try to put the jumbled outline back in its proper order. This helped him hone skills in sequencing. I love James Baldwin's notes because he was a very talented doodler. He drew faces in profile alongside his notes, which were often outlines for his speeches. Beatrix Potter's diary is fascinating because she wrote it in a cipher so sophisticated it took scholars over a decade to crack.

What might beginning writers be surprised to discover in the notebooks of a deeply accomplished writer?

Octavia Butler used her notebooks to record motivation. She didn't have formal training or mentors to support her. So, she had to support herself. She wrote out a series of visions for herself. In a notebook, she wrote "Every day / In every way / I am becoming / A better / More successful / Selling Writer" (Butler). Toni Morrison's brilliant writing is a result of ruthless editing. She went through at least 10 drafts while working on *Beloved*. Another great tip from Toni Morrison's notes is to start out with a précis—a little summary of what you want to write about. All of Morrison's novels were motivated by a single, meaty idea. This idea would inspire her to sketch out a précis. Each of her novels was also deeply researched. She kept files with annotated bibliographies of the books and articles she read as she prepared each novel.

What have you noticed about process across the many archives you've consulted?

Many writers have a practice of collecting small, seemingly insignificant ideas in their notebooks and recommend writers always carry a notebook with them. For example, in *Plotting and Writing Suspense Fiction*, Patricia Highsmith advises her readers: "Write down all these slender ideas. It is surprising how often one sentence, jotted in a notebook, leads immediately to a second sentence. A plot can develop as you write notes. Close the notebook and think about it for a few days—and then presto! You're ready to write a short story" (Highsmith 1990, 36).

Similarly, Agatha Christie found inspiration at random moments and always had notebooks on hand. In her autobiography, Christie remarks,

> Plots come to me at such odd moments: when I am walking along a street, or examining a hat-shop with particular interest, suddenly a splendid idea comes into my head, and I think, "Now that would be a neat way of covering up the crime so that nobody would see the point." Of course, all the practical details are still to be worked out, and the people have to creep slowly into my consciousness, but I jot down my splendid idea in an exercise book. (Christie 2019, 451)

JILLIAN HESS is a Professor of English at Bronx Community College, CUNY where she coordinates the First-Year seminar. She is the author of *How Romantics and Victorians Organized Information: Commonplace Books, Scrapbooks, and Albums*. Additionally, she writes a newsletter, *Noted*, all about how brilliant thinkers take notes.

Image credit: Jillian Hess

Teaching revision across the life cycle of a project

Although not every course will foreground revision to the same degree, we propose that all creative writing classes can be taught with a revision mindset: an emphasis on writing as discovery and an expectation that any project will move through an iterative process of intuitive exploration, critical attention, and deliberate experimentation. In other words, an expectation that all writing involves rewriting.

Macro revision: exploring "what ifs?" and making messes

When does revision begin? When you've completed a poem? When you have a full draft of a short story? As we see it, revision can, and often should, start earlier.

With the aim of helping students feel looser, less precious, and less attached to what they first set down on the page, we begin with generative structured exercises (**Chapter 3**) that invite students to make material: an image, a scene, a dialogue, a character sketch, a metaphor, a list of memories. By the time they put together a draft, they're already selecting from a wealth of material and weighing choices. In other words, they're already revising.

Documenting revision journeys: shifting focus from product to process

When teaching revision, we notice that students tend to rush toward a "finished" work, often seeming to feel "locked in" to initial structures or choices made without a great deal of awareness or intention. In response, we set out to design assignments that invite questions like: What is this? What could this be? What do I want this to be? Why did I do it this way? What happens if I try this instead?

Revision might look like work on the page—cutting, adding, rearranging. It might also involve rewriting by hand, using a computer program to remix text to see it differently, or freewriting about what is at the heart of a project. We wanted to make all forms of revision visible, to value exploration and experimentation, even when a specific technique didn't lead to demonstrable improvement in the text at hand. Busy students understandably prioritize what's assessed and graded. How could we shift focus from the revised work as a final product to the process of revision itself?

A revision as exploration log asks students to choose from a list of radical revision strategies designed to expand, contract, remix, or reimagine the body of work drafted in the course. Here are a few sample options:

- Select bits and pieces that feel most "alive" from the material produced so far and experiment with expanding and arranging them.
- Identify two or three keywords. Look these words up in the *Oxford English Dictionary*, and draw on their etymology and history to deepen your work.

Rather than submitting only their final revisions, students complete and share a log with an entry for each revision strategy that discusses and documents process (What did you try? How did it go?) and shares insights (What did you notice?). Keeping a log shifts focus from product to process and allows an instructor to respond to students' intentions and realizations as well as what is happening in their work.

Exploring parallel paths: making space for non-linear revision

A potter must choose to glaze a bowl in blue or in black. As writers working with computers, however, we have other possibilities available to us. We can save multiple versions of a draft and experiment. We can try both: glaze in blue and glaze in black and test which we prefer. The original remains untouched and available to return to if we ultimately decide an experiment is not working. Yet, developing writers can be reluctant to take full advantage of possibilities of testing and considering divergent choices.

Writers who explore parallel paths do so with the knowledge that some work will ultimately be discarded. And yet, we can also learn to experience a transgressive pleasure in undoing, reversing, or exploding our careful work (safe in the knowledge that it persists unharmed in a separate document). As Monica Youn said in our conversation, "When students have one version in the bag already, any further play can feel relatively low stakes. They feel free to take bigger risks than they might've taken with the original, less pressure to be authoritative or get it right."

A revision log offers students a great supportive structure for testing out multiple revision approaches with the same draft, either sequentially or divergently.

- Students in poetry might experiment with different ways to arrange a single poem on the page: short lines and long lines, couplets and long stanzas, field composition and numbered prose sections, normative orthography and irregular typography, with and without punctuation.
- Students in narrative genres might rewrite a scene in past tense and present tense or from multiple points of view. They might test setting a scene in several different locations to see what possibilities and pressures each setting offers.
- Students in multi-genre classes might reimagine an alternate version of poem as comic, story as song, or picture book as screenplay.
- An instructor might dedicate class time to a revision "lab session" and set up stations for different types of engagement.

Assignments that foreground non-linear revision and value process can help students:

- See their work as malleable. For many students, changing a piece of writing has only ever been a response to a correction or critique, motivated by a desire to fix or improve. When students are invited to change their writing as an experiment, they can inhabit a different relationship to the act of drafting, one that understands the initial draft as contingent and open to change.
- Become aware of choices they didn't even know they made. Students often write in present tense or in first person based on a vague assumption that poems or contemporary stories are "like that" rather than a deliberate choice. Exploring other possibilities offers them a low-pressure way to make these choices more intentionally (or to make other choices).
- Think about writing and skill development across multiple projects. When a revision log asks students to share insights and observations about the specific text they're manipulating but also about themselves as writers, how language works, or their creative process more broadly, they consider the long horizon of skill development and record insights that might support their future writing even when a particular experiment doesn't improve the text at hand.
- Embrace reflection and metacognition for themselves. Students come to see reflective writing not just as a way of showing your work for the teacher but as a tool most working writers rely on. Documenting progress and observations allows writers to notice more things and to consolidate vague impressions into clear language we can carry forward and apply. In sharing examples of process logs and reflective writing from published writers or our own practice, we also show how reflective writing helps us attune to our own cycles and stories. These practices become especially crucial for sustained projects, as we discuss in **Chapter 11**.

Monica Youn on generative revision

In a recent essay, you contrast "zero-sum" with "generative revision." What is this?

Generative revision is the idea that multiple versions of a poem can co-exist, that one doesn't have to supersede the other. You can have the original, but then continue to go back to that original as source material to do spin-offs, sequels, prequels, remixes, as artists across different art forms have done for ages. I might ask students to take an existing poem and do a version of torrin greathouse's "Burning Haibun" and see what happens when you try to distill your own poem down to its core or just one isolated angle. A popular variation is a detail study, where students take a detail from an existing poem and expand it into its own poem. Or I do a formal study where students take eight to twelve phrases from their own work and arrange them into a pantoum and see what possibilities emerge through those juxtapositions. Exercises like these let students get their hands into what they thought was finished and just arrange it. I say, "Look, this isn't going to impact the finished work, and it's still really fertile ground that you can keep playing with."

How might generative revision operate differently at different points of development?

At an early phase, I'll often have students do something I call an "exhaustion exercise." We read Wallace Stevens' "Thirteen Ways of Looking at a Blackbird," and then I tell students to take one topic and come up with thirteen different takes. Maybe they ultimately land on one that's more persuasive than the others or has a gravitational force that pulls the other variations into it. Or maybe they end up with a "thirteen ways" poem, which might offer a different approach to a difficult or multifaceted topic. For graduate students, I might take this further and say, "Pick one topic to write about all semester." They'll end up exhausting everything obvious or top-of-the-mind and getting into these very interesting subconscious levels or unusual takes that lead to the best poems. One student started with the word "egg," and it turned into this complicated exploration of femininity, fertility, and outer space. "Egg" became a symbol that just kept deepening and drawing more and more things into itself. It's good to start with something physical. At first, you write the obvious things about eggs, like "You eat them for breakfast" or "They come from chickens." But by about take eleven, you're having to mine deep and unearth new meanings.

When you ask students to practice generative revision, what visions of writing are you up against?

You're up against the perfectionist mode of writing, like "I have one poem to write about my difficult relationship with my mother, and I've got to nail this in one take, and everything has to be absolutely right." Students end up trying to balance aesthetic factors, emotional factors, societal responsibility factors in one poem, and it becomes a tightrope act where they're afraid to set a foot wrong. Generative revision allows more leeway for error. Even if you stray a little too far in one direction, you can balance it out with the next take. I especially find it helpful for writing about difficult topics like personal relationships, race, or gender. I hope that students leave the course with a freedom with words as a medium that other artists have to play with their media. Just because words have a more direct relationship to meaning than other media may historically have had doesn't mean that words have to be locked into one meaning. You can keep playing and exploring with words and ideas and find them inexhaustible.

How might instructors in genres like fiction or screenwriting build on these approaches?

I've had people from fiction writers to playwrights try this approach. You might explore a different character's points of view. You might explore different endings. You might take one detail from a story and make it into its own story. You might have one seed story that creates a constellation of stories that surround it. You might have a *Rashomon*-like film that explores a scene from different angles. What if a choice that swung one way swung in the other direction? What would have happened? How would the characters have responded? Again, it's trying to get away from the idea that there is one authoritative take and one central focus and one camera angle that is absolutely right. To see what happens if you leave the door open for other possibilities.

MONICA YOUN is a Professor of English at UC Irvine and a former constitutional lawyer. She is the author of four poetry collections, most recently *From From*, a finalist for the 2023 National Book Award.

Image credit: Beowulf Sheehan

Bringing non-judgmental curiosity to work in progress

After the flush of excitement in completing a draft, reality sets in, and with it, a tendency to view our work critically, perhaps to a degree that we neglect to see the good in it. Bringing a non-judgmental curiosity toward our work—seeing what's there and what's not and where it aligns with our initial vision—allows us to imagine how the work might develop and start formulating a plan of action. Writers across genres have discovered a range of tools for getting out of the "trees" of their writing to get a sense of the broader "forest." Here are a few that can work well in the classroom.

Reverse outlines, diagrams, maps, and inventories

Whereas some writers work with extensive outlines before beginning a draft and others prefer to jump straight in with freewriting, anyone working on a sustained project can benefit from some reverse outlining. If an outline is a plan for something you want to make, a "reverse outline" charts the moves and turns of what you've already drafted.

Reverse outlining creative work can take many forms. Students might use Scrivener, Post-Its, index cards on a table, a giant sheet of paper taped to the wall, or a whiteboard. Students working in prose forms might draw a horizontal straight line across a piece of paper and mark the major moments (scenes) in the work from beginning to end. In noting what's present, students identify not only key events but also gaps in their work: something needs to happen between moment A and B, moments C and D are similar and can be collapsed into one scene, moment E is inert and needs further work. They can begin to add, cut, or collapse moments to flush out the entire narrative.

A few other approaches:

- **Says/Does Chart.** Make two columns: "Says" and "Does." Move through a personal essay or play scene by scene or piece by piece. Briefly describe each piece in the "Says" column, and then attempt to articulate its function within the larger structure in the "Does" column. For example: Says: "Joe and his mom argue when he wants to borrow the car." Does: "Establishes tension between freedom and safety in their relationship."
- **Network Maps.** These might chart dynamics between characters, character motivations, or anything else that works in relationship.
- **Central Questions.** Identify 2–3 central questions at the heart of a story and graph scenes that speak to each one. Questions might relate to plot and suspense (i.e., Will Sophie find friends at her new school?) or to central ideas or themes (i.e., How do differences in social class inflect friendship?). Are there scenes that speak to multiple questions at the same time? Are there questions that "fade out" for long stretches?
- **Listening Inventory.** Ask students to choose something to track as they listen to peers read their drafts out loud. A student might record the presence of color language, food, changes in verb tense or point-of-view, or any number of other formal or thematic elements.

Students might resist this work when they struggle to see anything other than making new words as "writing" or fear the gaps and flaws that such mapping may reveal. We can remind these students that while outlining, they are still "writing" and "working" on the manuscript, that they are capable of finding solutions for any issues they uncover, and that they're testing out another tool to use when it serves them.

Using color to visualize

Color highlighting offers another strategy for bringing curious attention to our work. Seeing concrete visual evidence of our patterns and choices enables us to recognize and act on them. These exercises can help students diagnose and experiment with work in progress without a single word of feedback spoken. Here are a few highlighting strategies across genres:

- **Poetry: The Sentence and the Line.** Highlight each sentence of a poem in a different color. See what you notice about the relationship between the sentence, the line, and (if relevant) the stanza. Students working in prose might also highlight sentences to get a visual sense of sentence variation, structure, and complexity.

- **Fiction: Action, Description, Dialogue, Interiority**. Select a scene and highlight action, description, dialogue, and interiority, each in a different color. Some may notice an absence of description, others a dearth of interiority or long sections of dialogue uninterrupted by action or description.
- **Personal Essay: Scene, Summary, Reflection**. Use a crayon or highlighter to draw lines down the margin of an essay or memoir indicating shifts between scene, summary, and reflection to become aware of how these three modes work together.
- **Any Genre: Themes Or Emotions Across a Project of Any Length**. Use color highlighting to track emotion, tone, or theme across a project, from a single page of song lyrics to a full book manuscript, like Heather Christle, who describes using graph paper to chart themes across her braided essay *The Crying Book*: science was green, literature was yellow, autobiography was blue, with the shade deepening based on chronology. "At last," Christle writes, she could see, "the gaps and oversaturation in the pattern" (Lithub 2019).

Freewriting "next to" a draft

We encourage students to practice freewriting across all stages of a project. When the draft itself feels tangled and messy (or alternatively tightly woven, but still not quite right), students can find it freeing to work "next to" their draft rather than in it. They might freewrite draft material on a separate sheet of paper or a new document outside of the draft itself, where they're likely to feel more freedom to mess around. Or they might freewrite based on a question like, "What core memory is at the heart of this poem?" "How does the relationship between these two characters change across this novel?" or even "Why do I feel stuck on this section of my comic?" Students who freewrite around central questions or problems often find a surprising twist or unexpected solution emerge seemingly out of nowhere as their hand keeps moving.

When John worked with the playwright Joan McLeod, she described writing a soliloquy for each major or minor character in a piece of fiction, stage play or screenplay. Freewriting in this manner can help unlock character yearning, sharpen voice, lead to new discoveries in dramatic turn, or capture lines of truth. Although much of this writing may ultimately be discarded, the insights garnered will serve the entire work.

Micro revision: discovering the pleasures of obsession and practicing being a finisher

We see clear value in inviting students to experiment with detail-oriented micro revisions, equally essential for a working writer as exploratory macro revisions. As writers near the end of a writing process, more and more of the work on the page has been carefully considered and fully claimed. The intuitions and happy accidents of early drafts give way to deliberate technique and choice. As we tell students, "You don't need to know why you did it, but you need to know why you kept it."

At this point, students sometimes struggle with a writing paradox: engaging with their writing in a technical—even mechanical—way can lead to changes with significant emotional repercussions. To illustrate this paradox, we might share a video clip of Stephen Sondheim coaching a young singer on "Send in the Clowns" (2007). Sondheim is encouraging and patient, but absolutely meticulous. He identifies several issues in her singing: "ought to" is blurred when the two separate "t" sounds of "ought" and "to" should be distinct, there should be a small resigned pause after the "well," and emphasis should fall on the "next" of "maybe next year." The singer repeats the short section, clearly focused on the pause after "well" and once again slurs together the "ought" and the "to." Each time, Sondheim sends her back to the top with a smile and clear confidence that it's worth getting right and that the singer is capable of doing so.

When asked what they notice that they might apply to revision, students point to cognitive load. They see how difficult it is for the singer to focus on all three issues at once and how multiple passes, each focused on a particular element, can then be combined into a final version. It's not a huge stretch to imagine how their work might benefit from iterative attention to word choice, structure, sound, syntax, and so on, all of which contribute to a final composite effect. We can't hold everything in our minds at once. Thus, we need to toggle between intense focus on a single granular detail and experiencing the whole as an interconnected totality.

What students don't always notice, however, is Sondheim's warm, supportive tone. In revising their work, students might think of themselves as both Sondheim and the singer. There's a beauty and a pleasure to meticulousness that in no way undoes the importance of kindness and compassion, including self-kindness and self-compassion, as we discuss in **Chapter 11**. "Let's do it one more time. It's good for you!" Sondheim says, and the singer smiles and begins again.

In a recorded panel discussion (2014), poet C. D. Wright talks about the need, first, to develop "tremendous resistance" to external inhibitors and, next, to develop our own internal inhibitors. Wright describes external inhibitors as the nagging anxieties that might rise up to stop us. We need to learn to ignore them. Equally important, Wright insists, is evolving our own sense of the thematic concerns and formal gestures of a project. Building our own internal inhibitors means developing discernment, becoming intentional with all of the elements that shape how a text makes meaning. Without individually chosen inhibitors and parameters, a supposedly "free" piece is simply a piece at the mercy of external inhibitors of which its writer remains unaware. Micro revision practice offers students a chance to move from "I've always done it that way" or "That's just how stories work" to "I made this choice because I want to create a particular effect."

To practice building this discernment muscle, students might once again work with an experiment-based menu of micro revision lenses. Acknowledging the cognitive load challenge, this approach offers explicit permission to focus on one thing at a time: word choice, character relationships, chronological pacing, beginnings and ends, to name just a few possibilities.

Finally, although writing is endlessly perfectible, students benefit from having the chance to declare a piece done, finished, complete (or at least done-for-now). Opportunities to craft a final chapbook of revised poems, to share a **Revision Presentation** with the class, to submit an end-of-term portfolio, or to perform a story as part of an open mic give students a chance to practice that vital final step of releasing work into the world and moving on to something else.

Sample Assignment

Revision presentation: the story about the story

In your verbal presentation to the workshop, take us behind the scenes of your revision and the choices you've made. Tell us how your story came into being, what inspired your work, how you evolved through different drafts, writing experiments handed out in class, writing exercises done in-class, readings (both assigned and on your own), guest authors, talks in class, and so on. Address the question of how real life and fiction intersect in your work, regardless of sub-genre you're working in. And address how your story, in this version, fulfills and transcends your original design.

Identify and discuss 2–3 common problems you've had to address in this piece: emotional veracity and depth, character development, antagonism, cliché, point of view, unnecessary detail, lack of detail, scenes that only convey information and lack drama (i.e., conflict), narrative voice, or other issues.

Your presentation should be approximately 15 minutes. You can bring in samples of work, exercises, Post-It notes, scene notecards, outlines, readings that were helpful, images that inspired you, or other materials. The presentation should include a detailed examination of the choices and process you followed in your revision.

Revision and the voices of others

At any point—often at several points—in the process of moving from macro explorations to micro revisions, writers receive and integrate feedback from readers. Reader feedback allows us to see how our intentions are received, to encounter different perspectives on what resonated and what was confusing, unsatisfying, or incomplete. Yet, sharing work, whether for the first time in that project or the tenth time, comes with myriad challenges: uninformed or culturally insensitive readers, overzealous editors, reluctance to change anything, or eagerness to satisfy each conflicting request. As teachers, our feedback strategies and peer workshop structures aim to help students develop the skills to navigate these challenges with confidence.

Responding to student work across the revision process

The temptation to jump in and start offering detailed feedback on early work is something most instructors experience. We might see flaws in the language and sentences, lack of execution, flimsy structure, weak dialogue, thin characterization. But the value of early feedback is in a light hand—the work is not yet ready for a plethora of questions that might overwhelm the writer and send them in directions more in keeping with a reader's vision than their own inchoate intuition.

Across stages of completion, we see dialogue as foundational to the feedback process. Any time we plan to comment on or assess student work, we assign a statement, question, or agenda set by the writer. This allows us to get a sense of where the writer is (in relation to aesthetic inclinations and awareness of craft choices, but also in relation to something like intense subject matter) and calibrate our responses accordingly. It also means that the feedback process feels (both for us and the writer) like a conversation about the work where the student has power, rather than a situation where they've produced vulnerable material and submitted it to our judgment.

Students might, for example, respond to the following questions about their revised work before an individual conference meeting to discuss their project:

1. List three changes you've made in this draft from the original and say a few words about why you made them.
2. What are three questions that the new draft raises?
3. What areas feel over developed? Underdeveloped? What is the central idea, vision, or question of the work?
4. How is this supported?
5. What are your next steps?
6. What would you like to discuss or think through together when we meet?

Having observed the value of individual conferences to support revision, we often schedule at least one per term. The choice to make this a requirement, rather than an option, is guided by the observation that individual students have very different:

1. Feelings about what it means to approach a professor in an optional office hour.
2. Degrees of knowledge of what office hours are for and how to make use of them.
3. Time available during a set weekly open office period.

Students who attend a required individual meeting are more confident in seeking support outside of class, not just from us but also from our colleagues.

Peter Ho Davies on revision as close reading ourselves

You've written about revision as a process of close reading both our work and ourselves. Can you talk about this distinction?

Close reading our work asks us to bring the insight we bring as readers/critics of others' work to our own. Close reading ourselves might be more akin to the scrutiny we apply to characters, their motives and psychology. In the first mode we might note that a scene is elided or truncated; in the second we might ask why? "What am I, the writer, shying away from here? What are my motives? Was I just rushing for a deadline, did I leave out something I already knew, or might I not want to confront something?" The latter especially implies there's something more to discover in revision.

What metaphors do you return to (as a writer or teacher) for the work of revision?

There are countless ways of framing revision metaphorically, most obviously ideas of seeing and re-seeing. I like to reach for other less obvious examples. The idea of exploration might approximate the way we sometimes look around in the environment of a video game, searching a chamber for a hidden door, or buried treasure. Lately, I've been borrowing that old programmer's line, "It's not a bug, it's a feature," to reframe revision as less about problems, more about opportunities.

Students often ask how to tell when something is "done." How can we support students through the varying stages of "doneness" as they grow in their craft?

There's a natural tendency to rush toward doneness, a corollary of class schedules and deadlines in some cases, but also of the typical impatience of young, talented writers. We're used to the idea of impatient youth, but all writers prize talent and our instinct is to see talent as an accelerant, a shortcut. You don't need patience if you have talent. Flaubert's famous line, "Talent is long patience," which I take to mean that patience is a talent, is a helpful corrective here, albeit when I read it as a young writer, I'm not sure I was ready to believe it. What persuaded me was experience, the long, slow gestation of projects, and so I try to share those experiences, and those of other published writers, with my students.

PETER HO DAVIES teaches in the MFA program at the University of Michigan. His most recent books are *A Lie Someone Told You About Yourself* and *The Art of Revision*. Other books include *The Fortunes*, *The Welsh Girl*, long-listed for the Booker Prize; and two critically acclaimed short story collections. He was born in Britain to Welsh and Chinese parents.

Image credit: Lynne Raughley

From overwhelm to agency: coaching students on workshop feedback and revision

After workshopping a draft, students are awash in comments: they may have any combination of written notes on their manuscript, a letter from each peer, instructor comments, and notes they write themselves to capture parts of the conversation that resonate with them. Understandably, a student writer might struggle to parse and implement all of the feedback. We can coach students on crafting good questions and guiding a workshop discussion to make it as useful as possible. Still, feedback triage remains necessary. Beginners are often surprised to learn that not all feedback requires a response in their revision. John remembers advice a professor once gave: "80–90% of the feedback won't be of much use, but it's the 10% that can make a difference if you can find it." The point is, not all feedback, well-intentioned as it is, will help a writer develop a plan to revise their work.

Responding to feedback is a learned skill. While all writers discover their individual variations in what works best, we give students a chance to practice these basic steps:

1 Collate, synthesize, vet
2 Identify next steps
3 Take action

Step 1: Collate, synthesize, vet

In this step, writers gather all of their feedback into one place. When we collate feedback into one document, it's easier and quicker to assess at a glance what resonates and what doesn't. We might encourage students to suspend judgment for a time, simply collating and organizing impressions as if the feedback applied to someone else's work. Where do people agree? Where do impressions diverge? Patterns begin to emerge as comments are synthesized.

Students might go next through the document with a highlighter and identify the comments that feel especially compelling, while deleting any comments that feel off the mark. As they work through the collated feedback, they start to narrow and vet it. This process asks students to confront some difficult truths ("What I had hoped was coming through in this draft, isn't yet") and trust their intuition ("This feels like an important comment that I need to consider further").

Step 2: Identify next steps

Having synthesized and vetted their feedback, students are ready to articulate possible actions to take in response. If readers don't see the need for a minor character in a script or story, the writer might decide to give this character more space in the narrative or cut the character entirely. In translating feedback into action, a student might write "Decide whether to cut or expand character X" or even "Test by expanding and cutting character X in a scene and see how each feels." Action steps may also include scheduling a conversation with a writer friend, tracking down a study on harm reduction, or re-reading a craft essay about point of view. These action steps can then be sorted into columns or lists: "Major/significant revisions," "Micro or relatively painless revisions," "Language/prose/style revisions," "Revisions requiring research," "Undetermined/TBD," or whatever else suits the particular project.

As they weigh and prioritize next steps, students begin to craft a revision plan, which might be an elaborate spreadsheet or simply a bulleted list of key priorities. This can also be a valuable time for individual coaching meetings, as students' workshop impressions may be distorted by past histories or anxieties. When students risk becoming "frozen by indecision, unable to start revision," Peter Ho Davies recommends starting with "a suggestion that excites the writer, something they want to do to the story, which avoids the sense that revision is a chore we're doing for someone else." We might also encourage students to prioritize items from the "Major/significant revisions" list, as these are likely to have the greatest bearing on the remainder of the work. Students who work on this column steadfastly often learn that points in other columns resolve themselves and are no longer required as the piece develops.

Step 3: Take action

At this point, students can play and experiment guided by the feedback they have identified as central to their emerging vision. Of course, this process is iterative. Students might then offer the revised draft up for another round of feedback and repeat this three-step cycle each time, honing and refining the work and with it their patience, tenacity, discernment, and skill.

Developing an individual process

Various courses might offer students opportunities to hone technical revision skills, explore what-ifs, visualize work in progress, experience the pleasures of obsessive fine-tuning, and practice being a finisher. Ultimately, our goal is to help students develop an individual iterative process solid enough to sustain them beyond their studies and flexible enough to shift and adapt as they try out new genres, encounter new responsibilities, or adjust to new schedules.

Developing an individual process has both a highly pragmatic side and an intensely emotional side. Pragmatically, writers must figure out if we prefer drafting by hand or on the computer; if we like to revise in Word, Google Docs, Scrivener, or elsewhere; when we benefit most from a close track-changes edit or a free-wheeling big-picture conversation. We must develop protocols for saving back-up copies and keeping track of revisions and versions. This becomes especially important as we receive track-change comments from three writer friends in different documents, make brilliant edits on a printed page and then forget where we put it, or open a folder to find five versions of a document with the word "final" in the title.

On the emotional side, we must come to terms with the sustained duration of revision and make peace with its inherent inefficiency. We also need to develop strategies for moving through inevitable moments of frustration, disappointment, and self-doubt. As Helen Sword discusses in **Chapter 11**, writers benefit from exploring process metaphors. Revision might feel like gardening or cooking, like a journey or surgery. A need for pruning does not make a plant "bad." Facing a crossroads and making a choice is an unavoidable part of a journey. Process metaphors can help us reframe steps that feel like a failure or fault as natural and necessary. They offer breathing space, perhaps a little humor, a chance to see our efforts and struggles from a new angle.

Revision can also ask writers to do deep identity work. Danny Ramadan (**Chapter 5**) spoke of trying "to write a Canadian novel (whatever that means!)" as a Syrian refugee in Canada:

> I was truly occupied with what my audience would think, and how to approach them in a way familiar to them, and what they would want from me. I abandoned a lot of the poetics in exchange for plot; deleted many dilations in exchange for scenes, and opted for a much more straightforward narrative, with linear storytelling. But at some point, it all felt completely foreign to me.

For Ramadan, revision ultimately meant finding a structure that would allow him to access his own "authentic, representative, truthful ways of meandering."

We sometimes hear people say they don't like revision because they're bored with a piece—they want to move on and write something else. These writers often have folders filled with half-baked pieces, false starts, unfinished projects. And maybe some projects need to be just that. We all have them. But we ask students to question the tendency to say, "I'm bored with it," or "It's done" too quickly rather than digging in. As Carl Phillips writes, "I now see how much more powerful stamina can be than talent; or to say it another way, how powerless talent is, on its own, without stamina" (2022, 18). Revision asks us to practice sustained curiosity, to dwell in the messiness of our work with both humility and ambition.

9

Inquiry and Research

The role of research in creative writing

Students can be surprised when asked to engage in research in a creative writing class, which some see as a domain of pure expression or unfettered imagination. Yet, research is crucial for creative writing in any genre, not only for achieving precision and accuracy, but also for uncovering the true depth, complexity, and beauty of our subjects.

Still, research is often left off creative writing syllabi for all of the usual reasons like short, packed semesters and overwhelmed instructors sticking with what they know works. Some fear that research will let the air out of the creative writing classroom and come across as dry, boring, unappealing, and dare we say, too academic. Writers, who often rely on self-taught and idiosyncratic methods, may associate research with serious scholars in other disciplines and understand their own odd noodling or obsessive rabbit holes as something else.

Having observed just how idiosyncratic, immersive, and sensorily rich creative inquiry can be, we propose that research is just as important to teach as scene craft, story structure, similes, or syntax, and that it can be integrated into any assignment or activity. In conversation with the writers, scholars, and librarians we interviewed, we invite instructors to integrate research strategies and practices that lend both weight and spark to students' writing.

Nalo Hopkinson on research and speculative fiction

People might think of speculative fiction as the domain of the imagination. What place does research play in your writing process?

Research is especially important in the literatures of the fantastic because they're based on something. If you're writing science fiction, you're extrapolating into the future from existing science. You're not just making it up whole cloth. If you're writing fantasy, you're basing it in existing belief systems. So, you need to figure out what stories are told there.

You're responding to the canon and to current discussions, and you're responding to readers who are really knowledgeable. Many will have a grasp of the sciences. Many will know their folklore. So that's the level you need to be at. A story needs to have an internal logic. Research helps you create the narrative that holds it all together.

What fictional question launched an inquiry process for you?

In my novel *Blackheart Man*, I knew the ending early on: I wanted the character to jump off a cliff. And I knew I didn't want him to die, that something was going to have to hold him up. At first, I made it a country where men do a lot of needlework, so he always has crochet with him. I thought, okay, he'll use that as a balloon and he'll jump down that way. As I was getting to the end of my final revision, I thought, wait, how does that work? Can you actually hold up a piece of crochet, which is full of holes, and sail down? Well, no, you can't.

Since this thing was set roughly in the eighteenth or nineteenth century, I needed to look up period innovations in flight or floating. I've learned that whatever you can think of that you need humans to have done in a story, bunches of people will have tried it. And indeed, I found out giant man-kites were a thing. The Chinese even used them in construction so that workers could go from floor to floor before the stairs were built. Then I had my answer. The research doesn't get in the way. It enables your story. You remember: human beings have been ingenious since we were drawing bulls on cave walls.

How much research is enough?

In world-building research, you go beyond what the story needs. But you only need to put in just enough where the characters literally touch something or where they're intersecting with social mores or laws or, you know, this is how we wear our shoes. Show the world as much as you can in use, in action, rather than stopping the story to turn to the audience. I've learned to have faith in the reader's ability to play the game with me. Readers engage more if they have to pick up on clues to build the narrative and build the world in their own heads.

How do you approach research in a fiction class?

When students submit their stories for a workshop, I ask them to list two or three sources of research. We talk about how research can be everything from an encyclopedia to your mom's family photos. If I'm teaching fantasy, I assign a piece drawing on folklore from one of their own cultures. It's amazing: people find stuff they've never heard of and they come away really engaged. Same thing with historical fiction. If I challenge them to go talk to their grandparents, they'll come in excited. I once took a bunch of students to the Toronto archive to look at digitized historical photographs. People were able to find the streets where their families had lived. Students were phoning their moms. I try to teach research so it doesn't feel dry. And I try to engage any students who are historians in the class, because they'll have a bigger body of knowledge. Or psychology majors, scientists, engineers. I invite them to explain what they care about in ways that their peers and I can understand.

What's the most unhinged internet search you've ever looked up for a writing project?

I wanted to know what, if any, underwear nineteenth-century Parisian sex workers would wear, just in the course of their day. Not very much, apparently.

NALO HOPKINSON is a Professor in the UBC School of Creative Writing. She is the author of many books, most recently *Blackheart Man*. Born in Jamaica, she moved to Canada in 1977. In 2020, Science Fiction Writers of America made her its 37th Damon Knight Memorial "Grand Master," a lifetime achievement award in recognition of her writing, teaching, and mentorship.
Image credit: David Findlay

Inquiry as engine

Writing can start with curiosity, with a process of inquiry that draws on our full resources and capacities. As we discuss in **Chapter 3**, courses can cultivate inquiry-driven writing by:

1 Helping students generate material they feel a genuine connection to (versus what they think instructors want to see or what they believe serious writers do).
2 Leading students through exercises and assignments that help awaken their curiosity and invite them to venture beyond the edges of their certainty.

Inciting curiosity

Students sometimes need explicit encouragement to follow their own interests, which might feel too weird, too personal, or insufficiently academic. We can begin classes with exercises that—directly or indirectly—ask questions like:

- What are you obsessed with?
- What memories—no matter how insignificant they feel—continue to resurface in your mind?
- What is making you angry, frustrated, pissed off?
- What do you have mixed, tangled, or complicated feelings about?

Once students have a subject, a focus, some material (however they get there), we can help them tap into curiosity to deepen and develop this material. As Alex Marzano-Lesnevich mentioned in our conversation, "Students often show up in the classroom with an experience they want to write about or an issue they want to address. Often, they feel like they should have a settled thing to say about it. Sometimes they start the semester thinking that creative nonfiction is the genre they'll use to deliver that settled thing, that answer." Not only does this "place enormous pressure on them," Marzano-Lesnevich observes, but it also "circumvents their thinking just when it's getting started."

We can shift this impulse through activities and assignments that foreground inquiry, helping students see their writing as a way of getting to deeper questions, not getting to an answer. A few possible in-class guided exercises:

- Students identify a key character, place, or situation, and freewrite starting with "I know … " "I don't know … " and "I want to know … "
- Students dig into what's contradictory or unresolved in a seemingly settled thing by asking a new "Why… ?" question emerging from their material multiple times and seeing what comes up each time.
  - Example: "Why did my father join a new-age religious order after planning to become a doctor?" "Well, maybe he was disillusioned with medicine." "Okay, why was he disillusioned with medicine?" And so on.
- Students explore a different perspective or point of view in their piece—something or someone present or involved but not central.
  - Regardless of how much material makes it into the draft, an exercise like this can bring nuance to what's flattened and shed light on what's ignored.
- Students embed a pivot for digging deeper.
  - Drawing on Erika Meitner's poem "Dollar General" (2016), for example, they might use the phrase "What details am I leaving out?" or working from Brenda Shaughnessy's "Blueberries for Cal" (2019) they might pause to ask "That's not the most real feeling I'm feeling, is it?"

Inquiry can then lead to action, driving a project forward. Students who struggle to extend or develop their work, who may feel blocked or stuck, can use inquiry to take a moment or scene, even a glimpse or fragment, and explore its latent possibilities. Here are a few avenues for further inquiry:

- **Contiguity.** What is happening alongside or around this?
- **History.** How did this come to be? What led to this?
- **Narrative.** What happened next? Why?
- **Closeness.** What might getting closer reveal? What bodily sensations? What details?
- **Distance.** How does this fit into a larger picture? What broader social/cultural/political forces are in play here?
- **Speculation.** What might this lead to in the future?
- **Counterfactuals.** What might have happened if things had gone differently?
- **Expectations.** What expectations are raised by the existing material? (based on genre, context, etc.) How might you satisfy, complicate, or subvert them?

These questions show how a single moment can dilate out into a series of possibilities, any one of which might offer a spark for further investigation.

Sample Assignment

Proposal questions for an inquiry-driven project

As we move from generative exercises and exploration to a sustained project, use these questions to reflect on your work in preparation for our individual conference meetings.

1. What question or questions do you want to explore through your writing?
2. How does this project build on writing you've already done?
3. What is your personal stake in this question? How are you connected to it?
4. How does this question reach beyond you?
5. What research might enrich your writing on this question?
6. How do you want to approach this project in terms of form or style? What appeals to you about the formal approaches/gestures you're drawn to?
7. What text (from class or elsewhere) offers an example of the kind of piece you want to write?
8. What can I (as your teacher) help you think through or offer support with as you embark on this project?

Deepening inquiry

Eventually, no matter what genre or mode they're working in, students will hit points of unknowing or uncertainty: What was that tree on my childhood street? How do people celebrate the New Year in Naples? Do my received ideas about alphas and betas actually correspond with what scientists know about how wolves behave in groups?

When we take up the call to explore the gaps in our knowledge, we enrich our writing. In trying to figure out which tree was in their childhood yard, a student might:

- Look through an old family photo album and find themself re-immersed in sensory memories of childhood.
- Ask a family member and hear a story about the year their dad pruned a pear tree so severely that it looked like it would never recover and what a bumper crop came in the following year to everyone's surprise.
- Check out a botanical history book where they discover a detail about the etymology of the tree's name or the history of its geographic movement that perfectly illustrates or complicates an element in the piece they're writing.
- Dig into local archives and read town meeting debates about a controversial tree-planting initiative.
- Try any or all of these and still not find an answer, but stumble across something else that catches their attention and curiosity.

An inquiry process doesn't merely provide an answer to fill in the blank space (sometimes it doesn't provide an answer), but rather deepens the work by introducing context and complications. Driven by curiosity and discovery, a writer moves past superficial impressions or facile conclusions into something more strange, more specific, more inclusive of multiple perspectives, more self-aware, more historically grounded.

Unsatisfying writing comes when students hit these points of unknowing and brush past them. This is when writing becomes, at best, generic, and at worst, actively misinformed or harmfully reliant on cultural stereotypes.

Research in the classroom

Any creative writing course can foreground an attitude of "let's dig in and see what we can find out," treating research as a natural and expected part of a writing process, when an instructor:

- Invites students to identify potential areas for research in their own work or the work of peers.
- Pauses during conferences to look things up together and talk about different sources or approaches.
- Schedules an interactive session with a librarian.
- Gives examples of research (variously understood) from published writing, our own projects, or the work of visiting guests.

Depending on the focus of the course and the time available, we might choose to help students hone specific skills, such as:

- **How to recognize opportunities for research**, seeing gaps not as signs that something is wrong but as an invitation to dig in.
- **How to engage in research**, including archival and embodied research, as we discuss in the following section.
- **How research with a goal of making art or conveying experience differs from research for an academic essay**, where the goal may be crafting an argument or accumulating evidence.
- **How research can take place at the level of language itself**, and the value of tools like the *Oxford English Dictionary* and *Roget's International Thesaurus*.
- **How to cultivate pleasure in research** by engaging in playful activities like making a playlist a character might listen to or watching favorite childhood cartoons in search of a counterpoint image for a difficult poem about childhood.
- **How to return to writing**, for those who can't stop researching once they start.
- **How to incorporate the fruits of research into a draft**, and ways both *how* and *how much* can vary from project to project or genre to genre.
- **How to engage a reader**, even when the subject falls outside their typical interests, by establishing stakes (the "So what?") and connection (the personal angle) at the heart of research.

Any course that involves a sustained project (essay, story, screenplay, song cycle, group of poems) might ask students to complete a writer's research portfolio in which they gather literary models (and countermodels) and research sources of all kinds and briefly reflect on what each model/source has to offer in terms of information, critical vocabulary, context, and/or stylistic approach. Likewise, assignment structures like the revision logs we discuss in **Chapter 8** give students the chance to explore deep dives or go down rabbit holes by keeping the assessment focus on process.

Though conviction and commitments can and must inflect our writing, there's a rigidity to writing driven by certainty. Rather than an experience of dynamic movement, leading to a sense of humanity and insight, readers experience a monolithic consistency, dry, dull, didactic. Ultimately, we write into mystery, write to find out what we think and feel, not merely to record what's known. Assignments that explicitly foreground research teach students to make time for inquiry and expect change—in their knowledge, their perspectives, and their writing.

Alex Marzano-Lesnevich on spelunking for deeper questions

How do you incorporate research into an assignment for creative nonfiction students?

In the podcast *The Memory Palace*, Nate DiMeo digs up small-town newspaper articles from the past and spins a tale out of them. It's a good separation of what Vivian Gornick in *The Situation and the Story* calls the situation—whatever's in that newspaper article—and the story—that larger inquiry or push toward meaning-making. I have students listen to an episode called "Every Night Ever," in which three guys out for a drink one night believe they've found the body of an alien (or hoax their small town into believing that they've found one). It's this incredibly empathetic take where DiMeo asks, *What if they just wanted to shake up their small town?* It becomes this beautiful piece about how we approach surprise and mystery, about our desire to live in a narrative.

We listen to that episode and use the transcript to break it down and ask, "Where might this research have come from?" Students can quickly see solid details that weren't drawn from the newspaper article. To make this beautiful layered thing, DiMeo had to do additional research into the town, the time period, how widespread belief in aliens was at the time. I send them into the special collections in the school archives to look at local small newspapers, or they can find online archives from the place they grew up. Many end up writing essays that take a tiny news story that happened when they were kids that they didn't have any context for. One student had deer take over the town when he was growing up. He wrote a beautiful piece exploring who the land belongs to. He really saw the larger story in it.

When you're teaching through questions and curiosity, how do you incorporate craft lessons?

I introduce frameworks for different craft ideas, like the ladder of abstraction, drawing on Roy Peter Clark's *Writing Tools*. Clark points to a word that's concrete, singular, specific, you can touch it, and on the other extreme a word you can't touch, taste, smell, an abstraction. But a ladder has many different rungs. So, the bottom of the ladder is singular and specific, something concrete, the middle is summary, and the top is abstraction. And we need all of it! We map a piece and the moves a writer is making up and down the ladder across the essay. Students quickly see that most writers are moving every sentence or every half sentence. They're moving a ton! Students tend to rely on summary too much, especially in personal essays where the writer assumes that the reader already shares the same world and forgets that they have to rebuild the world for the reader. When students practice this analytical skill on a published piece, maybe a piece they love and see as a magic trick, they can then turn to their own piece and suddenly see where they are moving, but also where they're not and could be.

A research process involves exploring but also narrowing. How do you go about this as a writer? How do you teach these skills?

The metaphor I use for the early stages of research is spelunking, going into the deep cave. I don't put much of a limit on my spelunking initially, precisely because I don't yet know what I'm going to be curious about. I'm looking for the research not to answer the questions I have, but to introduce me to new questions, deeper questions. Here's a quick example from an essay called "Futurity": I was thinking about the concept of the future and I looked up the word "futurity" and found that it's also the name for a horse race. So, there I was off on a dive into horse racing! Which turned out to be a profoundly useful metaphor for gender because it's a race that horses are entered into before they're even born. A perfect metaphor for gender that I never would have found if I'd rushed!

But a time comes when you have to say, "Okay, Alex, you're not writing an essay about horse racing." And that's when I then start to think about the narrowing: this must be a finite entity, so what boundaries and limits am I comfortable adopting? I've had to accept that there is no actual end to the research. You're just a mortal being and you have to call it done someday. I talk to students about this all the time. At a certain point, you have to let this piece not be all the pieces you could possibly write. Instead, you have to let this piece be the version that you can write today. And trust that you'll live to write another day. If this topic is still fertile to you, you will come back to it.

ALEX MARZANO-LESNEVICH is an Assistant Professor in Creative Nonfiction in the UBC School of Creative Writing. They are the author of the award-winning *The Fact of a Body: A Murder and a Memoir*, and their essays and journalism have been published in *The New York Times* and included in *The Best American Essays*.

Image credit: Beowulf Sheehan

Embodied research: archives, interviews, field observations

What counts as research? Students accustomed to completing research papers may think first of databases, scholarly articles, encyclopedias, and information accessed through a computer or book. While these methods can be useful for writers, so can embodied forms of inquiry and investigation such as visiting archives, conducting interviews, or engaging in field observations. When we understand research as whatever adds authenticity, emotional truth, depth, meaning and credibility to our work, research can take the form of leafing through old letters, cooking a family recipe, or recording playground sounds and sketching a leaf. Books like Philip Gerard's *The Art of Creative Research: A Field Guide for Writers* (2017) and Thomas Mullaney and Christopher Rea's *Where Research Begins* (2022) invite us to think broadly about the forms research can take and the pleasures our students might find in it.

Archives

Many universities and colleges have archival collections and librarians happy to lead student workshops. Instructors working at colleges without their own collections might reach out to museums or larger universities to arrange a visit. Local public libraries or historical societies can also have a wealth of letters, records, or ephemera to interest students. In our conversation, Nalo Hopkinson described the pleasure of such visits: "Sometimes I'm going to a tiny archive of, I don't know, hats of the southern US. You learn stuff there, you get as close to hands-on as you can. Honest to God, sometimes the research is more fun than the writing." We also spoke with Melanie Boyd and Jason Brown-Nisenson to learn about their archive-focused creative writing courses.

Melanie Boyd and Jason Brown-Nisenson on research as adventure

When you hosted the symposium "Integrating Library, Archives and Special Collections into Creative Writing Pedagogy" where we met, you sent participants an envelope with a high-quality reproduction of an archival document. How do these envelopes connect to your teaching philosophy?

Jason: That exercise—investigating and responding creatively to an archival item intentionally divorced from its context—is central to our methodology. It makes the connection to the object personal and intimate, more likely to engender wonder and curiosity.

Melanie: This "message in a bottle" simulation is students' first experience with us. We never begin by teaching information and methods that might lead to judgment of themselves or the material. "Am I getting this right?" is an attitude we don't want to nourish.

How do you guide students through their first encounter with historical/archival materials?

Melanie: Our entire pedagogy draws heavily from the Focused Conversation Method, which stimulates attention, introspection, and participation. It's based on open-ended questions that fall under four categories: **objective**, **reflective**, **interpretive**, and **decisional**. So, students spend their first class with an archival item and a worksheet of **objective** questions about the item's materiality and content. These who/what/where/when questions act as a metaphorical microscope. Details pop and become grist for the second class. It's a focused conversation based on the remaining categories: **reflective**, related to feelings (What surprised you?), **interpretive**, related to meaning (What insights did you have?), and **decisional**, related to action (How will you apply this to your creative writing?). Only a few such questions will spark thoughtful responses and keen listening. We've never encountered silence!

Students may think that an idea comes first, and then research follows. How does an archive-centered Creative Writing course turn that expectation on its head?

Jason: Faced with just enough detail to whet their curiosity, students begin creating immediately into the void. Give them a taste of something evocative—two pages from a 1969 corporal punishment record book, for example—and let them follow whatever path interests them. We ask: What is this? Who's it about? Where are they? They can't really know for sure, so they begin creating answers out of the details in front of them. The idea is that their creativity, their invention of fact, will drive them willingly further down an individual path of research where they ask: What more do I want to know?

What roles might serendipity, curiosity, or playfulness take in a research process?

Melanie: They're all key and interrelated—something we set out to model in an assignment called Serendipitous Sleuthing. We met students in the library and gave them no verbal instructions, just a sparse worksheet. It told them to go into the stacks, pull a book and turn to a page at random, then write a twenty-five-word summary of the page and two questions arising from it. Students posted photos of their book spines and pages, summaries and questions. In a follow-up class, some students mentioned they'd never had an assignment that allowed for such freedom and discovery.

How do you approach students embarking on a creative project who feel that research is not required?

Melanie: We know "research" is fraught, so we lean into words like adventure and discovery and challenge ourselves to develop pedagogy that embodies them. What experiences can we offer students to catch themselves delighting in their own minds? Where even fact-checking is exploration, not drudgery. Where they get this notion: If I have an idea and start writing, I'm already engaged in research—mining my own knowledge and experience.

While we aim to show-not-tell them that research is valuable, it's important for students to come to that realization themselves. The process is surreptitious, and it builds. At a certain point we do teach research skills, but even that is discovery-based and hands-on.

MELANIE BOYD is an Associate Librarian Emerita, University of Calgary. Her poems have been published in numerous Canadian literary journals.
Image credit: Melanie Boyd

JASON BROWN-NISENSON is the Archivist for literary collections at the University of Calgary. His short fiction (as Jay Brown) has appeared in many journals and magazines across Canada.
Image credit: Jason Nisenson

Interviews

Students can dip a toe in interview-based research with something as simple as calling a sister to ask what she remembers about a childhood vacation for a personal essay or asking a roommate how he saw Miami change during the years he lived there as research for a story. Some students may find an interest and aptitude for interviews and start reaching out to larger groups of people, contacting strangers, or getting in touch with experts. Our colleague Tanya Kyi, for example, writes middle-grade nonfiction and often reaches out to biologists or sociologists to confirm that she's correctly understood their published research on insects, sleep, or stereotype threat. Bronwen's former colleague Adam Johnson showed students stories and pictures from a research trip where he interviewed and rode along with UPS drivers in Louisiana after Hurricane Katrina. At the time, Johnson wasn't sure if he'd write essays or fiction based on this material, which ultimately showed up in his short story "Hurricanes Anonymous."

Of course, interviews—especially with survivors of a traumatic event like a hurricane—require thought and care to be done ethically. Erika Meitner discussed her interview-based poetry work in our conversation (**Chapter 7**): "I do large-scale documentary poetics projects where I interview people and represent their voices, so I'm always asking, *Am I implicated in this poem? Is my context clear? How is this work going to move through the world?* I tell students there's certain work I would never present as a one-off piece or without a process essay." *The Art of Creative Research* includes a chapter on interview skills, and Robert Weiss' *Learning from Strangers: The Art and Method of Qualitative Interview Studies* includes enlightening analysis of interview transcripts. Our colleagues in anthropology, sociology, and other disciplines that engage in qualitative research involving IRB approval, have much to share with us on this score (and can be terrific guests to bring to our classrooms).

Field observations

Rather than speaking with UPS drivers on the phone or meeting them in a diner, Adam Johnson asked to ride along on their delivery routes. Being "in the field" allowed him to take in the full sensory experience and make his own notes.

Students might experiment with field notes in small non-threatening ways. For example, songwriter Dar Williams describes how she "drove to the local community garden one night and watched the moon for a while" and "made observations" and "explored additional themes and metaphors as [she] sat and watched" (2022, 69–70). Likewise, students might pick a spot near home to return to and observe seasonal changes week by week, or might sit in a crowded space like a train station or shopping center and observe how people relate to the built environment, or might revisit the site of a transformative life event to see what specific memories arise from the sensory experience of *being there*.

Sample Assignment

Learning research through readings

Tanka walks inspired by Harryette Mullen's *Urban Tumbleweed*

In her introduction (2013), Mullen writes, "So I began the diary despite being able to recognize only the most common creatures, and feeling that I lack a proper lexicon to write about the natural world, when what we call natural or native is more than ever open to question" (viii).

- How does Mullen navigate the categories of "natural" and "native" (as she mentions in the quote above)? Locate a poem that is clearly dealing with "nature." Locate a poem that in some way calls into question divisions between the natural and the artificial.

- To what extent is Mullen in dialogue with traditional Japanese haiku/tanka?
- How does Mullen use metaphor?
- Where do we see environmental crisis explicitly addressed in this book?

Take several tanka walks as Mullen does. Walk around campus or anywhere else you happen to be. Look, listen, and compose at least five short poems drawing on your observations.

Walking and observing is already a form of research. If you wish, supplement this field work with resources to develop your lexicon of place and sharpen your attention to details and differences.

Exploring context through research with Anne Boyer's *The Undying*

In *The Undying*, Anne Boyer describes Aelius Aristides' *Hieroi Logoi* as "an autobiographical account of what it is like to have a body in a specific time and place" (2019, 23). She also writes,

> The system of medicine is, for the sick, a visible scene of action, but beyond it and behind it and beneath it are all the other systems, *family race work culture gender money education,* and beyond those is a system that appears to include all the other systems, the system so total and overwhelming that we often mistake it for the world (66).

Drawing on research (broadly understood), offer your own autobiographical account of a body situated within a specific time and place, intersecting with institutions.

You may write about intersections with the system of medicine or other systems, such as law, education, or work. Let your account show how we are, as Boyer puts it, "marked by our historical particulars, constellated in a set of social and economic relations" (30). Write about these social and economic relations and their "costumes, machines, sounds, rituals, and architectures" (70). Boyer writes about discussion boards where "people were turned into patients with handles and signatures, agonies, neologisms, and encouragements. Mets. Foobs. NED. I was afraid, on the first day, for my vocabulary" (26). Pay attention to the specific vocabulary of what you're writing about.

Information literacy and navigating sources

While we're interested in a broad understanding of research, we're also keenly aware of the importance of information literacy and the hard work of helping students learn to locate and assess sources. As Bridget Whearty said in our conversation, "Information literacy means knowing where your information comes from, when your information comes from, and who your information comes from. Information is created in particular times and places and always ages. That's true whether you're talking about the latest physics or how we think about the Crusades."

The internet has placed vast amounts of information at our fingertips. In doing so, it has also flattened our media landscape. A student searching for vaccine statistics may struggle to differentiate a peer-reviewed study in a reputable journal from an official-seeming website. In addition, as AI-generated websites and browser summaries proliferate, online searching can become an echo chamber of misinformation. Information is never neutral. "Everyone involved in gathering and procuring information does so as an embodied person with filters and interests and positionalities and biases and agendas," Whearty emphasized. AI carries bias from its designers and from the vast swaths of data on which it has been trained. We agree with Whearty that "Anybody who writes needs tools to locate and vet sources properly."

To locate sources, students will benefit enormously from some experience with how search terms operate (for example, the value of Boolean operators "AND", "OR," "NOT") and how to use library search systems (filtering by date, for example, or leap-frogging from a Library of Congress subject heading to find other similar sources). Most importantly, students need to know what questions to ask and where to look for answers to assess sources. We can help students learn to ask questions like:

- **Who made this?** What group or individual wrote or compiled this? What expertise or credentials do they have on this specific subject?
- **Who published this or made it available?** Did this source undergo peer review or another vetting process? What do we know about the publisher, journal, or institution involved? Where does their funding come from?
- **Who was this made for?** Is this source speaking to fellow experts or to a broader audience? What background might I need to follow it?
- **How old is this?** Is it still relevant? Has more recent scholarship challenged these findings/views?

Our best tip is to work with librarians. As Whearty put it, "Librarians have been thinking about how to teach students how to find good information for centuries and working rigorously on information literacy instruction since at least the 1960s." In our experience across institutions, librarians leap at the chance to work directly with students. At many institutions, you can meet with librarians who will review your syllabus, discuss your assignment structure, and design a session specifically aimed to support your students in their work. We've seen students leave library sessions with concrete search skills, excitement about possible directions for their work, and confidence that they can reach out to librarians for help along the way.

A few other tips:

- **Acknowledge the difficulty.** Searching, navigating, and assessing are hard! When we let students know that we also struggle with these things, we remind them that having a hard time isn't a failure or personality flaw.
- **Encourage students to follow up with experts across the institution.** While we don't want to overwhelm our colleagues with requests, a raccoon behavior expert or subject librarian in classical Chinese might be happy to hear from a curious

creative writing student and eager to direct them to sound sources or even meet for a consultation or interview.

- Here's a little example from our own work: we wanted to write about the video of Stephen Sondheim coaching "Send in the Clowns" in **Chapter 8** and wondered if we could find a more reputable source than a random YouTube channel (or at least learn a bit more about the recording). We fired off a quick email to UBC Music Librarian David Haskins. Within an hour, Haskins replied with confirmation that the clip aired on *The South Bank Show* on May 20, 1984 and a link to The Paley Center for Media listing the performers. Over the following days, he reached out with details about *South Bank Show* production materials held in University of Leeds Special Collections and instructions on how we could purchase a digital copy of the episode from the ITV Film archive (for £145, unfortunately beyond our budget). Just one example of generosity, enthusiasm, and sleuthing superpowers you and your students can benefit from when you collaborate with expert scholars, and, especially, librarians.

- **Practice searching and navigating together in class or in one-to-one conferences.** Information literacy can feel like a fun puzzle when students work together to brainstorm possible search term combinations or search for author bios.
- **Give students the chance to learn from one another through research presentations.** Research process presentations invite students to share questions they've asked, methods they've employed, sources they've consulted, and ways they plan to incorporate their findings into their creative work. Students take inspiration from peer tenacity and ingenuity, along with ideas for their own work.

Bridget Whearty on information literacy and the beauty of details

It might be obvious why information literacy is important for a journalist or researcher—why is it also crucial for a novelist, poet, or screenwriter?

The power of creative writers to shape our understanding of the world cannot be overstated. As a Medievalist, I see a lot of terrible information about the Middle Ages in screenplays and novels. The stakes are high for people who do creative work! The reach of a good historical novel is so much bigger than the reach of a very niche academic article.

The success can be dazzling. I'm thinking of *Hild* by Nicola Griffith, a historical novel about an eighth-century woman named Hild of Whitby. We know basically nothing about her beyond little references in an ecclesiastical history of the British people by Bede. But Griffith has done the most amazing job mastering what we can learn from Bede, connecting this to other sources, digging up wonderful details. There's a scene where Hild and her mother have a political conversation while making eye salve, and the recipe that rattles through in the background is actually connected to the Ancient Biotics Project, which made huge waves in Medieval studies about eight years ago. It's one of those moments where getting the past right is beautiful. Hild is also queer, and Griffith has done some amazing research, including drawing on love letters between medieval nuns, to show that in a way that's true to the sources and to the needs of readers today. We can see how a duty to the past and a duty to the present are entirely compatible.

Why is it important to get things right?

The truth is richer and weirder and so much more complicated and interesting. There's an ethics of getting it right, but there's also a beauty to getting it right. A study came out a couple of years ago involving fragments of blue stone found in a woman's skull. It's lapis lazuli. And the best explanation is that she was a highly skilled painter working with the most expensive materials. What a beautiful concrete example pushing back on broad generalizations like "women couldn't read back then." Well, some women couldn't. Some men couldn't. Some women were artists working with semi-precious stones that had to be imported from Afghanistan.

That's also where writing comes alive. As teachers, we need to talk about ethics, but we also need to help students see the beauty of reveling in true details. Think of a poetry collection like Melissa Range's *Scriptorium* that engages with medieval manuscripts and pigments. A text like that can show students how much fun it is to dig into research. It's not just "If you write a novel and your peasants are eating potatoes, by God, I'll smite you because they couldn't have eaten potatoes before 1492." No, it's the beauty of the questions: *If they couldn't eat potatoes, what would they have eaten?* If they can't grow corn, what would they grow? The word "corn" existed in Middle English well before 1492, but it doesn't mean what we mean now. Just reveling in the language and the scene creation and the world building. Everything gets weirder and therefore more fun.

What makes it hard for students—and, well, everyone—to assess a source and know whether it's trustworthy?

- If you're dealing with sources written by experts, you can lean into expertise and forget to notice the age of the source. A recent newspaper article referenced Phillipe Ariès' theories about how medieval people didn't love their children. Ariès did incredible groundbreaking work, but some of it is outdated now.
- People forget that you can be a specialist in one area, but that doesn't mean you're accurate about something else.
- Sometimes experts don't do a great job making information accessible to non-specialists.
- The information that's easily accessible is fragmentary. I was looking at the Wikipedia article on homosexuality in Italy the other day, like you do. They cite a condemning passage in Dante's *Inferno*. And that is accurate. But they leave out Dante's passages in Purgatory where queer people are at the very top of Purgatory about to be cleansed of their final sins and make it into heaven.

What is an activity or assignment you've designed to guide students engaging in research?

In advanced classes, I do an experiment that's always interesting and sometimes makes people angry. Part of information literacy is understanding that who you cite is a statement of power and who you don't cite is a statement about whose voices don't matter. I ask students to look at the demographics of who they cite in their essays: How many people are dead? How many people are white? How many people are men?

And then I ask, "Are you comfortable with the arguments you're making about authority?" This always causes a lot of discussion. Some people feel offended by the assignment, but it's important to consider that who you cite is an endorsement. Who you cite is a treasure map for your readers, so who's a treasure that you want to include a map to?

Before training as a Medievalist, you were an undergraduate creative writing major. Looking back, what do you wish had been part of your creative writing studies?

I had some amazing workshop teachers, but research for creative writers was never really taught. As an undergraduate, I thought about my work in history and my work in creative writing as completely different things. When teachers help students see how the world and knowledge and information and wisdom can interpenetrate with their creative work, cross-pollinate and enrich it, that's a real gift. Our understanding of the past is always growing richer and weirder and better. Details and specifics are beautiful. They're not a penalty. They're not one more hoop to jump through. They're where creative writing lives.

BRIDGET WHEARTY is an Associate Professor at Binghamton University. She is the author of *Digital Codicology: Medieval Books and Modern Labor* and is working on a new book about three twelfth-century queer love letters.

Image credit: A. Spaulding

Writing beyond your experience

In **Chapter 5**, we discussed the value of helping students consider how the material they're engaging connects to their own lived experience and how it reaches beyond them. We've noticed that some students are frozen at the fear of "getting it wrong" when it comes to writing beyond their experiences and identities, whereas other students dive in with more confidence than care. In both cases, we recommend the same solution: research.

Research can allow the stuck student a path forward, a reassurance that an ethical way to write beyond the self is possible. And research can offer a check on the overly confident student, perhaps a confrontation with a detail that disrupts their received ideas, and, hopefully, a pleasure in the richness of the actual that deepens their work (or, at times, allows them to realize that this is someone else's work to make). The moment of "I hadn't seen that coming" is the moment when a song (or story, script, poem or essay) has the opportunity to rise to the complexity of its material. We repeatedly return to the questions Paisley Rekdal lays out at the conclusion of *Appropriate: A Provocation* (2021), particularly:

- What kinds and types of interactions have you had with the communities you wish to represent?
- In what small and large ways have those interactions informed your research, your perception of your characters, and your writing?
- Which books, films, and art have you studied by the identities you wish to represent? Which ones are most relevant to your project? (194).

Ways of drawing on research involve further ethical choices and complications, which vary from genre to genre. Alex Marzano-Lesnevich discussed asking students to "see their positioning as narrator as an explicit choice that shapes their essay." Fiction students face their own choices of point of view, focalizing character, interiority, and so on, whereas poets may reflect on persona poems or polyvocal poems or how to represent moments of encounter with otherness.

Erika Meitner (**Chapter 7**) shared an example from her teaching practice: "A lot of people take public transportation in Madison, so students wanted to make art about that. I had students writing bus poems populated by other people that crossed racial lines, or crossed class lines, or represented individuals with disabilities." Rather than addressing this issue individually or through a workshop, Meitner "put out a call on social media for public transportation poems," which she shared with students to "see how a range of poets handled writing other people, and talk about what the class felt comfortable with and what they didn't." This approach allowed the class to "discuss the ethical questions of representing the other without a student's work as the focus."

When we lead with an expectation of positive intent and an invitation to talk, many students will respond eagerly. We don't want to approach an individual or a group with a tone of "you're doing it wrong" that may lead to shame, defensiveness, or avoidance. Instead, we want to simply say "research is one of the many challenges of writing, and I'm here to help."

10
Assessment and Grading

The challenges of grading

What creative writing instructor hasn't felt a twinge of unease when settling down to grade a stack of student projects? Sure, there's the daunting prospect of the stack itself, thicker and more time-consuming as teaching loads and course enrollment caps increase. But we might also feel a fundamental lack of fit between the demand to quantify and rank our students and the care we feel toward their creative efforts and growth, their courage and vulnerability in attempting to transform a difficult experience into writing for the first time.

Students have a range of priorities and reasons for taking our courses. For some, the course is a requirement, for others an elective, for others a central part of their degree. Students also vary widely in the time and resources they're able to dedicate to their coursework. Many juggle full course loads with one or more part-time or full-time jobs, long commutes, child and/or elder care, or participation in clubs and Varsity teams. And yet, we are asked to score and rank their work as if these differences didn't exist. Other reasons we feel uneasy around grades, especially when it comes to creative work, include:

- Grades and grading have been shown to cause problems, such as decreased intrinsic motivation and increased cheating (Bolton and Elmore 2013; Kohn 2013).
- Grades have been shown to increase anxiety in students and lower their willingness to take risks or stretch beyond their comfort zone (Butler 1988; Pulfrey and Buchs 2011; Stommel 2023). An instructor's role as someone responsible for measuring and ranking students can feel in direct opposition to the encouraging coaches we wish to be.
- Grades make learning feel transactional. As Asao B. Inoue said in our conversation later in this chapter, "I found that the presence or expectation of grades in my course focused students' attention on the grades or points, not on their learning or my feedback."
- Grades and what they mean are arbitrary. An 80% may be an A– in one context and a B– in another. Grades don't necessarily measure or predict meaningful things, especially future success as a writer, which may require entirely different

rhythms and habits from those mandated by an academic schedule of attention divided across multiple subjects.

- Learning is unpredictable and surprising. In trying to nail down learning objectives and figure out how to assess them, we can feel like we're circumscribing something that should be fluid and responsive to emergent growth and discoveries.
- Grading is time-consuming for instructors, and this time doesn't always feel well spent in terms of student learning.

Faced with all of the problems with grades and grading, we may be tempted to tell our students "Grades don't matter! It's the work that matters!" or "Don't worry about grades in this class. Just do your best!" Although learning, growth, and art-making can be more important than a grade, such messages easily come across as disingenuous and provoke frustration among students for whom grades have clear material repercussions in the form of scholarships and funding, entrance to competitive degree programs, and access to graduate study or work opportunities. In asking for students' amorphous "best," we assume infinite available time and resources students don't have. A student working three jobs while caring for an ill parent needs clear expectations, not platitudes about effort and aspiration.

Declining to offer grading clarity:

1 Relies on tacit knowledge about expectations that some students might have and others don't.
2 Unfairly prevents students from being able to make informed decisions about how to spend their time/energy.

Instead of pretending grades don't exist or telling students that grades don't matter, we might say, "Your grade is not the only thing that matters," and try to create a course where this feels true.

Institutional factors and guiding principles

In making decisions about grading, we have to consider the broader ecosystem of the program and institution. For example:

- A large university may have a strictly maintained target grade average for all entry-level courses.
- Failure to norm grades across a program might mean that merit-based scholarships disproportionately fall to students who have studied with a specific faculty member.
- A course with a reputation for high grades can attract students who are looking for a GPA boost but aren't particularly interested in the course itself.
- A course with flexible due-date policies may become the lowest priority even among interested students as courses with stricter policies rise to the top of their to-do lists.
- Instructors with many students spread across many sections need to make sure that grading can fit within the time they have available.

It's also worth noting that a learning management system (LMS) like Canvas, Blackboard, or Brightspace can have its own insidious effects on our grading choices (and what choices are available to us). An instructor unable to apply different due-date policies to different assignments in the LMS may shrug and accept a more punitive late policy across the course because it's easiest to manage. An instructor might realize only at the end of the term that students have been able to view their grades but not the rich written annotations included with each grade unless they knew to click a certain button. We may find ourselves reluctant to try out a new pedagogical approach when we think of all the nested modules and networked links we'll need to update as a result. As writers, we know that no tool is neutral; the technologies we use shape the choices we make. We need to keep this awareness at the front of our minds and maintain a critical scrutiny toward our options and choices or we can easily find ourselves designing courses guided by the constraints and affordances of a particular LMS.

In making decisions about grading and assessment, we should consider not only institutional factors and technological nudges, but also our particular skills as instructors, what we have to offer to students, and where we want to devote our time. Teaching across institutions, levels, genres, and modalities, we've needed to adapt and adjust over and over. We've also developed the following core principles that guide our decisions when setting up a grading approach:

- Invite students to identify and articulate their own goals among—and alongside—the explicit learning goals for the course. In a small class, student goals (at the level of the assignment or the course) might be used as assessment criteria.
- Make grades as clear and transparent as possible so that students can make informed choices. Note: this doesn't imply constant grade updates (i.e., a running online attendance grade), which might make students feel more surveilled than supported.
- Align assessments with the real goals of the course (while acknowledging that learning is unpredictable).
- Grade based on what we can clearly articulate and see demonstrated.
- Offer clarity around expectations while remaining aesthetically plural (i.e., avoid rubrics that privilege lyric poems over experimental poems).
- Offer multiple pathways to success (i.e., demonstrating engagement by taking notes for absent peers as well as by speaking up in class—see the interview with J. Logan Smilges in **Chapter 1** for more on this).
- Make assessment part of an ongoing conversation through artist statements, reflections, and conferences.
- Include significant amounts of completion-based work (20–60%, depending on the class).
- When possible, give students a voice in the focus and modality of feedback they receive.

Ultimately, we don't think the unease we feel around grading can be undone, even with the most carefully designed courses and the most thoughtful pedagogy. Grading unease is the result of participating in systems rife with inequity under a capitalist structure that treats people as sources of value to be extracted. We can get to "better" grading approaches, and we put significant thought and care into designing them, but we don't expect unease to disappear. Instead, we're honest with students about the structures we work within, the efforts we make, and our hope for what can happen in their learning and art-making that transcends grades.

Alternatives to traditional grading

How do we design a course where a student's grade doesn't feel like the only thing that matters? The options available to us will vary depending on the institutional context, the specific student demographics, and the structure of the course. We're far from alone in experiencing grading unease, however. Here are a few solutions instructors have come up with:

- **Ungrading or self-grading.** Ungrading involves asking students to grade themselves, in part or in whole, sometimes with a possibility that an instructor may overrule (up or down). Self-assessments are often reflection-based and rely on student integrity and a shared understanding of what constitutes strong work. Our conversation with Jesse Stommel (later in this chapter), author of *Undoing the Grade: Why We Grade and How to Stop* (2023), digs into some advantages and challenges of this approach.
- **Pass/fail or complete/incomplete grading.** Students receive a "pass" or "complete" on the basis of meeting a handful of clear parameters. This approach can be especially useful for generative exercises and process-based work.
- **Contract grading and labor-based grading.** These approaches remove qualitative assessments in favor of benchmarks for each grade tied to measures of student labor (demonstrated by word count, number of revisions, and so on). Shortly, we discuss this approach with Asao B. Inoue, author of *Labor-Based Grading Contracts: Building Equity and Inclusion in the Compassionate Writing Classroom* (2019).

Books like *Grading for Growth* (Clark and Talbert 2023), *Ungrading* (Blum 2020), and *What We Know About Grading* (Guskey and Brookhart 2019) consider other approaches, including standards-based grading, specifications-based grading, competency-based grading, and mastery grading, and explore ways to apply these approaches across disciplines. Aspects of any of these grading approaches might have something to offer, depending on your values and teaching context. We encourage instructors to explore and experiment—perhaps starting with small interventions—rather than becoming overwhelmed by options or hung up on precise distinctions.

Asao B. Inoue on labor-based grading

What is a labor-based grading system, and what does it look like in your classroom?

Labor-based grading is a system that takes grades, numbers, and letters out of the classroom and off of all activities and assignments. The practice focuses on how much labor or work students agree to do for an agreed-upon final course grade. While the teacher still provides feedback and assessments on student writing and other performances, nothing is graded. The system can look different in different courses and with different teachers. The key elements of my practice are:

- Students negotiate the terms of our grading contract, how much labor will be required for each final grade possible, and how completion of labor is determined.
- In preparation for our contract negotiations, students learn about the historical practice of grading, research on its detrimental effects on learning, and how labor-based grading addresses these issues.
- Students still receive feedback and respond to it, but they are not obligated to do what I say or please me as a reader. They are obligated to listen thoughtfully and compassionately to me and their colleagues.
- Students must also create labor plans for each unit (about 2–3 weeks of work), and track their labor for all work in the course, usually through things like labor logs or labor tracking documents.
- Students periodically reflect upon their labor and consider the lessons they can draw from their labor as a practice over time.
- Students learn about and draft a charter for compassion, which lists compassion practices that we all promise to use in our course labors.

What changes for students when assessment shifts to their labor?

In my experience, many students who have been hurt by conventional grades on their writing are able to experience their own languaging in, dare I say, more liberating conditions. They get a chance to write without worrying about the grade. The conditions afford them the chance to focus on learning to write better, on understanding their own languaging in ways that are not deficit-based. They can write and learn from conditions that treat their languaging as assets they bring to any communication or learning situation.

ASAO B. INOUE is a Professor of Rhetoric and Composition at Arizona State University, and the 2019 Chair of the Conference on College Composition and Communication. He has published many books on anti-racist writing assessment, race, and racism, which have won national-awards.

Image credit: Asao B. Inoue

Assessing product, process, and performance

A syllabus communicates what's important to students through its key terms, its tone, and, most explicitly, through its assessment breakdown. Across various chapters, we've considered questions like:

- Should workshop engagement be a graded component of a course?
- What message do we send when we tell students generative work is important but only allot 5–10% of course assessment to low-stakes writing?
- If we expect students to revise their stories, should the first draft receive a grade?

Each question grapples with decisions about how a course articulates its priorities and values—explicitly or implicitly—to students. Decisions must also take into account logistical and structural challenges: How do we measure workshop contributions fairly? How many drafts do we actually have time to offer feedback on? In conversations with colleagues, we've noticed a couple of common challenges:

How to communicate the value of process

Final products can be the easiest to grade. Does this final story or script demonstrate strong work with plot, character, setting, dialogue, and so on? If so, great! It's an A. If partially, it's a B. If barely, it might be a C or lower. Given this clarity, faculty sometimes weigh final product assessment heavily, expecting that students will still recognize the value of an engaged process necessary to get to a strong final product. But students, caught up in the urgent triage of a long homework to-do list, may not get this message. How, then, does a course substantiate its commitment to process? Here are some solutions we've seen work:

- Give space in class and in the assessment breakdown for process-based work. Examples: give substantial weight to process components, offer dedicated time for process-focused conferences, or assign presentations where students share process efforts or research findings.
- Turn the process into a product by asking students to document and reflect on their process. You'll find examples of this throughout the book, such as the revision logs discussed in **Chapter 8**.
- Consider alternative assessments, which can open up new possibilities and shift a student's relationship to the work. An early draft might be assessed complete/ incomplete based on word count or other clear parameters but not assessed qualitatively until the student has had a chance to receive feedback and revise. A course might set up a Contract Grading schema where students receive credit for booking a consultation with the instructor at whichever point in the process they feel would be most useful to them.

How to balance flexibility with clarity

Appreciating the value of things like class conversation, workshop engagement, craft readings, and in-class writing, an instructor may decide to lump a number of loosely defined activities into a broad category called Class Participation. "I don't want to count how many times someone talks during a workshop," they might say, "So I'll just rely on my holistic sense of student performance." While this reluctance to define and pin down is understandable, we've found that students can feel expectations are unclear when it comes to "big vague bucket" grades, which they worry may be determined by whether the instructor "likes them" or "thinks they're smart/talented." How can we offer students clear expectations while remaining open to the different ways they might demonstrate skill? Here are some approaches we recommend:

- Review what's included in the "big bucket" of Class Participation. Would it make sense to unspool any of these components and make a separate category? For example, a course seeking to hone peer feedback skills might create a category for "Peer Responses and Support."
- Push yourself to identify and articulate expectations—explicit and tacit—and confirm that they're aligned with your values and support student growth. Consider both quantitative and qualitative parameters and keep inclusion and accessibility in mind. What might respectful attention look like for different learners? Is it important that students write ten peer responses or would it be better to have them write three with a higher expectation of nuance and attention?
- If a course has multiple pathways for demonstrating skill or engagement, make sure students are aware of these options, and offer them a chance to reflect on their performance and growth (and share examples that may not have been immediately apparent to you).

John C. Bean and Dan Melzer on non-graded assignments, self-assessment, and peer response

Not all assigned writing needs to be graded, responded to, or even turned in in order to be useful to students. What are some guiding principles instructors might use to make these decisions?

John: To understand my guiding principles, it helps to know why I started building non-graded writing exercises into my courses. When I first studied pedagogy, I read an article on "wait time." The author's point was that teachers don't wait long enough after they ask a question before they call on students for answers. The author was concerned that our educational system doesn't help students distinguish between deep questions that promote critical thinking and "right answer" questions where the teacher knows the answer.

Suppose, for example, that I wanted to ask my class "Why does Shakespeare include the graveyard scene in *Hamlet*?" Students are trained to think that this question has a right answer and that the teacher knows it. But my graveyard question is an authentic question—a true puzzle—that requires wait time for pondering. When I read that article, I was also learning from my composition colleagues about the generative power of freewriting. I started posing an authentic deep question and asking students to explore the problem through ten minutes of freewriting before I opened the discussion. I found those ten minutes of silent freewriting enormously powerful in sparking a better discussion. It never occurred to me to collect the freewrites and try to grade them. Their value was immediately apparent in the enriched discussion.

My first guiding principle for using non-graded assignments, therefore, is to appreciate the way they help students see themselves as makers of knowledge rather than memorizers of knowledge. To put it another way, non-graded assignments give students continual practice in doing the intellectual work of our disciplines. Students are motivated by seeing how non-graded exercises build knowledge and thinking skills they need for a downstream graded project. In *Engaging Ideas,* Dan and I provide dozens of ideas for developing prompts for non-graded assignments, building them into a course, and rewarding students for doing them. The key is that these tasks should never appear to students as "busywork." They are always connected to authentic disciplinary questions and build the knowledge and skills used by disciplinary experts.

***Engaging Ideas* has been a teaching influence and a model for this book. The most recent (third) edition introduces chapters on self-assessment/ peer review and on alternative grading. What's exciting about these new developments?**

Dan: The new edition of *Engaging Ideas* encourages teachers to place students in a more central role when designing responses to student writing. In my class, self-assessment is integrated from the first day to the final portfolio. My first writing activity asks students to take a literacy inventory where they reflect on their past writing experiences, their strengths and challenges as writers, and their goals for the course. Students write a process memo for each peer feedback session and teacher conference, reflecting on the strengths of the draft and mentioning questions they have for readers. For the final portfolio, students write a reflection letter that considers ways the contents of their portfolio show evidence they have met the learning outcomes for the course.

Revisions to the new edition of *Engaging Ideas* reflect recent empirical research on student self-reflection and peer response that has found when students are more involved in the response to writing that happens—both through critical self-reflection on their own writing and providing feedback to their peers—they make greater gains as writers and become more self-aware of their own writing processes.

JOHN C. BEAN is a Professor Emeritus of English at Seattle University. He is the author of *Engaging Ideas* [third edition co-authored with Dan Melzer] as well as co-author of three widely used composition textbooks—*Writing Arguments, The Allyn and Bacon Guide to Writing*, and *Reading Rhetorically*.

DAN MELZER is a Professor and Director of First-Year Composition in the University of California, Davis University Writing Program. He is the author of books including *Assignments across the Curriculum* and *Reconstructing Response to Student Writing* and co-author with John C. Bean of the third edition of the book *Engaging Ideas*.

Choosing an assessment approach for graded assignments

With each course, we make choices about what to assess and how to assess it. We also make choices about how and when to communicate that assessment to students. We've seen a wide range of approaches: some instructors decline to discuss grades throughout the term and give a final letter grade based on their holistic assessment of a student's performance; others have detailed rubrics for each assignment and offer students a running total of their precise grade. We've experimented with different approaches as we've encountered diverse teaching contexts: graduate classes, asynchronous classes, undergraduate large-lecture classes.

On one hand, putting a number or letter on student work immediately shifts attention from the work itself to the assessment. We find rubrics inherently alienating and worry that they risk being "fake-accurate," pretending to measure something as nuanced as creative writing with more precision and objectivity than we really can. On the other hand, "holistic" grading introduces a significant risk of bias. How can we make sure we're not assessing based on culturally conditioned (often racist, sexist, classist, or ableist) impressions of "who seems capable" or who we remember "doing good work"? Given all this, how do we approach graded assignments fairly and transparently without making grades the central focus?

We've developed some policies we maintain across courses and levels: giving a clear percentage breakdown for assessment categories and setting explicit expectations for fixed and flexible parameters. As we've mentioned, we use complete/incomplete grades or contract grades for process-based assignments and generative exercises across levels and contexts. But for graded assignments, we've found that the most apt assessment approach depends on the course level, size, and subject; the specific assignment; student needs; and our own capacity. Here are three possible options:

Option one: A brief assessment statement and a personal response

For small classes working at a high level with flexibility around grades, we find it sufficient to include a short statement of assessment parameters and give a holistic assignment grade and a personal response. Particularly in a graduate course, we're most interested in helping students articulate their own goals and key terms for their work and see our role as creating a generative and responsive structure. We want to be in conversation with students about their work, and the grade is a structural requirement we acknowledge but minimize.

Option two: A single-point rubric

For classes with a broader range of performance, and for assignments with a high number of fixed parameters, a single-point rubric can be useful. A single-point rubric, like the example in Table 10.1, spells out expectations for criteria or components in strong work. A single-point rubric might be tied to points (i.e., 10 points for this component and 5 for this one) or not. It might leave space for individual comments for each criterion—perhaps indicating how the work rises above or does not yet reach proficiency—or simply space for a check/plus/minus notation followed by a personal comment at the end. The goal is to establish clear accountability for fixed parameters while leaving space for personalized notes.

Option three: A grid rubric

For large undergrad courses with a wide range of student performance, and especially for courses with TA support or a target grade average, we may opt for a grid rubric. Whereas a single-point rubric spells out criteria for proficiency, a grid rubric, like the example in Table 10.2, articulates performance across a range of levels. A grid rubric pushes us to clarify the difference between stellar performance and solid performance. It obliges us to articulate the minimum acceptable standard for receiving a passing grade on the assignment.

A grid rubric can be helpful when any of the following are true:

1 We need to set a realistic expectation for the range of grades students will receive.
2 Students have a pressing desire to know why they got the exact grade they got.
3 We want to offer students clear ample information about their performance as efficiently as possible.
4 We're trying to norm a number of TAs to grade consistently.

A grid rubric can offer students the clarity they want while leaving the instructor (or TA) time to write a brief personal note.

Table 10.1 Single Point Rubric for a Peer Mentorship Assignment

Criteria	Comments
Log Sections The log includes clear detailed notes that address all five interaction points (Initial Consult, Pre-Workshop, Workshop, Post-Workshop, Portfolio Preparation).	
Supporting Materials The log includes and clearly labels all supporting materials: peer's pre-workshop memo, workshop précis, peer's post-workshop memo.	
Engagement with Developing Support Skills Notes and reflections show evidence of deep, kind, and supportive engagement in peer's work. Log shows evidence of developing abilities as a mentor (which may also include setting boundaries on time and energy).	
Reflection on Experience with Your Own Mentor Reflection thoughtfully discusses experience as a mentee and insights garnered from taking on both roles.	

Table 10.2 Grid Rubric (from the Revision as Exploration Log Assignment Discussed in Chapter 8)

Extending Skills	Applying Skills	Developing Skills	Attempting Skills
You've chosen revision strategies with intention that reveals a keen and growing awareness of your poetic aims. You take up the radical invitation of the assignment and go beyond small tweaks to explore new possibilities for your work. Reflections push beyond WHAT you notice and get into the HOW and WHY of poetic form and process. Insightful observations serve the current project and reach towards future writing.	You've chosen revision strategies that support your writing goals and interests. You engage in the radical possibilities of the assignment to explore new possibilities. Reflections demonstrate curiosity and close attention to language.	Any of the following is true: (1) You've chosen revision strategies but have not made fully clear why these particular strategies were selected or how they connect with your goals. (2) The work does not fully respond to the call for "radical revision" and shows mostly small changes. (3) Reflections, although adequate in length, would benefit from deeper curiosity and closer attention.	Any of the following is true: (1) You've chosen revision strategies, but these choices seem randomly selected or favor strategies requiring minimal time and effort. (2) The work does not respond to the call for "radical revision" and makes only minor changes. (3) Reflections do not dig deeply into the particularities of process and form. (4) Depth/degree of completion is inconsistent across strategies.

Fixed and flexible parameters in grading

Any assignment involves some fixed parameters (which may include length, genre, technique, process, etc.) along with many flexible parameters (such as tone, setting, plot, style, etc.). As we discuss in **Chapter 2,** clarifying fixed and flexible parameters allows students to focus on their work rather than on trying to read the instructor's mind. An effective instructor communicates both parameters clearly and assists students in identifying and claiming spaces of agency and creativity within the fixed parameters of each assignment. To set clear expectations, we tell students not just what we're asking them to do but what will be assessed and how. An assignment sheet that reads "Assessment: Wow us!" may be greeted as an open field for play by some, but will certainly be a source of needless stress and anxiety for others.

What does a mix of fixed and flexible parameters mean for assessment? In courses with highly motivated students and no particular grading pressures, we can focus on responding to the work individually. But in classes with a wide range of performance levels or a strict target average—classes, in other words, where we might choose to use a rubric—a couple of common issues can emerge.

Assessing flexible parameters as if they were fixed

Sometimes, in an effort to be clear, instructors end up with a rubric that narrows assignment parameters in ways they don't intend or treats flexible parameters as if they were fixed. Genres with a wide range of practice, such as lyric writing or poetry, present particular challenges. We recommend reviewing your rubric closely and asking: Is this something I expect to see in all student work or only some? Am I narrowing options without meaning to?

Terms on a rubric we can't define or point to

We've seen a lot of rubrics over the years with terms like "creativity," "originality," or other words we might see in blurbs on the back of a book jacket. We get it—creativity, innovation, and originality are qualities we hope to see in student work. But these terms are also hard to pin down, highly contextual, and deeply subjective. As experts in our genres, we may be able to say "I know an original TV show when I see one," or "I can tell the difference between a film script where a student is flexing their creativity and one where they're not." Perhaps. But what does this mean for students? Does "creativity" on a rubric point a student in a useful direction? Would we be able to give a clear answer if someone asked "What does originality look like here?" or "How do you measure creativity?" Here's what we recommend:

- Leave vague or abstract terms like "creativity" and "originality" off your rubric. Instead, nudge yourself to clarify what you mean by "creativity" in this specific context. If you arrive at something tangible, that might go on the rubric instead.
- If these terms feel important to you, open them up for group conversation. Invite students to present work they consider "original" for the genre and talk about why. Ask students to share their understandings of "creative" and consider how they align or diverge. At the end of a conversation like this, you might even work with students to create a shared definition of "creativity" that everyone's happy to have on a rubric.

A few more notes on rubrics

- **Using rubrics to assess process-based work.** When we include process-based components in our assessment, a rubric may include terms like "agency" or "engagement" that we can't point to in the script or memoir in isolation, but can assess by reviewing the work in conversation with documentation or reflective statements.
- **A fixed parameter in a rubric doesn't have to imply a fixed parameter in a genre.** As we discuss in **Chapter 5**, we find it useful to distinguish between fixed parameters for a specific assignment (i.e., "this short story has a clear inciting incident" on a rubric) and universal "rules" for a genre (i.e., all short stories must begin with a clear inciting incident). We can ask students to work with high-structure assignments or a large number of fixed parameters without adhering to a falsely universalizing stance. Like our colleague, Nancy Lee (interviewed in **Chapter 6**), we believe in "tools, not rules" as our baseline pedagogy. We offer structured exercises with fixed parameters as explicit opportunities to explore choices and results in preparation for making decisions with greater awareness and agency.
- **Using assessment to build on strengths.** Across levels, students often benefit from coaching in how to use assessment to support their growth and future work. For many, the initial impulse is to cringe and look away from a low grade or sigh in relief and move on from a high one. We might invite students to look over a past assignment and respond to questions like: What are you good at as a writer? How can you carry your strengths forward into your next project?

Jesse Stommel on motivation, trust, and ungrading for busy instructors

In your ungrading approach, students complete self-reflections throughout the course and assign themselves a grade at the end of the term. How do you support a buy-in on learning rather than an impression that students won't have to work to earn an A?

I have conversations with students about assessment, and I ask questions like:

- How does it feel to be graded in this course versus how you're graded in other classes?
- What kind of space does it create for your work?
- What's motivating you? Where do you feel demotivated?

Usually, the students themselves very quickly notice that their motivation works a little differently in a course that's ungraded. They start to say things like, "I'm not really worried about the deadlines like I am for my other classes, but I actually go deeper into the material and I get caught up in wonder." I want them to have space in their education to invest themselves and care about the topics and about their own learning and the work that they're doing. I don't want them to do busywork.

People often ask, "Do they work on stuff for other people's classes before they work on yours? Do they prioritize other classes?" And I say, "Yes, but they prioritize differently, not necessarily more." Students might be more likely to get something in on time for one of their other classes, but for my course they might be more likely to really sit with something in a troubling, complex, curious way. And to me, that's a success.

Trusting students is at the heart of your pedagogy. What happens when this trust is tested or broken by students who lie, cheat, or do less work if it's not being "rewarded" with a grade from the instructor?

I start with careful, thoughtful trust. I don't start from a place of suspicion. How does trust develop and how does trust grow stronger? What gets called cheating might be understood as students brushing up against our boundaries. When that happens, there's an opportunity for conversation. And those important conversations are exactly how we deepen trust. Students might test boundaries when we don't set them clearly enough or when the boundaries seem arbitrary. Why would someone obey or respect an arbitrary boundary if they don't understand why it's there and what it means?

These moments become an opportunity for us to get closer to students. To be clear, there are certain boundaries like respect for someone's humanity, and if a student crosses that line, there isn't always a productive conversation we can have. But mostly when we're talking about things like cheating or plagiarism, the vast majority of incidents are unintentional. And so that means they really are opportunities for getting closer, developing trust, and ultimately opportunities for us to teach students.

You've written about the value of self-evaluations such as process letters. How would you approach these assignments in a large class where you don't have time to respond to each person individually?

These are even more important in larger classes. Students' process letters, self-reflections, or self-evaluations give me invaluable information that I wouldn't have access to otherwise. But we don't have to carefully pore over every single word of self-reflections and respond to every one individually. Trusting students also means that not every piece of work students do has to go across the desk of the teacher.

Instead, I skim and read selectively. I flip through them, and I read one really carefully. I read part of one, a couple paragraphs of the next one. I'm trying to get a sense for what's happening in the class, a sense for the hum in the room. Then, I write one letter to the entire class that addresses what I'm noticing: here are some common questions, here are answers to things I saw come up repeatedly. I'll often include a note that says "Is there anything specific you want me to address?" About 10% might include specific questions, and about half of those questions might already be answered in the large letter to the class. So, then I might write individual notes to the 5% of the class who had specific questions not answered by the larger letter.

JESSE STOMMEL is a faculty member in the Writing Program at University of Denver and co-founder of *Hybrid Pedagogy*. He is author of *Undoing the Grade: Why We Grade, and How to Stop* and co-author of *An Urgency of Teachers: the Work of Critical Digital Pedagogy*.
Image credit: Jesse Stommel

GenAI and academic integrity

Along with writing instructors everywhere, we've been grappling with what the rise of GenAI means for ourselves and for our students. The creep of AI into the technologies we've already integrated into our lives means that unless we actively block them, we're given AI-generated summaries in our internet search results and AI-supported autocomplete suggestions in our email clients.

What is taken from us—and from our students—through these supposed labor-saving shortcuts? The work of thinking, considering, choosing. The work of intention. How refreshing a piece of paper and a pen can feel these days. *Finally, I'm alone with my thoughts.* Writers strive to arrive not at the most statistically probable next word, but at the most apt, the most peculiar, the most devastating, the most satisfying. As teachers, we share this difficult and rewarding striving with our students. While thought-provoking uses of GenAI in art-making exist (as we discuss with A. E. Osworth in **Chapter 2**), a poem, scene, or "response" to a peer draft lifted directly and uncritically from a large language model text generator does not demonstrate them.

Student use of GenAI can be most confronting at the point of grading and responding. Like many others, we've felt that sinking feeling when you're trying to bring supportive, curious attention to a draft and find yourself wondering: *Did a student even write this? Am I putting my finite time into trying to support something made without thought in five seconds by a machine?*

While it may seem obvious to an instructor that an assignment is fully AI-generated, AI use is difficult to prove, and an academic misconduct process is time-consuming and often fruitless. This process also places instructors in a role of suspiciously policing students that can feel antithetical to our purpose. When university guidance around AI and integrity seems to range from bland statements that each instructor can set policies for their own classroom to unreflective embrace of each new technology (or even requirements that all instructors incorporate AI into their pedagogy), we can start to wonder what we're even doing here.

We would argue, however, that while not every student will be in a place to be able to receive it, what creative writing courses have to offer is more essential than ever. In a world of slick slop and automated products, we can invite students to be curious about their own minds. To experience the deep satisfaction of making something difficult and meaningful. Along with our solidarity, we offer these pragmatic suggestions:

1. **Give clear policies and rationales.** Communicate (and be as specific as possible) in the syllabus and reinforce throughout the semester prohibited and/or permitted uses of GenAI in students' academic work and the rationale for these decisions. Students are likely navigating differing levels of GenAI permissions in all of their courses, so communicating expectations in a clear and straightforward manner is important.
2. **If you choose to allow GenAI use, foreground choice, ethics, and responsible citation practice.** An instructor teaching a course like Writing for New Media may decide that GenAI experimentation is relevant to course learning goals and have the skillset to design assignments that give students options to use (or not use) GenAI. And to articulate their choices in relation to pleasure, curiosity, and risk-taking, as well as environmental impact, intellectual property rights, Indigenous data sovereignty, and other ethical concerns. We encourage these instructors to discuss responsible disclosure and citation practices for work that draws on GenAI.
3. **Convey to students that what they think and create and how they write matters.** Making songs, poems, stories, and comics allows us to deepen, question, and share what we experience and imagine. In offloading their making to AI, students effectively devalue themselves.
4. **If you choose not to allow GenAI use, design assessments and rubrics that emphasize human qualities.** In your rubrics, foreground human elements like specificity or positionality that you hope to see in student work. When AI-generated work performs poorly on the rubric, students are disincentivized from relying on AI for future assignments without an instructor needing to call out the work as AI-generated.

5 **When your capacity allows, have conversations with students who cross a line.** When we asked Jesse Stommel how he might approach a student, he said, "What I would say to the student is, 'Well, you used AI, but what AI produced was not great, so let's talk about that. Let's talk about why it failed to produce something useful. Did this help you? How did this help you and why did it not help you, ultimately, to use this tool for something like that?' It's about creating conversations."

6 **Keep in mind the various reasons students may turn to GenAI.** Asao B. Inoue spoke with us about how "students may view such technologies as ways to get 'better writing' or English, which frames their own Englishes as deficits because they will inevitably be different from what the technology produces." The more our courses can value a plurality of Englishes and reward students for evoking their unique lifeworlds on the page, the less likely students will be to see their articulations as deficit-based and turn to GenAI solutions.

7 **Remember that many students are hungry for genuine intellectual and emotional stimulation.** When we hear about the elaborate puzzle-like processes teen GenAI-cheating influencers share with their followers, we can't help but think: what if students brought this tenacious puzzle-solving energy to their actual writing? Over and over, we can invite students to claim their writing and make it their own, rather than seeing it as busywork for a grade.

8 **Don't let a handful of bad actors become your pedagogical (and emotional) center of gravity**. It can be so demoralizing to confront AI-generated work that it's easy for teachers to lose sight of the bigger picture. But in any class, we also have students who genuinely want to make art and who care deeply about their work. Let these students guide your pedagogy.

Grading strategies to support students and still have a weekend

Instructors are constantly confronted by the constraints of time. In course design, we weigh which assignments to include and which to omit. Week by week, we make decisions about how to divide class time between discussion, in-class writing, lecture, workshop, and other options. But perhaps the most difficult time-based challenge we encounter lies in grading: how much time should we spend responding to student work?

We've both struggled with this as we've moved between institutions and across levels. We've found ourselves balancing between two extremes:

1 The impulse to let grading and commenting take the time they take and find pleasure in this thoughtful work without rushing.

2 The imperative to contain what can easily expand to almost infinite proportions.

When we set strict timers or attempt hourly quotas to push through grading efficiently, we can start to feel like assembly line workers and wonder why we ever decided to become writing instructors. But without checks or containers, we can easily look up to find we've spent an entire afternoon on a single feedback letter.

From our challenges with time and marking, we've realized that we do ourselves and our students a disservice when we fail to maintain boundaries and become holier-than-thou fatigue warriors. We can offer invaluable mentorship and guidance to our students without commenting on every line break or each sparkling (or dull) verb.

Here are a few strategies we've explored to offer useful feedback while acknowledging the constraints on our time and energy and the limits of what students can usefully absorb:

- **Quick checks.** For low-stakes or process-based work, a quick confirmation that work satisfies requirements might offer students clear accountability and be all that's necessary.
- **Comment on some each cycle.** If students are completing a number of generative exercises, we might choose to comment on a set number each week, such that everyone gets comments every other week or every three weeks.
- **Self-Assessment.** Depending on the course and level, students might assess their own work. Especially in advanced courses, we've explored weekly self-assessments for assignments like Commonplace Books (**Chapter 6**) to give students privacy to explore and accountability to indicate that the assignment matters.
- **Instead of make-ups, consider skips.** Inevitably, things come up and students miss low-stakes assignments. Rather than negotiating make-up policies and drawing out your marking, do yourself and your students a favor by allowing a proportionately appropriate number of "skips" using the "Drop the lowest score" function available in your LMS.
- **Adopt policies that offer students grace AND respect your time.** In a large class, for example, you might set an assignment due date and offer a week-long grace period during which students can turn the assignment in late and receive rubric comments and a grade without penalty but also without an additional personal note. (See **Chapter 2** for more on due dates and policies.)
- **Bring the feedback into class.** Instead of leaving individual comments on a stack of student reflections, consider synthesizing issues and questions students raise and sharing this synthesis at the start of class.
    - You might offer some notes or suggestions that apply to multiple students or use this synthesis as a way to launch discussion. A task that might take several hours each week becomes not only quicker but also a way of creating community and connection within the group.
    - Likewise, you might notice a recurring issue in student work (like vague language or unintentional slips in verb tense) and choose to focus a class on this issue rather than leaving individual comments (Jesse Stommel discusses a version of this).
- **Consider templates and/or comment banks.** Especially with beginning students, templates or comment banks can help an instructor move through a stack of student writing efficiently.

  - Pasting in a basic comment on replacing vague nouns with concrete specific ones might leave you time to review the stage play or personal narrative and pick out a perfect example of a strong specific noun to point to as a model.
  - A template might be as simple as a Post-it that says "I noticed … I was struck by … I wondered … As you move forward with this project … " to remind us of the basic moves we want to make in our responses.
- **Opt-in feedback.** Opt-in feedback requires students to take an active step to request it.
  - We might offer opt-in feedback on an early low-stakes assignment by telling students to ask a question about their work if they want notes.
  - A final revision or portfolio can be another occasion for opt-in feedback. Some students are eager to keep revising and would welcome in-depth feedback; others just want to be celebrated for completing their work or receive a few tips for future projects.
  - When making choices about opt-in feedback, we keep in mind that how entitled a student feels to instructor time and energy can vary based on gender, cultural expectations, or class background and we take steps to mitigate any reluctance.
- **Choices in feedback focus and/or modality.** We also invite students to take the lead on what type of feedback would best support or challenge their work.
  - A process statement or writer's introduction (which we often assign) can include a note to the instructor specifying feedback a student is looking for, often in the form of questions.
  - In a small class, we might also give students a chance to select a preferred modality—one student might prefer line-level comments they can review at their leisure, whereas another might prefer a face-to-face conversation where they can ask follow-up questions.

Some final thoughts on writing feedback and grading

Over time, we've developed response strategies that work for us: checking due dates for various courses against a calendar to make sure we haven't set traps with multiple assignments all coming in at once; establishing daily quotas and scheduled times for this work (rather than expecting to somehow squeeze it in at the margins); identifying points in our schedules where we're neither depleting our best writing energy nor dragging ourselves forward on fumes at the end of a packed day; and, most importantly, designing assignments that lead to work we're genuinely eager to read.

We advocate for taking regular breaks while grading—go for a walk, make a cup of tea, deal with some email or a low-energy admin task. Regular breaks help us return fresh to the work and be more considerate in our tone, which may start to show impatience when we're tired. These tone-checks are vital, as the sheer volume of student work can elicit a range of emotions that might unintentionally leak into our notes. Finally, we try to remember that yes, grading is serious business because grades are important to students, but it's our comments that accompany the grades that can have a profound and lasting impact (positive or negative). The more levity, grace, and patience we can offer ourselves in this work, the more generosity, kindness, and clarity we can bring to our students.

11 Supporting Thesis and Capstone Work

Capstone courses and thesis supervision

What happens when students tackle a sustained project like a thesis? Often, they begin with energy and joy: finally, a chance to write that novel with the characters they've been obsessing about for months, to bring that screenplay to life, to write the poems they *really* want to write. Soon, however, new challenges emerge. The strategies that served them well in crafting powerful short stories may prove inadequate for planning and drafting a longer work of fiction; writing a feature-length script feels more daunting than drafting a treatment. Doubts and uncertainties can creep in. *Is this really the project I want to be working on? Am I capable of finishing it? Will anyone ever read it?*

A thesis process asks new things of students in craft, stamina, and personal growth. As thesis supervisors and mentors, we are likewise asked to develop skills and capacities different from those we rely on in classroom teaching: how to support students without the framework of assignments, when to encourage persistence and when to suggest a change, how to help students figure out their own process when their work habits or aesthetic goals may be radically different from our own.

Instructors may support undergraduate students crafting their first sustained projects in a capstone course that lasts a term or supervise graduate students through an individual thesis or dissertation over months or years. In a capstone course, the constraints of the term and the larger group necessitate some degree of shared structure. We may assign due dates for process components or ask all students to try out the same research tool. Still, there can be room for shared agency and flexibility. We may offer planning templates for students to adapt to set their own milestones or give the group a choice between frequent discussions of short selections of work in progress or less frequent deeper engagement with longer selections or full drafts.

With individual thesis supervision, we have the greatest opportunity to step back and support a student in setting their own agenda. Indeed, one-on-one mentorship offers considerable scope for student initiative, and we may find ourselves working quite differently with one student than another. As supervisors, we want to support students in making their work their own way. Often, however, students are still figuring out what *their way* might be. So we offer strategies, structures, and options, along with encouragement to experiment and observe. We also need to consider our own capacity and set boundaries. We start by establishing a clear and consistent way to communicate across the life cycle of the project. Here are some initial decisions to review and negotiate with students embarking on a thesis:

- How to keep in touch and who initiates contact.
- How often to meet (weekly, monthly, variable depending on stage of development).
- How to meet (phone, video call, in-person).
- Frequency and length of submissions (twenty pages per month during a drafting phase, nothing until the first full draft, outline materials and process notes).
- Time interval needed to read and respond to submitted work (a few days, a few weeks).
- Type of feedback, if any (a conversation, written notes on the page, a reading list, bullet points on a notecard).
- What happens if plans need to change.

Coaching creative project management

The first great challenge of any sustained project is this: we must plan and we must be prepared for our plans to change. As writers, we've grappled with this over and over (including while completing this book!). One student may show up with a firm commitment to a tightly honed outline. Another may begin with a desire to feel their way and a reluctance to commit to any plan or schedule. Each will wrestle with this challenge in their own way.

As mentors, we aim to get as much information on the table as possible, including known unknowns. In an initial conversation, we'll likely discuss:

- What a student knows about the project so far: genre, style, inspirations, approximate length, aesthetic goals.
- How fixed or flexible their timeline is. One student may need to complete a thesis and degree by a set date to start a new job or move across the country. Another student may wish to draw out the thesis process as long as we permit in order to receive continued support on an ambitious project. Institutions also vary in flexibility and funding available.
- Approximate schedule and time they'll be able to dedicate to thesis work. Any challenges they anticipate (work commitments, TA responsibilities, family care, health issues, isolation, and so on).
- Hopes and fears for the project and for the mentoring relationship, with reference to any past experiences with either sustained projects or mentorship.
- Any questions the student has for us about past student experiences, our approach, and what we can (and can't) offer.
- An initial plan for starting work together and a time to check in on how the collaboration is going.

We like to ask a lot of questions and take many notes during these initial meetings with two key purposes in mind:

1 To articulate a shared understanding of the project and the students' parameters.
2 To model for the student how they might plan for their next project, post-thesis, when they no longer have the formal support of a mentorship.

The next step is to ask the student to write up their thoughts in a document both student and advisor can refer to (and revise) as the project takes shape. This document may be a formal letter of agreement that both advisor and student sign to capture and recognize their shared commitment to the project. Or it may be an informal bullet point list of goals, plans, and open questions. While composing these documents can be challenging and feel a bit stilted or artificial, especially for those new to talking about their work, the push to articulate a description and a plan will serve students in clarifying and naming their goals, even though both project and plans will inevitably change. For some students, this process will also inform grant and residency applications as they graduate and start building a career.

In the initial meeting or shortly after, we review a calendar together and walk through some backward planning: a thesis submission in May means a thesis committee meeting in April, which means a revised draft by March and a complete draft by January, for example. We encourage the student to play with numbers here: how many weeks between today and January? If you're aiming for a 75K word draft, how many words per week would you need to produce to maintain a steady schedule? What about if you block out vacation, some work travel, some family commitments, and leave a safety buffer at the end? Students might draft a rough timeline in a live document like a Google Doc that both student and advisor can refer to as we move forward, adding scheduled meetings, video call links, and due date milestones as we go.

Both genre and subject inform how a thesis process takes shape. A thesis mentor supervising a screenplay might offer students an experience in producing industry-standard deliverables along a typical timeline. Students working in a modular genre like poetry, lyric writing, a short story collection, or a collection of essays might be able to count on gradual accretion of a project over time, while students working in novel or memoir will likely need more support with outlining and planning. Individual projects may require significant research, serious care with ethical concerns, or particular emotional fortitude. These are all important considerations to discuss early in a mentoring relationship. The deeper students can dig into potential challenges and how to face them, the more grounded and realistic they will be when starting out the most daunting creative project they've undertaken.

Scaffolding and the value of quota tasks

We encourage students to break their big ambitious projects down into manageable tasks. These tasks include completing chapters or sections of the project itself, but also activities like reading, completing research, diagraming, synthesizing, getting feedback, and so on. In our conversation in this chapter, Jessica Abel discussed the difficulty of breaking a big project into discrete pieces:

> How do you literally break down goals? How do you look at the next thing? How do you slot this into your day? How do you make decisions about what's important and what's not important? How do you face the dilemma of two things that are important and you don't have enough time? These decisions can be a struggle even for experienced writers. For students attempting their first sustained project, they can feel insurmountable.

When first setting milestone goals, students run into two common problems:

1. They don't break goals into small enough pieces.
2. They set vague goals.

"I want to finish the first half of my novel this summer," a student might say. But unless they take the time to define what "first half" might look like and map specifics onto a weekly calendar, there's a risk that each morning they'll simply look at the big daunting to-do list item "finish first half of novel" and find their willpower slip away. Likewise, a goal like "make progress on revisions" can leave a writer at a loss in terms of where and how to start. Fortunately, students facing either problem can be helped by calm and encouraging coaching: breaking down a big project into pieces, mapping goals onto a calendar, translating feedback into actions, or deciding where and how to start. "What is the first step forward?" we find ourselves asking students (and ourselves) over and over.

Like Jessica Abel, we've also seen the value of what she calls "quota tasks." A quota task is a task defined by time committed rather than progress accomplished. The benefit of this framing, as Abel said, is that "we have so much more control over deciding to show up and work for thirty minutes or two hours than over how much gets accomplished in that window." Particularly when a project feels daunting, we encourage a student to make a quota task goal (and to try their utmost to defer doubts and self-recriminations until they've put in the established amount of time). Again and again, we see that five focused hours truly *does* move the project forward.

Many writers—students and professionals alike—benefit from a time-tracking spreadsheet to stay accountable and recognize progress and patterns. A simple spreadsheet might include:

- Date
- Time spent on project
- Word count (if appropriate to the project and phase)
- Notes/Observations (i.e., what was hard, insights or discoveries)
- Where to pick up next time

Over the life span of a project, documenting quota tasks allows writers to gather rough data permitting us to make more accurate estimations for our future work (and help us make choices about what kind of work to take on, knowing just how long that type of work truly takes).

Jessica Abel on big projects and self-forgiveness

You work with creative people across disciplines. Where do people encounter gaps in their preparation for continuing to make creative work over the long haul?

Most people don't get any education about how to continue their work over the long haul. There's just an assumption that you'll figure it out. Often, we are trained into terrible habits through schooling: you get assigned big projects in six different subjects without enough scaffolding in how to break them down into steps. Students are essentially encouraged to pull all-nighters and burn the candle at both ends. There's also a lot of make-work, chug through, check boxes. At the same time, there's a built-in feedback system of grading and due dates. So, when you graduate and you're trying to do your own thing, you don't know how to pace yourself and create the structure for finishing something big. When there's nobody on the other end saying, "You did a great job, congratulations, you get an A," a lot of people just fall off a cliff. They don't know how to finish anything.

I teach a course where students conceive of and plan a semester-long project of their own—a thing they want to do, not that I'm giving them to do. We make a big whiteboard and they set weekly deadlines for themselves. The goal is to help them figure out how to put this kind of structure in place when they're working on their own. I want to set students up to be able to decide they want to do a thing and *do* it instead of thinking about stuff they want to do, dreaming about it, but not having any idea how to fill that gap.

What are the most valuable things a teacher can offer in a mentoring context such as thesis supervision?

Keep the focus on engagement with the process. To help students work on a sustained project, you have to work against all of the training they've had through their lives and help them turn off the part of their brain that's constantly telling them, "This next thing is due! No, pay attention to this other thing. No, switch gears to this."

Help students understand the importance of sleep and regular practice! I think teachers need to become less nervous about talking to students about their actual literal process. If students say they're not getting work done, you can help them investigate what is happening in their days and walk them through habit stacking. Like, what time of day are you trying to do this work? What else is happening during your day? When do you typically go to sleep? When do you typically get up? What's your morning routine like? What is the last thing you do in your morning routine every single day? Do you have time there? Can you put in a writing session at that moment? Sometimes it's helpful to get very concrete and actionable.

We can also help students accept that they need to make tough choices. Sometimes, they just literally don't have time in their calendar to do everything well. One unorthodox thing I've done in class is say, "You do not have time to do well in all your classes this week. You just don't. So, what's most important to you?" And if a student says, "Well, my painting class," then I say, "Great. Now, what are you going to suck at this week? Tell me what you're going to suck at." As mentors, we can model self-forgiveness and not beat ourselves up over productivity. How do you create a flexible container for your work that gives you enough structure to keep going forward, but also is responsive to the life you really have? If you start blaming yourself every time you don't hit your 500-word goal or whatever, you are going to stop writing because it's going to become poisonous to you. It becomes a source of shame. And when it's a source of shame, you run in the other direction.

JESSICA ABEL is the Chair of the illustration program at the Pennsylvania Academy of Fine Arts. She's an indie cartoonist-turned-founder of Autonomous Creative, a creative business coaching company, and author of many books, including *Growing Gills: How to Find Creative Focus When You're Drowning in Your Daily Life* and two textbooks about making comics.
Image credit: Maria Teicher

Context and process

Throughout this book, we've emphasized how writing is in conversation with other writing. As thesis advisors, we want to help students figure out who their project is in conversation with and who else they might read (or watch or listen to) to deepen and broaden this conversation or to approach their work more responsibly. Recent thesis conversations have sent us to our bookshelves and group text threads with questions like: What are some long poems with sustained narrative elements? Who writes about motherhood in new or surprising ways? What are some ways writers handle multiple languages when writing from and about diasporic communities? What writers are working mostly in summary and half scenes instead of full scenes? How do writers manage seamless transitions between prolepsis, analepsis and the fictive present?

The work of context also involves imagining audience. "Who is your ideal reader?" we ask students, "And how are you caring for that reader through your choices on the page?" As we discuss in **Chapter 5,** we may have much or little in common with a student's imagined reader. We raise these gaps directly with students, acknowledging our limits and ways we might stretch in service of their vision. "I can tell you what it's like for me to encounter Persian dialogue here," we might say, "But if you're imagining a bilingual reader, it would be great to get that perspective as well."

Even when we need to deepen our knowledge of IVF procedures or Toronto neighborhoods to be better readers of our students' work, we keep in mind that the main thing we have to offer is our knowledge of process, the accumulated experience that allows us to say, "That's a familiar phase many writers face at this point in a draft, and I trust that you can get through it," or, "I've had that problem, too. Here's a tool that worked for me."

Depending on the situation, we might suggest any of the reading, revision, and research tools we discuss in **Chapters 6**, **8**, and **9**. Often, though, we recommend that students keep a process journal or writing log. A process journal is a place to gather notes, sit with questions, and document progress. It's a book about the book you're writing that can also inform the next book you'll write. Students might include brief sketches of character work and images, or a hand-drawn map of the setting of the story to keep track of the geography. They might make a chart to clarify the pros and cons of the POV they've selected or end each writing session with a quick freewrite on a question like "What am I struggling with right now?" or "What areas of energy am I feeling pulled toward?" A process journal might share notebook space with or incorporate elements of a Commonplace Book (**Chapter 6**). It gives students an opportunity to keep a conversation going between themselves and the book over the lifespan of the project.

By serving as a repository of ideas and possibilities, a process journal can rescue a momentary flash of inspiration from being lost or allow a vague impulse to incubate into a major plot point. When students flip back through earlier pages, they start to realize that, although they're still wrestling with some of the same problems, they've found satisfying solutions to others (and, of course, uncovered many new ones). A process journal can help a writer recognize movement over the long haul of a project. Students who go on to publish their thesis and find themselves promoting the book at writing festivals and in media interviews often return to these notebooks to trace the origins of an unexpected solution or share in detail the doubts, swerves, and discoveries inherent in any sustained project.

Rajiv Mohabir on figuring out who you want to be in conversation with

How is thesis supervision different from classroom teaching? What skills or practices have you been called on to develop in the role of thesis supervisor?

Well, everything is so much more personalized and individualized. If I'm teaching a Poetry and Ecology workshop, the syllabus is based on my ideas of what students need to know. With a thesis it's more like: "What do you *want* to know?" My goal as a thesis advisor is to help students become independent in their thinking and writing. As soon as you're done with your MFA, you have to live in the world. Sure, you'll have your writer friends, but you need to trust your own voice. In a thesis, we can have conversations like, "What is some extra-literary thing that you're inviting into the space of your writing?"

On a practical level, I begin by asking students what they've been reading. I see this as building an inquiry base. I'll ask, "What do you notice about the organization of this book?" or "What are you connecting with formally here?" Sometimes they have clear answers, and sometimes they say, "I don't know. I just feel something here." So I'll say, "Let's slow down and look together at exactly what's happening here. Is it something about the line? Is it the dissonance between things that are brought together?" This is a lot of fun! I also have the students create their own writing experiments based on what they're reading. There's a forward motion to reading as a poet and deliberately allowing influence into your work. Of course, that can inspire anxiety sometimes. I try to reframe this as "Who are you in conversation with?" There's no such thing as original, you know. All of our ideas are connected through a web.

Craft challenges versus mental/emotional challenges. Is this a meaningful distinction? How do you help students figure out what they're dealing with and how to get unstuck?

I think many craft challenges are supremely emotional. I had a student who was writing these really long lines that didn't make sense for the poem. When I asked why she'd made this formal choice, she said, "I don't believe in line breaks." So, I pushed a bit, like, "Where is your breath when you read it out loud?" or "What is your purpose with the long line? Is it just because you want to contest something?"

Eventually, she said she was doing it because she'd read a craft essay on enjambment by someone she thought was a white supremacist. Here's a craft question that is also fully emotional. And I don't want to devalue her lived experience because craft writing can erase folks, but also, why this conversation? Why not be in dialogue with Fred Moten or with folks in *A Broken Thing: Poets on the Line*? Something that presents as a craft challenge could have emotional questions—about discourse community or about what kind of person makes what kind of work—at the root of it.

You've talked about the pressures faced by queer BIPOC writers to produce "queer BIPOC marginalization porn" or perform trauma in digestible ways. What might you say to a student who is feeling this pressure?

First, I'd say, "I totally understand." Then I might tell them a story, like how *Friction Magazine* invited me to submit work, and I sent some poems from *Whale Aria*, which are not very clearly about colonization but are also very much about colonization. I got a rejection that said "Please submit to us any time!" I replied, "I'd be happy to send you more poems. What would you like to see?" The editor wrote back, "The board says they were looking for poems about colonization." I looked up the board and saw a bunch of cis white folks, and I was like, *Oh, you want to mine me for something*.

I'd tell the students this story, or another story, and just be really frank: in the US, trauma porn sells for folks of color, right? People are so thirsty for that. I would also tell the student, "Look, anyone can write a trendy poem. In five years, where's that poem going to be compared to a poem where you're actually writing what you want to write, what you believe in, instead of trying to perform for people?" I think of Haunani-Kay Trask, how she worked to create a platform for people, sometimes in the face of incredible silence. If you're making work and you feel like the system or the academy doesn't want it, you have choices: Do you stop? Do you perform? Or do you make space, do the invisibilized slow work of creating a platform for your people, whoever your people are?

RAJIV MOHABIR is an Assistant Professor of poetry at the University of Colorado Boulder. He is the author of four poetry collections, including *Whale Aria*, and has been a finalist for the National Book Critics Circle Award.
Image credit: Bryan Kamaoli Kuwada

Supporting sustainable habits

To complete a thesis, students need to develop work habits that fit their lives—Do they write mornings or afternoons? Draft by hand or on the computer? Seek out silence or thrive on coffee shop bustle? All of these fall under what Helen Sword calls "behavioral habits" in *Air & Light & Time & Space* (2017), and, along with artisanal, emotional, and social habits, they determine our ability to sustain a long and pleasurable life as a writer. Artisanal habits, which we might be more likely to call "craft habits," are a natural extension of our classes: How do you get better at whatever you're trying to do as a writer? When we recommend craft essays, suggest models, or introduce a new tool, we're supporting our students' craft habits. When approached with respect and delicacy, emotional and social habits can also have a place in the advising conversation.

Emotional habits and common challenges

While it takes discipline to show up to the page day after day, discipline alone is not sufficient. We need ways to find pleasure in writing and strategies for dealing with inevitable frustrations. We need to become aware of the stories we tell ourselves about how writing works and what kind of writers we think we are, and, often, we need to learn to hold them more lightly.

A student who is working diligently to establish a consistent writing practice (a behavioral habit) and hone their skills with scene-building (a craft habit) may be surprised to be asked to identify and experiment with their emotional habits as well. Emotional habits can feel inseparable from core identity and impossible to shift intentionally. But just as we can get better at not opening email before starting to write, we can get better at things like maintaining perspective when faced with rejection, reframing the unkind things our brains tell us when writing gets hard, and contextualizing and resisting big cultural myths about who can be a writer and what subjects are worth writing about.

Thesis writers often benefit from practicing the emotional habit of shifting between two equally valid perspectives and inhabiting the one that feels most motivating in the moment:

- **Perspective #1**: This thesis is the draft of my book, and I want to use the thesis process to fulfill my ambitions and make it as strong as I can.
- **Perspective #2**: This thesis is an academic exercise within a particular context, and it's fine to see the thesis as a step on the way of a longer journey.

It's great to have big ambitions for a thesis, but if high expectations lead to freezing, the second perspective might allow a student to lower their expectations enough to move forward. We also remind students that not everything they learn through the thesis process will manifest fully in the thesis itself. That doesn't mean that learning isn't happening or that the thesis process isn't worthwhile. Here are a few other common challenges we encounter as thesis supervisors.

Unrealistic expectations

Students sometimes start the thesis process with unrealistic expectations, imagining that, as thesis writers, they will magically transform overnight into efficient and productive writers, waking at 4 a.m. to hammer out pages of gorgeous prose before breakfast. "I'm finally working on my dream project," they might say, "So why does it still feel so hard?"

But writing *is* hard, even when we're making work we care about. And lives, responsibilities, and personalities don't suddenly change just because we enter a new phase of writing. When students are frustrated with their failure to instantly transform into their imagined ideal of "the productive writer," we advise self-compassion, realistic confrontation with historical habits and actual schedules, and, especially, finding the pleasures in writing that will build into positive feedback loops. We also invite students to review their early notes and agreements from our initial meeting, and to assess how their work has evolved and diverged from their original plans. Some will realize that they have, in fact, made more progress than they'd thought. Others may notice that they haven't followed their initial writing schedule and weigh whether they want to adjust their weekly schedule or their overall thesis timeline. These reassessment conversations help cultivate self-awareness that will serve students long beyond their degree.

To support self-compassion, we might ask a student: "What do you notice yourself thinking when you don't meet a goal you set out?" Often, the self-talk students report is cruel and unfair, words they would never say to a friend. We might work with students to reframe or revise these thoughts that rise up. Instead of "I didn't hit my word goal today. I'm never going to finish this," perhaps "Today was very full, and I still showed up to write anyway." Instead of "I should already know how to do this—what's wrong with me?" perhaps "This is hard because I'm trying something new. I'm working at the edge of my comfort zone because I want to grow."

Pragmatically, we might also look together at the goals they're setting and how realistic they are. If you struggle to wake up when your 8 a.m. alarm goes off, maybe a 5 a.m. to 8 a.m. writing goal is not the one for you, even if that's how your hero finished her book while working full time. If you're taking two classes and TAing, you might only have one afternoon per week to devote to thesis work, so there's no point feeling surprised and guilty each new day that goes by without opening that document. Instead of saying "I missed my two hours today, so I need to do four hours tomorrow to make up for it," we suggest the opposite: aim for one hour tomorrow as a way to get back on track and create momentum once again.

When we suggest lowering a goal, we do so with positive feedback loops in mind. In our conversation in this chapter, Helen Sword described a "broaden-and-build" cycle:

> This is an idea from Barbara Fredrickson that if you come to a task in a positive frame of mind, you're more likely to be successful at that task, which then reinforces your chance of success for the next time around. Each iteration of the task, you're broadening and building on your success. Of course, if you flip that helix over, it can become a narrow-and-collapse spiral.

In other words, a student who writes for one hour and feels accomplished is more likely to show up tomorrow in a good writing mood than a student who aims for four hours and stops after two feeling like a failure.

Setting realistic goals we can meet is one way to bring a positive frame of mind to our work. Another might be to cultivate pleasure in writing by using a beautiful pen, making coffee in a favorite mug, or listening to a song that calms or motivates you. Sword even mentioned watching a short video of "penguins jumping into the water" as a mini-intervention to start her writing with laughter. She also underscores how important it is "for teachers and supervisors to be aware of their place on that broaden and build spiral," noting the many stories she's heard of "the devastating effect of one negative comment, something likely intended to be helpful but received as complete criticism." In contrast, she described the power of encouragement from a mentor that's grounded in deep attention to the work, praise "that challenges you, that invites you to see yourself moving towards your goal."

Along with coaching students on compassionate self-talk, realistic goal-setting, and finding pleasure in writing, we also remind them there's a lot we don't know about other people's productivity, and especially the family money, spouse making dinner and picking up the kids, or college connections that might allow writers to achieve the success they do. And we remind them that no one else can make *their work* the way they can.

Doubt chasms and doom spirals

Time away from a draft is essential both for pacing energy over the long haul and for returning to the work with the new perspectives and insights distance offers. We encourage students to take vacations and to use the window after they've completed a draft (while we're reading and preparing our notes) to step fully away from the thesis: work on a different project, read and explore, attend to their personal lives and reconnect with friends and family. Students consistently return from deliberate time away with renewed energy, and often with new clarity that cuts through previously unresolvable problems.

Yet, sometimes, students find themselves dealing with a different kind of gap. What starts as busyness or preoccupation with more pressing to-dos can become anxiety and avoidance. The longer such a gap persists, the more it fills with doubts: *What if I reopen the document and everything I thought was good is actually terrible? What if this was a bad idea and it's unsalvageable as a concept?*

When writers are "outside" of their writing, they risk disconnection from the constant problem solving and imaginative work of active creation. They may find themselves in a doubt chasm where everything is theoretical and struggle to get traction on specifics or solutions. Like any other bad feeling, the doubt chasm risks generating a negative feedback loop. A student may avoid sharing doubts with the advisor out of shame and spiral further and further into visions of failure, convinced that they've let everyone down.

Rather than waiting for this kind of issue to emerge, we recommend taking preventative measures like maintaining regular contact and normalizing struggle, such that the conversation is easy to enter and doubts can be voiced. A short note with a reading recommendation or check in can keep a student connected and communicative. More importantly, regular communication lets the student know that they are supported and if things begin to go sideways, they can ask for help.

"There's a line for me between creating a situation in which people feel shame and creating a situation in which people feel an expectation they can reasonably achieve," Jessica Abel said. Like Abel, we're honest about timelines and the consequences of missed due dates, but we have no interest in guilt trips or the "I'm disappointed in you" talk. Instead, we encourage students to expect change, build flexibility into their plans, and get in touch when they're not sure how to take the next step. Often, we can be most useful by helping students articulate the next small thing that will allow them to re-enter the project: Just open the document? Read a few pages? Write a short scene? As soon as they're back inside the work, they return to the realm of concrete problems and tangible solutions: the wheel turns, the project moves forward. We remind students at every step that these situations are inevitable, and that the difference between keeping on and giving up lies in learning how to navigate them and manage the emotions they raise.

Switching projects mid-stream

Every so often, a student shows up in the office or Zoom room and says, "I think I want to do something else." It may be month two or month ten of a thesis process, with only a handful of words written or many. In either case, we try to respond with calm curiosity. The feeling of "wanting to do something else" could indicate clarifying aims that can, in fact, be realized through revising and sharpening the project at hand. But this feeling can also be prompted by grappling with the mess and stress inevitable to the middle of a big project, which a student may imagine an enticing new idea to be free of. The desire to change projects might also be the result of peer conversations or perceived market pressures: "Everyone else is writing contemporary, so what am I doing with this historical novel?" or "My friend said that only celebrity memoirs get published." And, of course, there's always a chance that a student has been laboring away on the project they thought they *should* write and has finally become brave enough to pivot to what they really want to be working on.

Fortunately, we don't need to solve these feelings and the dilemmas they raise for our students. Instead, we can focus on listening and helping them get to the root of what's prompting the impulse for change. We can remind students that no sustained project is completed without moments of serious doubt and that publication markets are a moving target at best and hard to predict. And we can offer a reality check about what a big change might mean for time-to-degree—and perhaps the need to switch to a different supervisor. But most importantly, we can listen without judgment as students speak their way to greater clarity.

Helen Sword on process metaphors and embodied writing

Why are process metaphors so important when we write? How might we approach them intentionally?

Metaphor is a natural language we reach for when we're trying to communicate emotions, and it offers people a way to ground complex emotional experiences in something familiar in the real world. Just last week, I did a workshop with a bunch of judges, and I was looking at a sea of mostly white men of a certain age thinking: Is this going to work? I talked about the power of metaphor to take you through the hard parts of a writing process, and we looked at some examples from Mihaly Csikszentmihalyi's book, *Flow*. He uses the metaphor of a sailor with the perfect wind or a painter watching a painting take shape on the canvas. I asked about times in their lives when they'd experienced flow and then asked them to choose a metaphor for their writing practice: a profession, an art or craft, a sport. One picked surfing, another mathematics.

A metaphor connected with something fundamentally enjoyable and fulfilling can help us get through the negative sides of writing. Say, a gardening metaphor: we understand that you're going to have compost, you're going to need to prune the bush. We don't need to be afraid of these negative processes, negative emotions. We need to have strategies for moving through them, but also ways of recognizing them as completely necessary and even enriching and fulfilling parts of our writing practice. Metaphors can help.

Writing is an embodied act. What does it mean to take this seriously as a teacher and mentor?

There's a real suspicion of embodiment among scholarly writers, that old mind-over-body hierarchy. There's also a suspicion of anything playful or fun, as well as a suspicion of beauty, of aesthetic pleasure. Combine all of those things together, and academic writers believe they're expected to live in this colorless, cognitive, completely abstract realm where writing means black words on a white page. And of course, that's a really limited way to think about writing!

The more research I've done with writers who have expanded their practice, the more I've come to value strategies for bringing the body to your practice, bringing physical objects, notebooks, pens, bringing color. I often use color as a way of seeing patterns in the writing. These are all embodied practices, as are things like thinking about your writing on a walk. In the creative writing sphere, there may be a bit more leeway for the idea that writing can be multimodal. Yet, at the same time, I suspect there's still the idea that, "Only writing is writing, and anything I'm doing that's not words on the page is wasting my time." There's an embodiment to writing in a notebook by hand, typing with your fingers on a keyboard, walking your dog and thinking about your writing, talking to somebody about a project. There's no way not to be embodied as a writer! But each fires up a different part of the brain. So, the research-informed thing to do is bring the body into our practice in multiple ways. And by body, I also mean the senses, things we see, things we touch, physical objects. How do we bring these into our practice intentionally and joyfully?

HELEN SWORD is scholar, poet, and master teacher whose research-based books on writing and writers include *Stylish Academic Writing*, *The Writer's Diet*, *Air & Light & Time & Space: How Successful Academics Write* and *Writing with Pleasure*. She is Professor Emerita in the Faculty of Arts and the Centre for Arts and Social Transformation at the University of Auckland.

Social habits

When students begin the thesis process, the built-in camaraderie of classes can give way to isolation. "I'm in my thesis cave," a student might say, "I haven't talked with anyone in a few days." While sustained projects benefit from deep solitary work, most writers work better (and more happily) with regular conversation and support from others grappling with similar challenges. Neither of us can imagine our writing lives without phone check-ins, group text threads, and friendly draft exchanges with writing friends and groups that go back over twenty years. There are many ways to bring our writing practice out of isolation. As mentors, we encourage students to form peer writing groups and offer support materials to help participants clarify individual goals and articulate the purpose and parameters of the group. Tools we've mentioned earlier, like the time-tracking spreadsheet, might be done as a group through shared Google Sheets, where group members (perhaps with wildly different schedules and no time to meet up) leave encouraging notes, questions, or tips.

At times, we've launched or led these groups ourselves, as when John hosted monthly one-hour Zoom sessions for his group of thesis students. This group involved no pre-reading or prep: students simply showed up to share struggles, brainstorm solutions, offer reading recommendations, and set goals for the month ahead. John also invited former thesis students to join the group and share the perspectives and insights time and publication offered them on the thesis experience. Students not only shared their challenges, but also built knowledge together. As they graduated and John went on sabbatical, the group continued to meet independently, sharing struggles and celebrating successes.

Professionalization and ongoing mentorship

The thesis process eventually comes to an end, and students submit their thesis and graduate. Institutions approach this conclusion in different ways: a formal defense with an external reader, a final committee meeting with an in-unit second reader, grad readings with family and friends present, a simple signed form to signify the requirements complete, or some combination of these. As students reach the end of the thesis process, we invite them to look back on their journey and forward to next steps. A final committee meeting can be an opportunity for students to deliver a presentation on how the work took shape—from earliest experiments to key choices to major revisions—and recognize just how far they've come. It's also an important moment to reflect on future goals and how to set themselves up for success.

Most students are keen to figure out how to actually bring their work to an audience through participating in public readings, pitching to agents, or submitting work to magazines or contests. As mentors, we try to strike a balance between resisting any narrow definition of success as a writer and demystifying the often-opaque processes of publication (along with grants, residencies, readings, and other aspects of a writing life). We might discuss key differences in pathways to publication between genres, talk about why a writer might prefer a small press to a large one, or recommend using the thesis abstract they wrote to fulfill university requirements as the starting point for a grant application. We often recommend interviews with writers about their publication experiences, along with books like Courtney Maum's *Before and After the Book Deal* (2020) and Beth Pickens' *Make Your Art No Matter What* (2021). We also ask questions like, "Who might you continue to swap work with after graduation?" or "What have you learned about yourself as a writer? How can you build on these insights to keep going without the structure of school?"

Particularly with thesis students, the mentoring relationship doesn't end with graduation. We tell students they are a part of our community, one that continues to grow and evolve with each group of graduates. Each season, we hear from former students requesting a reference letter for a job or a blurb for a new publication. Others get in touch looking for advice on whether to pursue a PhD, relocate for a temporary position, accept a publication contract, or try out a new genre. A student might email or stop by to ask the title of a book we recommended last term or share a publication that started as an exercise in a course we taught ten years ago. Conscious of the generous mentors who have supported our own writing lives, we set aside dedicated time for this work. And we set up structures—like reference letter guidelines—to help us give an enthusiastic affirmative to requests whenever possible.

Any instructor or mentor who remains in the profession long enough begins to see former students become colleagues and peers, like the generous former students who (along with others) have offered us thoughtful and critical feedback as we've completed this book. The role of teacher is contingent and temporary, and we know few greater pleasures than working alongside and learning from writers who've spent time in our courses and office hours.

12 Navigating Classroom Challenges

What does it mean to be the teacher?

Being the teacher means accepting responsibility to make a space where learning can happen. We don't have to know everything or be the biggest expert in the room. But we must create a structure with clear and equitable expectations, establish and maintain boundaries that will protect our students' well-being, and exercise our power ethically and intentionally. The challenges we encounter vary based on who we're teaching, what we're teaching, and who we are. A non-fiction instructor may have many students writing about unprocessed traumas, whereas a fiction instructor may be more likely to grapple with issues of cultural appropriation. An older white man may fit effortlessly into students' image of authority and need to make concerted efforts to decenter his power, whereas a young woman of color may need to work harder to have her experience and authority recognized.

This chapter reviews the balancing acts inherent in teaching writing, considers common classroom challenges and possible solutions, offers strategies for building on individual strengths as a teacher, and underscores the importance of self-advocacy and self-care for anyone who wants to keep teaching creative writing over the long haul.

Acknowledging our power, accepting our limits

As soon as we step into the role of instructor, we hold power. We establish norms for what's acceptable in the room. We intervene (or fail to intervene) in a moment of crisis. We may feel the clear weight of this power, or we may feel like we're sitting at a round table of peers. But failing to acknowledge our power doesn't make it go away. Instead, muddied responsibility heightens students' anxiety and can create a vacuum where dominant voices overpower others.

However, an instructor's power has limits. We can intervene in conflict in the classroom, but we can't control what one student says to another in the hallway during a break. In

Chapter 4, we discuss necessary conditions for meaningful gathering and offer strategies for co-creating community agreements. At the same time, we acknowledge the limits of safety within institutional spaces and the reasons our students may not find presence, belonging, or trust available to them, despite our efforts. We can aim to support students thriving through thoughtful policies, a welcoming attitude, and accessible assignment approaches, but we can't resolve all external circumstances or past experiences that mean students experience our classrooms and policies differently.

Beyond the challenges all instructors confront, creative writing involves its own particular uncertainties: what students choose to write about, how they respond to readings we assign, all the attitudes and intense emotions writing can bring up for students, whether they're writing about vulnerable material or testing out a new genre. It's easy to feel nervous, to walk into class with worries such as:

- What if I assign a text and everyone hates it and hates me?
- What if a non-Indigenous student is 100% committed to writing from an Indigenous character's POV and they go about it irresponsibly and offensively?
- What do I do if a student is writing vulnerable material and wants to talk about their experience rather than about the writing?
- What if a student keeps interrupting others?

Even our own behavior can be a source of anxiety and uncertainty:

- What if I assign something someone finds triggering in a way I hadn't considered?
- What if a micro-aggression happens, and I panic and don't respond in the moment?

To teach our classes with joy, confidence, and empathy, we need to find a balance between two practices that sometimes feel in opposition:

1. To prepare proactively and set up our classes to anticipate what could go wrong. We need to test assignments and texts and workshop methods and reflect on how they work and make changes as we go. We need to research possible scenarios and solutions and build response skills.
2. To accept the limits of our control and develop our ability to endure uncertainty. When we try too hard to prevent anything from ever going wrong, we risk shutting down the space of learning, not to mention making ourselves so anxious it impacts the way we interact with students. Above all, we need to cultivate a habit of self-compassion to help us learn rather than shrink when we make mistakes.

This book offers many tools to support the first practice: how can we research, learn, prepare, and do better? But we also want to think about the second practice: how do we make peace with the limits of our control and treat our students and ourselves with kindness?

Life after course evaluations

After a tech glitch or a discussion that falls flat, future course evaluations might flash before our eyes: "She's so disorganized." "They're boring and inept." "He didn't even know how to work the Zoom screen sharing."

Course evaluations, student experience of instruction surveys, whatever they're called, are known to reflect gender and racial bias (Baruch 2025; Heffernan 2021; Kreitzer and Sweet-Cushman 2022), yet institutions still rely on them for decisions about whether to rehire an adjunct, or who to promote or award merit. While faculty in stable positions can choose not to read their course evaluations, junior faculty and precarious instructors may need to discuss their scores with a Program Chair or include a summary in a teaching portfolio for a job application.

A class observation from a thoughtful colleague or frank conversation with students is more likely to give useful feedback on how to improve a course than an anonymous survey. Keeping a teaching journal (**Chapter 1**) throughout the semester can also provide us with invaluable feedback. Still, we might review student comments with a triage approach similar to what we use for reader comments on a draft:

1. **Some feedback is useful.** We might see a request for more time on a major assignment and think "Fair enough, I need to cut something to make space" or read a suggestion to include a field trip and say, "Ooh, interesting idea!"
2. **Some feedback reveals a need for clearer communication.** We might think, "Hmm, I said this, but it didn't come through. How can I say it differently?"
3. **Some feedback reveals frustrations with structures beyond your control or is based on bias and should be ignored.** When one student wants more class time and another student wants less class time (and anyway the amount of class time is set by the institution), or someone mentions your hair or boots or water bottle, you can discard these comments.

Tips:

- Don't read course evaluations right away. Even a week past the end of the term can offer some much-needed perspective.
- If you've had a rough term, or you expect your evals to include racist, misogynistic, or homophobic remarks, consider asking a trusted friend to review your course evaluations and make a synthesized précis that removes the poison and leaves you with feedback in neutral language.

Balancing preparation and presence

The more a course relies on student interaction and participation, the more variables it holds. The amount (and nature) of preparation necessary for a new instructor standing in front of a large lecture course may be quite different from that of an experienced instructor entering a small group workshop. But in either case, it's possible to cling too rigidly to a minute-to-minute plan or trust too sanguinely in our ability to "wing it." Each encounter involves a delicate balance between showing up with a plan (and perhaps a back-up plan) and paying sufficient attention to adjust that plan if something more pressing emerges or if the plan isn't working.

Teaching material that stretches us

If we're doing our job as instructors, we're teaching material that stretches us. A novelist assigned to teach a multi-genre intro course may need to brush up on poetry and screenwriting pedagogy. Certainly, we'll find ourselves assigning readings by writers with backgrounds, contexts, and aesthetics different from our own. As we encounter areas where we feel out of our depth, we can remember ways our past experiences make us ready for this new challenge. We may not know much about screenwriting, but we know how to design an assignment, how to pay close attention to formal elements, how to ask good questions, how to draw on the experience and expertise our students bring, and, especially, how to research. We can read a book on screenwriting and then ask a colleague to confirm our sense of the key principles to introduce to beginners.

Research is especially vital for white instructors assigning texts by writers of color. We've seen instructors attempt to diversify their syllabi by adding texts by writers of color (or queer writers, writers with disabilities, working-class writers, etc.) only to show up to class unprepared to do justice to the texts they've chosen. The excitement a Black trans student feels to see work by a trans writer on the syllabus quickly turns to frustration as they feel obliged to intervene when the instructor doesn't have the vocabulary to lead discussion responsibly. **Chapters 5** and **6** explore how to select, research, and introduce craft concepts and course texts thoughtfully, but we'll suggest writer interviews (in writing, and especially, through terrific podcasts like *Between the Covers with David Naimon* and *Longform Podcast*) as an inviting and often revelatory starting point (and one we can dig into while biking to work).

Remaining responsive

We also recognize that the impulse toward responsible preparation can become desire for control, an anxious perfectionism that sees any slip or mistake as unacceptable failure. Rather than hoping to anticipate and prevent any possible false steps, we try to build a classroom space where feedback (including critical feedback) can be expressed freely and where repair is possible. Here are a few classroom practices we cultivate with this mind:

Offer feedback opportunities

Use mid-term surveys, separate from official end-of-term evaluations, to get a sense of classroom climate. A simple mid-term survey might list classroom activities and ask students what they'd like to see more/the same/less of, along with inviting students to reflect on what the instructor, peers, and they themselves might do to support their learning. Individual meetings also offer students a chance to voice concerns they may not feel comfortable raising in class, especially if we show that we're genuinely open to listening and willing to make adjustments.

Respond with curiosity rather than panic when put on the spot

As teachers, we sometimes feel we always need to have an answer when students ask a question. Of course, this is impossible. If we can respond with curiosity rather than anxiety, we can model key learning behaviors: how to ask follow-up questions for clarification or how to acknowledge the gaps in our knowledge and take the time to research and return with a considered response.

Practice tolerating productive discomfort (especially our own)

We get better at what we practice. Often, we experience discomfort along the way. We can choose to acknowledge this discomfort, perhaps even voice it to a class, and move forward anyway when something feels important. A teacher might say, "In my own education, I was taught not to mention whiteness, even though it was always present and influencing everything, so it feels taboo and strange for me to name it now, but I'm doing so because … " or "This really matters to me, and I'm working on it, and I will probably make mistakes." Even being seen as "trying too hard" isn't necessarily a bad thing as long as we are inhabiting, not merely performing, the approaches we bring to the classroom.

While expressing vulnerability and humanity, instructors (especially white instructors) must exercise caution against expecting students to affirm their good efforts or reassure them when they mess up. To be clear, instructors must build and nurture our own support systems, people who can listen to us moan and beat ourselves up for a moment and then help us move into possibilities for repair and ways to do better next time.

Matthew Shenoda on grounding difficult conversations in scholarship

Tackling difficult conversations in the classroom takes courage, but it also takes skills. Can you talk about some of these skills and how to hone them?

Setting clear parameters around discussions and steering things back to the text or topic at hand is critical. It is also necessary to work at balancing the personal with the scholarly/historical: to not let personal opinion reign as the dominant form of knowledge or discourse, but to also to make room for the efficacy of lived experience. It's a constant balancing act guided by interjecting into discussion with specific questions and references.

It's also necessary to make clear what is acceptable in terms of how we engage issues of difference and that the goal is not necessarily that we "all get along," but rather that we all gain a more critical understanding of the topic at hand. The best way to hone this kind of skill is certainly through practice and trial and error, but also through a thorough and deep understanding of the topics you are engaging that are rooted in bodies of knowledge outside of yourself or your opinion. There has been a trend over the last several years of people feeling a need to address contentious social issues but diving into them without a great deal of knowledge themselves. It is important to remember when we talk about race, gender, sexuality, social structures, inequality, and so on we are talking about topics that have a significant amount of scholarship and study that have been dedicated to them and we should be aware of those bodies of knowledge.

Instructors often experience significant anxiety around the risk of "getting it wrong"—assigning a text that's surprisingly polarizing or failing to notice or confront a micro-aggression—what advice would you give to folks who feel this?

First, you will at times get it wrong, and in those moments, own it, be open about it, model it as a part of an iterative process. That said, I think it's necessary that instructors have an anticipated sense of how students may respond to a text, meaning that they should know the text well and have read some of the criticism around it, which would certainly hint at the various ways it can be read. It's necessary in these moments to have a fairly refined sense of the discussion and the ways it may go. If an instructor is themselves uncomfortable with the various facets of a text, they will struggle to teach it. I also think it is helpful to pre-empt some of these potential issues, to say from the outset, there are multiple readings/interpretations of this text, and we need to make space to discuss them all. The goal should be to critically engage a text not to assume or attempt to get your students to read it in only one way. We need to leave room for various readings and beliefs and address that polarization head-on.

It is a common, and I would argue faulty, liberal framing that teaches us that we can come to terms with deeply contentious issues in some universal manner. Difference is difference, which is to say we may have opposing views, and a class cannot necessarily reconcile that. What we can, however, hope for is that each "side" might have a clearer understanding of the position of the other even if they reject it. Finally, I think it's necessary that these kinds of moments of contention stay rooted in the text, not just in personal interpretation. It is necessary then for an instructor to guide the class regularly back to the text and anchor the discussion in the context of the work they are debating. Too often we open things up to a much wider conversation, which can be difficult to manage.

You've talked about the importance of being anchored in scholarship. What are a few essential readings on structural inequality that creative writing instructors would benefit from spending time with?

This is a vast question in so many ways and for me much of it is less about creative writing specifically and more about things anyone interested in engaging in these issues should know as people in the world. But maybe more specifically, Toni Morrison's *Playing in the Dark* and *What Moves at the Margins* seem like really essential texts to know. But I also think a running knowledge of things like Edward Said's *Orientalism*, Cedric Robinson's work on racial capitalism, Aimé Césaire's *Discourses on Colonialism*, the works of Sara Ahmed, George Lipsitz's *The Possessive Investment In Whiteness*, and James Baldwin's myriad essays are all hugely instructive. It's a long long list.

MATTHEW SHENODA is a Professor and Chair of the Department of Literary Arts and affiliated faculty in Africana Studies and the Brown Arts Institute at Brown University. He is the author of the poetry collections *Somewhere Else*; *Seasons of Lotus, Seasons of Bone*; *Tahrir Suite*; and *The Way of the Earth*. Shenoda is a founding editor of the African Poetry Book Fund.

Image credit: Josephine Sittenfeld

Common creative writing teaching challenges

A creative writing course invites meaningful and vulnerable work from people with different priorities, needs, backgrounds, and habits. What one student sees as useful structure, another may view as condescending micro-managing. Some students will welcome the chance to engage with a politically urgent text; others may find it overwhelming or complain that it's too intense. A seemingly small aesthetic difference can divide and polarize a workshop group. Here are a few frequent scenarios and possible strategies for approaching them:

Reluctance to engage

In a large class, some students will be intrinsically engaged with their writing, whereas others may choose a creative writing course as an "easy elective" or "grade booster." Many may be on the fence: cautious, curious, but not yet committed. When teaching these courses, we aim to create as many entry points as possible and welcome students who show growing curiosity and engagement at any point along the term. We talk early and often about purpose, choice, and agency, inviting students to find ways to make the course meaningful and useful for them, no matter how they got there in the first place.

We also remind ourselves to keep our egos in check. We're there to set a bountiful table and welcome everyone to eat: if students choose not to join the meal, that often has more to do with their lives and priorities than it does with us and our course design. We communicate clear expectations, design policies we can live with, and keep disappointment and guilt trips out of our messages to students.

In small courses, however, especially workshops where students are sharing vulnerable writing and discussing issues they care deeply about, a disengaged student can shift the atmosphere of an entire class. If a student seems checked out, we might try any of the following things:

- **Check your expectations.** Is the student simply demonstrating a more low-key affect, perhaps a neurodivergent difference in eye contact or body language? In other words, is this an issue or just a difference? An inclusive classroom must welcome a range of ways to be embodied together.
- **Reflect.** Ask yourself: What have I done to demonstrate to this student that their trust and engagement are welcome here? Am I assuming something that needs to be earned?
- **Look for an opportunity to speak with the student.** Perhaps in an individual meeting, seek to connect around what drew the student to the class/genre/topic and strategize around how they might claim greater responsibility in making the course what they want it to be. See if anything has happened outside your gaze (i.e., private feedback notes or out-of-class conversations) that might have caused the student to feel unwelcome or withdraw.
- **Use class time to shift the energy.** Get students moving around the room out of their calcified positions, maybe doing something a bit silly or messy, with the hope of shaking loose some stiffness and alone-ness through laughing and experimenting together. Annie Murphy Paul in *The Extended Mind* (2021) describes an experiment where two groups of students were tasked to solve math problems. One group sat at their desks while they worked, and the other group was free to move around. The students' cognitive load "considerably increased under the instruction 'not to move'," and the study concluded that "sitting quietly is not necessarily the best condition for learning in school" (48).

Variations of resistance

Sometimes, a student is not just checked out but openly resistant. They may question the purpose of every reading, roll their eyes as we explain instructions, or argue that each assignment doesn't work for them and they need to do it differently. When we encounter resistance, we try to pause and figure out: What kind of resistance is this? Where is it coming from? What action (if any) is needed? Here are some versions we've encountered:

- **Resistance as need for differentiation.** Some students, especially those on the tail end of adolescence, have a deep need to establish their identity through differentiation. For these students, the need to resist structure is more important than the specifics of any given structure.
    - An instructor's role is simply to remain unflappable, point to opportunities for choice and agency within any constraint, and provide a container that offers the student space to grow toward maturity.

- **Resistance as self-protection.** At times, resistance comes from students who fear risk, perhaps because they've experienced harsh criticism or undermining in previous experiences with writing or art-making.
  - We can support these students by talking about why writing *is* difficult and risky and why it's still worthwhile. As Felicia Rose Chavez suggests in **Chapter 1**, we might invite students to list their fears and declare "But I will write anyway."
- **Resistance due to lack of clarity.** Resistance or reluctance can be an indication that students haven't grasped the purpose behind course design choices. For example, students used to a non-structured workshop approach might see something like Critical Response Process as uncomfortably constraining, even infantilizing.
  - We've discussed the importance of transparent course design throughout this book. Still, a conversation—individually or as a class—might let us get into student goals, why we designed the course the way we did, and whether they can find a pathway through it that they can take interest in (or at least suspend skepticism long enough to try).
- **Resistance due to lack of fit.** Sometimes a student signs up for a course expecting one thing and is surprised to find another. Perhaps they expect a course focused entirely on workshopping peer work with only two due dates for workshop submissions and instead find a generative course with weekly due dates and very little time dedicated to workshop.
  - If a student wants primarily to work on their own project without frequent structure or deadlines, another course might be a better fit. As we discuss in **Chapter 1**, having a clear purpose means not trying to be everything to everyone (which isn't possible anyway). A frank discussion of options can help the student make an informed choice to stay or go.
- **Resistance to a genuine flaw or oversight.** We're human, and we make mistakes.
  - It's always possible that a student has noticed an issue (a contradiction, omission, oversight, or problem) with the course that we need to reflect on and correct if we can.

Reflecting on her experiences as an MFA student, Jasmine Sealy (**Chapter 3**) said that there's "a fine line that creative writing instructors must walk between helping students to foster creative practices that feel comfortable and applicable to them, while also pushing students to try new methods, and attempt work that is perhaps uncomfortable." Often, we want to help students find *their* way to approach a writing challenge, or encourage them to go deep on what works for them. But sometimes, we ask them to try something new, strange, possibly uncomfortable. We've found that vocal resistance doesn't necessarily indicate a problem. Sometimes complaining is what lets us do hard things. We've taught classes where students groan-laugh something like, "I hated this, and I can't believe you made me do it." And then we might say, "I know, isn't it hard? You never have to do it again if you don't want to. Let's go around the room and see if anyone found something useful here."

Charged subjects and difficult conversations

If students are writing about things that matter to them, they will inevitably touch on charged subjects. Writing on gender-based oppression, police violence, ecological disaster, geopolitical events, and economic exploitation, to name just a few, emerges inevitably out of students' lived experiences. Any sense of a writing classroom as somehow "neutral" or "focused on craft, not politics" strikes us both as undesirable and untenable. Equally inevitable are the differences in positionality, perspective, and opinion within any group. How can a course hold space for people with different views and perspectives? How can it simultaneously protect the most vulnerable students? Building on our conversation with Matthew Shenoda and others, we identify four crucial, often challenging, responsibilities for instructors here.

1 We must prepare for difficult conversations by setting ground rules for engagement and demonstrating that we will hold the class accountable to them. (See **Chapter 4** for a discussion of community agreements.)
2 We need to develop a practice of regulating our nervous systems during heated conversations so that we can respond rather than react. Box-breathing, or slow deep breathing, can help in the moment. In the long term, instructors benefit from taking time fully away from work, identifying and working through our own sources of activation, and finding ways—from swimming to meditation to hugging a friend—to complete the stress cycle.
3 We need to value lived experience without acting like anecdotal or off-the-cuff takes hold equal validity with deeply researched positions in fields like critical race studies and disability studies.
4 We need to give students opportunities to be experts on their own experiences without placing unfair burdens on them to educate peers (and instructors).

A student perspective: RJ McDaniel on strong emotions and meaningful challenge

In our Teaching Creative Writing course, you did a project on responding to strong emotions in the classroom. Can you discuss a few key insights based on your research and your own experiences?

Sure! Students may have emotionally intense experiences in class for any number of reasons. Some may be within the instructor's control, or directly related to the content of the class; others might be completely unrelated to the course and out of the control of the instructor. Regardless of reason, it's important that students feel safe enough in the classroom environment to continue to show up; the other option is often absenteeism, and the worst possible thing for a student who is struggling is to be isolated. So in the moment a student becomes upset, it's critical that they not feel isolated by the instructor's response. Singling out the student—for example, by abruptly stopping the discussion to ask them what's going on, or if they're okay—can make them feel like they're being interrogated in front of their colleagues; ignoring them entirely can make them feel invisible. Becoming visibly upset in front of a room of colleagues is a really destabilizing and often embarrassing experience, and the polar responses of pretending it's not happening or drawing the class's attention to it can make everything feel worse.

Instead, it's important to let students dictate their own emotional needs. Instructors can give the student space to take a break outside of the class, and, if they wish to remain, allow them to continue to participate in the class discussion without being treated as a distraction. At a juncture that doesn't draw attention to the student, like a break in the class or at the end, the instructor can check in. Once again, interrogative questions ("Are you okay?" "What's happening?") probably aren't the most helpful. Instead, the instructor can offer less personal, more concrete interventions, like:

- Is there anything you need from me in this moment that would be helpful?
- Is there anything that came up in class that you'd like me to address?

Approaching the student in this way allows them to express what their needs are without feeling compelled to share anything personal. Sometimes students might not really respond to instructor inquiries. If they have a specific need that they communicate, or a part of the course that they say wasn't working for them (whether in the structure of the class, the nature of the feedback, or something they found harmful in the discussion), then the instructor can move forward with addressing that need.

But often, the response will be vague: "I'm fine" or "I'm just having a bad day." Although it might be difficult, in an environment built around trust and safety, trust has to go both ways. If a student has been given an opportunity to communicate a need and has declined that opportunity, that is their prerogative. Instructors, too, need to be conscious of their own emotional needs: being an emotional caretaker for a student in crisis is not part of the work of being a creative writing teacher. Follow-up with the student can be a simple email in the days following the workshop, letting them know again that they can feel safe to communicate any needs.

What did meaningful challenge look like to you as a student?

When people think of something being "challenging" in an academic context, often what comes to mind is desperately trying to memorize huge amounts of complex information, being up all night studying, staring in horror at the pages of an exam, or tearing out hair and rending garments. The difficulty—the challenge—is created by the artificial structural impositions of school, with its deadlines and exams and grading schemes, as well as the promise (or threat) of success at these tasks as the single determining factor of one's future happiness. It's a particular and sharp kind of stress that people very rarely encounter outside of school, which is why people who have been out of school for decades still have anxiety nightmares about showing up late for an exam.

Creative writing courses can offer an entirely different kind of challenge: the chance to really think about something in a new, unexpected way, with all the risks that come with entering the unknown. Here's an example: I avoided taking poetry classes (or even discussing poetry with anyone) for pretty much the entirety of my undergrad degree. My justification was that taking a poetry course wouldn't be useful or interesting for me as a writer. In hindsight, I see what was really going on: I was scared of being bad at something. As much as I believed that I didn't care about grades or being validated by the education system, I was still operating under the belief that it would be personally damaging to me, somehow, to risk failure.

I ended up unexpectedly having to take another creative writing course in summer 2020, and poetry was the only one available. I found myself immersed in this entirely new way of thinking, observing, writing. It was hard work, and sharing my writing in the course felt truly frightening! But I came out of it feeling excited to write, which I hadn't felt in a long time at that point. I realized how much the fear of failure had held me back from growing. By mostly sticking with classes with expectations I was sure I could fulfill, I had resisted being challenged creatively. I guess it comes down to this: the challenge posed by most graded academic courses is the challenge of seeking perfection. A great creative writing course can offer the challenge of abandoning it.

RJ MCDANIEL is the author of *All Things Seen and Unseen: A Novel*, as well as many essays about baseball.

Image credit: Emily Ann Garcia

Vulnerable material and intense emotions

Students write about pregnancies and terminations, experiences of childhood abuse, and sexual assault. They write about gender transitions, miscarriages, eating disorders, deaths, divorces, mental health diagnoses. These are the materials of life. Often, they're the watershed experiences students seek to interrogate and comprehend through their writing or the transformative moments that drive students to intervene in the cultural conversation.

It's a privilege to witness and support the powerful work of students excavating histories and inventing unimagined futures, sharing their fiery rage and hard-earned insights. It can also ask a lot of us as teachers. Sometimes, a student brings work to class that they're barely able to write, much less discuss with any degree of critical distance. Or a student makes thoughtful vital work that nonetheless runs roughshod over another student's triggers. Here are a couple of balancing acts we're always working on and some interventions we've tried:

1 Make clear to students that the creative writing classroom can handle any material they're ready to confront AND establish that students don't need to disclose trauma in order to make interesting work. Possible interventions:
   - Especially with introductory classes, curate a reading list (and perhaps a series of generative exercises) that foregrounds pleasure, delight, curiosity, humor, and inquiry alongside examples of struggle and pain.
   - Share interviews in which writers discuss their writing choices around trauma and disclosure and the different conclusions they arrive at.

2 Invite students to show up to class as full humans with messy feelings WHILE keeping the class from taking on a therapeutic role we're not equipped to manage safely.

A student might reasonably feel hurt if they brought a vulnerable personal essay to workshop and their peers immediately started coldly critiquing the syntax. Likewise, a class that jumps straight into discussing the assigned reading the day after a significant global event might leave students feeling alienated, as if school didn't operate within the all-consuming reality they're experiencing.

At the same time, a student might experience frustration if they brought an intensely emotional poem to workshop and peers just wanted to check in about their feelings rather than treating the work as art and engaging with it on a level of craft. And, as much as we may wish to create safe spaces for students to work through emotional difficulties, academic spaces can offer only limited safety. In fact, to create a "safer" space for students, we must be upfront about the limits of that safety and the reality of the institutional power dynamics and professional expectations in play. Possible interventions:

- Stay informed about the mental health resources available to students and be prepared to help students access them.
- Acknowledge major events that may be affecting students without necessarily derailing the class to focus on them.
- Offer students opportunities to discuss the emotional challenges of writing while ensuring that these invitations are open-ended enough that students can set boundaries aligned with their comfort level.
- Clarify that although there can be many reasons to write and many possible benefits of writing (including therapeutic ones), the creative writing classroom serves students best when it keeps a focus on the process and craft choices that are the instructor's area of expertise and fellow students' shared focus.

Problematic material: a case study

Instructors often ask about how to deal with "problematic material." But material can be "problematic" in various ways, and each asks different things of instructors. Our concerns and responsibilities also depend on whether the issue shows up in a short experiment turned in only to the instructor or in a major project the student plans to share with classmates. Our baseline response is to always treat the situation as a learning opportunity. As we're encouraging our students to take risks in their work, it's possible that they may need interventions and coaching to reflect on the risks they've taken.

Let's imagine a student writing about disordered eating. This student may be writing from personal experience or based on the experience of people close to them or by drawing on in-depth research or by uncritically repeating common cultural tropes. The writing could be problematic because:

- The student is writing about current eating disorder issues and needs support beyond what a creative writing course can offer.
- The student is writing about disordered eating in a way that glorifies thinness or offers an "instruction manual" to others, which classmates may find triggering or difficult to read and respond to.
- The student is writing about disordered eating in a way that flattens complexity or reinforces stereotypes.

A student's writing might be problematic because of any of these issues alone or some combination of them together. As instructors, we need to ask: Am I concerned about the student's well-being, care for other students who may be affected by this work, the ethics of what the student is attempting, or some combination? In any of these cases, we would likely reach out to invite a conversation with the student. But we would approach the conversation differently depending on the particulars. In this conversation, we might:

- Ask the student how they came to write about this material and what drew them to it as a subject.
- *If a student is drawing on personal experience*: Ask what they're doing to take care of themselves while writing and revising this material. Ask what concerns they have in bringing work to readers.
- *If the student is not drawing on personal experience*: Ask what research or preparation they've undertaken to write responsibly about a subject that can evoke strong feelings or responses. Ask what models they've considered of writers handling this content in ways they find ethical and effective.
- *In either case*: Ask what their goals are in making this work. Ask how they have/plan to take care of readers who may find the material difficult—both in the text itself, and if relevant, in sharing the material for group critique. Ask how prepared they are to receive feedback, including critical feedback, on the work.

This may seem like a lot of asking, but in practice the meeting should feel like a supportive conversation, not an interrogation. It's an important crossroads moment for the student, who can either feel supported and learn from it, or feel defensive and shut down. Our role, we remind ourselves, is to teach and support while encouraging students to think critically about their creative decisions and gestures. We want students to feel that we are on their side and believe in their capabilities even when we're pushing them to think more deeply about their work.

Other common challenges

In the chapters they connect to most directly, we address other common challenges, such as:

- Writing beyond your experience and cultural appropriation (**Chapters 5** and **9**)
- Workshop friction (**Chapter 7**)
- Generative AI and academic integrity (**Chapters 2** and **10**)
- Balancing student voices (**Chapter 4**)
- Challenging materials and content notes (**Chapters 4** and **7**)

Building on your strengths as a teacher

There's no single way to be a good writing teacher. Individual strengths and commitments guide effective course design. Likewise, our attempts to build a classroom climate of collaboration and respect—and our responses to teaching challenges—will be most successful when grounded in practices we can inhabit with authenticity. As James M. Lang (**Chapter 4**) observed in our conversation, "I've read enticing descriptions of creative icebreakers, but I hate icebreakers. If I am tempted to try one in my classroom, I might do so unconsciously assuming it will fail, which means it probably will fail. It might work wonders for my colleague next door, but it doesn't fit with my teaching persona." Icebreakers are not for everyone. Just because an activity or approach works beautifully for a colleague doesn't mean that everyone else needs to incorporate it into their teaching. Still, we agree with Lang's emphasis on remaining open to new experiments:

> I would argue that we should always be experimenting, but it's the nature of experiments to fail sometimes. So try something new, and if it fails but seems promising, revise and try again. If it fails again, move on. But a commitment to experimentation is essential for maintaining one's passion over the course of a lifetime of teaching. Teaching is demanding work, and boredom and dispiritedness wait always in the wings; trying, failing, and trying again keep a teacher's brain and emotion engaged.

In short, growing in our teaching practice means finding ways to identify and build on our strengths while remaining open to other approaches (and to new strengths that new modalities, genres, or contexts may invite us to discover). Along the way, we keep asking:

- Which teaching activities feel uncomfortable because they're stretching me in a productive way, and which ones feel uncomfortable because they're "just not me"?
- What do I have to offer students (because of my background, lived and teaching experiences, brain chemistry, or education)?

Balancing authenticity and professional boundaries

As teachers looking to form authentic connections with students, we may share messy early drafts, discuss professional struggles and setbacks, or be open about our own challenges with self-criticism or motivation. By showing up as full human beings, we can help push back against myths of effortless success and reassure students that the difficulties they're experiencing are part of the writing life. For the well-being of students and teachers alike, we offer four guidelines for balancing authenticity with professional boundaries.

1. **Be honest about the power dynamics in the room.** At times, the gulf between teacher and student can feel immense. At other times, it may feel like a matter of chance or temporary arrangement who plays which role. In either case, acknowledge and respect this power difference responsibly.
2. **Never put students in a position of needing to take care of you.** In sharing struggles or vulnerable experiences, we need sufficient equanimity and distance from the pain points of these experiences to discuss them without looking to students for reassurance. In moments of repair, this is particularly important. We must acknowledge a misstep without relying on students to comfort us about our good intentions.
3. **Beware the need to feel needed.** The work of teaching can be thankless, and it's gratifying to see ourselves as useful and feel our work matters. But we must not rely on the ego boost of feeling needed by students, which can easily tip into unhealthy dependence and blurred boundaries.
4. **Set boundaries that won't cultivate resentments.** It can be hard to maintain boundaries like not answering email after dinner, or keeping student meetings to the days we've set aside for them, especially when we see how helpful that extra Friday meeting was or how much a student appreciated the extra comments via email. Yet, if we're not attentive, these seemingly slight overrides of boundaries can leave us feeling depleted and resentful. Our recommendation: don't give what you'd feel like a martyr to see left on the table. If a student misses a scheduled meeting or tosses comments into the trash, we still need to feel okay. If we feel resentful when a student flakes, that's a sign that we're extending farther than we should be.

Sara Graefe on self-compassion and repair

How do you apply the same compassion you advocate for students toward yourself?

It's really easy as instructors who care and are compassionate to forget about ourselves in the mix. Our students are complex people, bringing their whole selves into the room. We have to remember that's us, too. We can't lose sight of our families and our wider lives outside of the job. We're also writers; we can't lose sight of our own writing. To be at our best in the classroom, we need to have a vital writing life and show up at the page for ourselves.

This is challenging: showing up for your students but also taking time for yourself. Not working around the clock, making sure you're sleeping well, making sure you're exercising, making sure you're writing. Having boundaries around the times you check email. Deciding when to call it a night knowing that the work will be there for you tomorrow. It's basic stuff, but it's really important. I have a colleague who says that it doesn't matter if you're teaching one course or a full course load, the teaching can easily fill all of your time. But it's okay not to think about students after a certain time of night, to have quality time with your family and make sure you're getting a good night's sleep so that tomorrow when you're back in the classroom, you can care about your students when it's time to care about them.

How can teachers stay grounded, respond thoughtfully to crises, and repair when necessary?

The big thing is just to breathe through it. It's so hard because our flight, fright, freeze response gets activated and we're just there having this physiological reaction, right? If I feel my mind racing and I'm just like, *oh my gosh, what should I do?* I try to remember *breathe, focus on your breath, breathe through it, listen*. Sometimes it's a matter of listening to both sides, calling for a time-out to let people de-escalate. Sometimes it's calling time-out and then dealing with students individually. But in the moment, the most important thing is to breathe and buy yourself some time before you respond. As a rookie teacher, I was so afraid of conflict that I'd be tempted to think, *Did that really happen? Do I let this go or do I act on it?* But you can't let stuff go. You've got to respond. You're the facilitator in the room. It's your role to step up.

Repair when necessary. I think that's really key because, again, if we're practicing a pedagogy of compassion, we're going to recognize that we're human and we're fallible. We're not perfect. We try to respond to the best of our ability in the moment and, still, we may mess things up. When things haven't worked out the way I'd hoped or are still messy or left hanging, it's possible to go away, reflect some more, and return and repair. Often, it's about repairing with individual students one-on-one as well as with the whole group to maintain a sense of safety.

SARA GRAEFE is a faculty member in the UBC School of Creative Writing, where she has taught since 2006. A playwright, screenwriter, and essayist, she is editor of *Swelling with Pride: Queer Conception and Adoption Stories* (2018), selected for the American Library Association's 2020 Over the Rainbow Nonfiction Long-List.

Image credit: Yung Adetiba

Self-advocacy and self-care for teachers

Higher education across the board relies heavily on precarious contingent labor (a trend that is likely to persist as universities across North America continue to make dramatic cuts in their budgets and replace core faculty with adjuncts). Based on our experiences across positions, institutions, and working conditions, we have a few thoughts on self-advocacy and self-care to share. Some of these recommendations are of particular relevance to aspiring teachers just starting out. Others are reminders we keep pinned to our bookshelves to this day.

The sunk cost fallacy

This is the phenomenon where we tell ourselves "Well, I've already put so much time into this, so if I stop trying now, all those efforts will be wasted." Often, writers who want to teach accept terrible working conditions because they want to get the experience on their CV and they hope the bad job will lead to a good job. Sometimes this works out. But often it doesn't. And once we start thinking this way, it's hard to quit. We recommend only saying "yes" to a teaching opportunity if the position is worthwhile for itself (however you define that). If the time comes when the opportunity will only be worthwhile if it leads to something better, it might be time to say "no."

Don't scrutinize the void

Although graduate advisors should know that getting a "good job" (like getting published) relies as much on luck and connections as it does on skill and experience, we've still heard advisors trying to figure out "what went wrong" when someone doesn't get a job. It can be hard to admit just how bad things are, just how beyond our control a "good outcome" really is. Bronwen remembers her intensive job search at the end of her PhD and the professor who told her, "Don't scrutinize the void." And sure, this can be taken too far. Sometimes it's useful to think about strategy or re-evaluate an approach, but so often decisions are made based on factors we'll never know about.

Claiming your priorities and deal-breakers

It's not easy to get a full-time, well-paid job teaching creative writing. The scarcity of positions can lead to feelings of desperation and a sense that aspiring teachers should accept whatever they can get. As you consider possibilities, we invite you to identify your own priorities and deal-breakers.

- What draws you to teaching creative writing?
- Which teaching contexts/conditions would offer what you're looking for? Which would not?
- Do you hope to teach full-time, part-time, or on the side?
- What groups/levels/genres are you interested in working with?
- Do you want/need to make money from your teaching? How much money would you need to make for it to be sustainable and worthwhile for you?
- Are you willing to move for a teaching job? If so, are there places you'd love to move/decline to move?

The deadly exploitation triangle

When teaching as adjuncts, we knew that if we assigned a draft and a revision, we were effectively driving down our hourly wage by creating more work for ourselves. But we did it anyway. We also met with students in extended office hours, responded to their emails in detail, and wrote letters of recommendation. Why? Because we cared about our students, and we wanted to support them as we've been supported by mentors in our own careers. After all, they weren't the ones exploiting us. Here's the crux of the matter: our students deserve everything we have to give them. But the institutions that hire us only deserve what they compensate us for. We're not saying don't give your students extra, but we are saying to pay attention. No one else will set limits for you.

You're more than your job

Even teachers who are great at encouraging students to take care of themselves can be terrible at remembering that they too are embodied humans (not teaching machines) who need to sleep, eat, rest, and play. There is always more to do and we can fall into the trap of considering the work we do so essential or vital that it overrides our personal lives and relationships. "Let me just get through this stack of drafts," we say. Or "If I put in a few hours on Saturday, the week ahead will be so much calmer." But we will never "just get caught up." We need to take care of ourselves now by bringing a healthy dose of humility and frankness to deciding what we must do now, what can wait, and what's not ours to take on. Books like Oliver Burkeman's *Four Thousand Weeks* (2023), David Gooblar's *The Missing Course* (2019), Maggie Berg and Barbara Seeber's *The Slow Professor* (2016), Tom Rademacher's *It Won't Be Easy* (2015), Bill Coplin's *The Happy Professor* (2019), and Sarah Jaffe's *Work Won't Love You Back* (2022) can help situate these individual struggles within a broader context of productivity culture and burnout.

Hold space and don't be consumed

Students bring raw vulnerability and intense feelings to their writing. It's a privilege to share this intimate art with one another, to support writers in grappling with what's painful. But it can also be a lot to process. We aren't therapists, yet we often need to practice the counselor's skill of listening and being present with pain, and then letting go. To keep showing up for our students, we need to find channels for releasing the vicarious stress and suffering that come to us through teaching. A quick debrief with a "battle buddy" who understands can help reground us after an intense interaction. A ritual—like changing into soft pants or logging out of email—can mark the moment when you energetically leave the teaching space (which can feel very fluid when so much can be done via laptop from your couch).

Continuing to grow

The best way to be an effective teacher over the long haul is to never stop being a student. The joy (and, at times, the frustration) of writing is that there's always more to learn: books to read, craft to deepen, perspectives to consider. The best teachers we know radically resist the idea that learning from others calls their authority or ability into question. Instead, they're hungry for new possibilities, eager to be stretched or challenged, open to rethinking a long-held position. And by trying new things—whether guitar lessons or marathon training—they give themselves opportunities to remember the awkwardness and difficulty of being a beginner and use these insights to design courses grounded in humility and reaching toward possibility.

In *Teaching to Transgress*, bell hooks writes,

> The classroom, with all its limitations, remains a location of possibility. In that field of possibility we have the opportunity to labor for freedom, to demand of ourselves and our comrades, an openness of mind and heart that allows us to face reality even as we collectively imagine ways to move beyond boundaries, to transgress. This is education as the practice of freedom. (1994, 207)

To face reality and collectively imagine beyond boundaries, we must be willing to "create a sense of creative discontent" and "instill a sense of freedom to question assumptions that have shaped students' identities and lives" (2012, 54), as George Yancy writes. Like Yancy, we seek to prioritize questioning over the false safety of the status quo.

We also take seriously the difficult feelings that can arise when long-held assumptions are challenged, mindful of how easily guilt or shame can lead to stuckness or denial, rather than action or change. We've found readings by Ross Gay, Leanne Betsmosake Simpson, Robin Wall Kimmerer, and others useful in helping students move through difficult feelings into spaces of greater possibility. Rather than positioning ourselves as authorities, we can remain open to difficult discussions, inviting our students to see both difference and connection, to share knowledge and experience, to question, to change.

As teachers, we look for opportunities to support our students, and, if we have some degree of stability, chances to shape the priorities and policies of the institutions where we do our work. None of this is easy. When we asked what advice he had for faculty, especially marginalized or contingent instructors hoping to find spaces of action and change, Matthew Shenoda offered these words:

> All I can really say is that one should know the context they are operating in, be clear about its possibilities and limitations, know yourself and your limitations, protect your health and your time, find meaningful and significant spaces *outside* these institutions to remind yourself of the vastness of the world and the fact that these places do not define the whole of society. Take on the opportunities to make real change whenever they present themselves and however small knowing it is always a risk and that the window is always short. Waiting has never worked; it only reifies the status quo. Be willing to take that risk or if you are not willing or you can't, be honest with yourself and the people around you about it. Realize the classroom is a far more transformative space than "the institution" and thankfully that is where we do the core of our work. Finally, find your people, create networks of support, build community.

Works Cited

Akbar, Kaveh, "Do You Speak Persian?", Split This Rock, posted February 2, 2018, www.splitthisrock.org/poetry-database/poem/do-you-speak-persian.

Awad, Mona. *13 Ways of Looking at a Fat Girl*. Penguin Books, 2016.

Baldwin, James. *The Fire Next Time*. Random House, 1995.

Barkley, Elizabeth F., and Major, Claire H. *Student Engagement Techniques: A Handbook for College Faculty*, 2nd ed. John Wiley & Sons, 2020.

Barry, Lynda. *What It Is*. Drawn & Quarterly, 2008.

Baruch, Oshrit Kaspi. "The Persistence of Gender Bias in Student Evaluations of Teaching: The Role of Gender Stereotypes." *Journal of Academic Ethics*, Vol. 23, pp. 279–303. 2025. https://doi.org/10.1007/s10805-024-09535-6.

Bean, John C., and Melzer, Dan. *Engaging Ideas: The Professor's Guide to Integrating Writing, Critical Thinking, and Active Learning in the Classroom*, 3rd ed. Jossey-Bass, 2021.

Berg, Maggie, and Seeber, Barbara K. *The Slow Professor: Challenging the Culture of Speed in the Academy*. University of Toronto Press, 2016.

Bernays, Anne, and Painter, Pamela. *What If? Writing Exercises for Fiction Writers*, 3rd ed. Longman, 2010.

Blum, Susan D. (Ed.) *Ungrading: Why Rating Students Undermines Learning (and What to do Instead)*. UBC Press, 2020.

Bolton, David L., and John M. Elmore. "The Role of Assessment in Empowering/Disempowering Students in the Critical Pedagogy Classroom." *Counterpoints*, Vol. 451, pp. 126–40. 2013. www.jstor.org/stable/42982087.

Boyer, Anne. *The Undying*. Farrar, Straus, Giroux, 2019.

Brand, Dionne. *The Blue Clerk: Ars Poetica in 59 Versos*. Penguin Books, 2019.

Brookfield, Stephen D., and Preskill, Stephen. *Discussion as a Way of Teaching: Tools and Techniques for Democratic Classrooms*. Jossey-Bass, 2005.

Brown, Jericho (Ed.) *How We Do It: Black Writers on Craft, Practice, and Skill*. Hurston/Wright Foundation, 2023.

Burkeman, Oliver. *Four Thousand Weeks: Time Management for Mortals*. Penguin Books, 2023.

Butler, Octavia. n.d. manuscript. OEB 1512. The Huntington Library. San Marino, CA.

Butler, Ruth. "Enhancing and Undermining Intrinsic Motivation: The Effects of Task-involving and Ego-involving Evaluation on Interest and Performance." *British Journal of Educational Psychology*, Vol. 58, pp. 1–14. 1988.

Carroll, Lewis. *Alice in Wonderland*. Dover Publications, 1993.

Chavez, Felicia Rose. *The Anti-Racist Writing Workshop: How to Decolonize the Creative Classroom*. Haymarket Books, 2021.

Christie, Agatha. *Agatha Christie: An Autobiography*. HarperCollins, 2001.

Christle, Heather. "On the Patchwork Approach to Piecing Together a Book." Lithub, November 5, 2019. https://lithub.com/on-the-patchwork-approach-to-piecing-together-a-book/.

Clark, David, and Talbert, Robert. *Grading for Growth: A Guide to Alternative Grading Practices that Promote Authentic Learning and Student Engagement in Higher Education*. Routledge, 2023.

Clark, Peter Roy. *Writing Tools: 50 Essential Strategies for Every Writer*. Little, Brown Spark, 2008.

Coplin, Bill. *The Happy Professor*. Rowan & Littlefield, 2019.

Corral, Eduardo. "Eduardo C. Corral reads 'in Colorado My Father Scoured and Stacked Dishes,'" posted December 19, 2013, by strandbookstore, YouTube, 2 min., 48 sec., www.youtube.com/watch?v=ULqXR7_jtHQ.

Creeley, Robert, "The Art of Poetry, No. 10," interview by Lewis MacAdams and Linda Wagner-Martin, *The Paris Review*, Fall 1968. www.theparisreview.org/interviews/4241/the-art-of-poetry-no-10-robert-creeley.

Davies, Peter Ho. *The Art of Revision: The Last Word.* Graywolf Press, 2021.

Dweck, Carol S. *Mindset: The New Psychology of Success*. Ballantine Books, 2006.

Elbow, Peter. *Writing Without Teachers*. Oxford University Press, 1973.

Elhillo, Safia. "Ode to Sudanese-Americans," Poets.Org, Academy of American Poets, January 7, 2021, https://poets.org/poem/ode-sudanese-americans.

Finn, Charles, and Stafford, Kim (Eds.) *The Art of Revising Poetry*. Bloomsbury Publishing, 2023.

Garner, Dwight, and Sehgal, Parul. "Close Read: 19 Lines That Turn Anguish Into Art," *The New York Times*, June 18, 2021.

Gay, Ross. "seeds to share: In His New Essay Collection, Inciting Joy, Prize-Winning Poet and Author Ross Gay Turns Our Attention to What Brings Us Together, Extolling the Pleasures of Collaboration and the Recognition of What Connects Us Rather Than Divides Us." Interview by Aimee Nezhukumatathil. 2022. *Poets & Writers Magazine* 50, no. 6: 30+. *Gale Literature Resource Center*. https://link.gale.com/apps/doc/A722919242/LitRC?u=ubcolumbia&sid=bookmark-LitRC&xid=39486cc1.

Gerard, Philip. *The Art of Creative Research: A Field Guide for Writers*. University of Chicago Press, 2017.

Gooblar, David. *The Missing Course: Everything They Never Taught You About College Teaching*. Harvard University Press, 2019.

Green, Chris. "Materializing the Sublime Reader: Cultural Studies, Reader Response, and Community Service in the Creative Writing Workshop." *College English*, Vol. 64, No. 2, pp. 153–74, 2001.

Groff, Lauren. "How Lauren Groff, 'One of Our Finest Living Writers,' Does Her Work." *New York Times*, September 11. Interviewed by Elizabeth Harris, 2023 www.nytimes.com/2023/09/09/books/lauren-groff-vaster-wilds.html.

Guskey, Thomas, and Brookhart, Susan. *What We Know About Grading: What Works, What Doesn't, and What's Next*. Association for Supervision & Curriculum Development, 2019.

Heffernan, Troy. "Sexism, Racism, Prejudice, and Bias: A Literature Review and Synthesis of Research Surrounding Student Evaluations of Courses and Teaching." *Assessment & Evaluation in Higher Education*, Vol. 47, No.1, pp. 144–54, 2021. https://doi.org/10.1080/02602938.2021.1888075.

Highsmith, Patricia. *Plotting and Writing Suspense Fiction*. St. Martin's Press, 1990.

hooks, bell. *Teaching to Transgress: Education as the Practice of Freedom*. Routledge, 1994.

Hurston, Zora Neale. *Their Eyes Were Watching God*. Amistad, 2006.

Inoue, Asao B. *Labor-Based Grading Contracts: Building Equity and Inclusion in the Compassionate Writing Classroom*. The WAC Clearing House, 2019.

Jaffe, Sarah. *Work Won't Love You Back: How Devotion to Our Jobs Keeps Us Exploited, Exhausted, and Alone*. Bold Type Books, 2022.

Jahoda, Susan, and Woolard, Caroline. *Making and Being: Embodiment, Collaboration, and Circulation in the Visual Arts*. Pioneer Works Press, 2020.

Johnson, Adam. "Hurricanes Anonymous," *Fortune Smiles*. Random House, 2015.

Johnston, Bret Anthony. *Naming the World and Other Exercises for the Creative Writer*. Random House, 2007.

Kapil, Bhanu. *The Vertical Interrogation of Strangers*, Kelsey Street Press, 2001.

Kincaid, Jamaica. *A Small Place*. Farrar, Straus, Giroux, 2000.

Kohn, Alfie. "The Case Against Grades." *Counterpoints*, Vol. 451, pp. 143–53, 2013. *JSTOR*, www.jstor.org/stable/42982088.

Kolb, David. *Experiential Learning: Experience as the Source of Learning and Development*, 2nd ed. Pearson, 2014.

Kreitzer, Rebecca and Sweet-Cushman, Jennie. "Evaluating Student Evaluations of Teaching: A Review of Measurement and Equity Bias in SETs and Recommendations for Ethical Reform." *Journal of Academic Ethics*, Vol. 20, pp. 73–84, 2022. https://doi.org/10.1007/s10805-021-09400-w.

Lang, James. "The Case for Slow-Walking Our Use of Generative AI," *The Chronicle of Higher Education*. February 29, 2024. www.chronicle-com.eu1.proxy.openathens.net/article/the-case-for-slow-walking-our-use-of-generative-ai.

Lang, James. *Small Teaching: Everyday Lessons From the Science of Learning*. Jossey-Bass, 2016.

Lerman, Liz. *Critical Response Process: A Method for Getting Useful Feedback on Anything You Make, From Dance to Dessert*. The Dance Exchange, 2003.

Lerman, Liz and Borstel, John. *Critique is Creative: The Critical Response Process in Theory and Action*. Wesleyan University Press, 2022.

Lerman, Liz. Commonplace Podcast Interview. September 21, 2022. https://commonplace.today/commonplace-podcast/episode-104-the-critical-response-process (min 1:20–1:22).

Longenbach, James. *The Art of the Poetic Line*. Graywolf Press, 2007.

Maum, Courtney. *Before and After the Book Deal*. Catapult. 2020.

Meitner, Erika. "Dollar General," *Oxford American*, October 28, 2016. https://oxfordamerican.org/magazine/issue-94-fall-2016/dollar-general.

Minh-ha, Trinh T. *When the Moon Waxes Red: Representation, Gender and Cultural Politics*. Routledge, 1991.

Mullaney, Thomas S., and Rea, Christopher. *Where Research Begins: Choosing a Research Project That Matters to You (and the World)*. The University of Chicago Press, 2022.

Mullen, Harryette, "Imagining the Unimagined Reader: Writing to the Unborn and Including the Excluded." *boundary 2*, Spring 1999, Vol. 26, No. 1, 99 Poets/1999: An International Poetics Symposium (Spring, 1999), pp. 198–203.

Mullen, Harryette. *Urban Tumbleweed: Notes from a Tanka Diary*. Graywolf Press, 2013.

Myers, David Gershom. *The Elephants Teach: Creative Writing Since 1880*. University of Chicago Press, 1996.

Nickerson, Raymond S. "How We Know—And Sometimes Misjudge—What Others Know: Imputing One's Own Knowledge to Others." *Psychological Bulletin*, Vol. 125, pp. 737–59, 1999.

Nordmann, Emily, Hutchison, Jacqui, and MacKay, Jill R.D. "Lecture Rapture: The Place and Case for Lectures in the New Normal." *Teaching in Higher Education*, Vol. 27, No.5, pp. 709–16, 2021. https://doi.org/10.1080/13562517.2021.2015755.

Palmer, Parker J. *The Courage to Teach. Exploring the Inner Landscape of a Teacher's Life*. Jossey-Bass, 2017 [1997].

Parker, Priya. *The Art of Gathering*. Riverhead Books, 2018.

Paul, Anna Murphy. *The Extended Mind: The Power of Thinking Outside the Brain*. HarperCollins, 2021.

Phillips, Carl. *My Trade is Mystery: Seven Meditations from a Life in Writing*. Yale University Press, 2022.

Pickens, Beth. *Make Your Art No Matter What*. Chronicle Books, 2021.

Pound, Ezra. "A Few Don'ts by an Imagiste." *Poetry*, Vol. 1, No. 6, March 1913, pp. 200–06. www.jstor.org/stable/20569730.

Pulfrey, Caroline, Buchs, Céline, and Butera, Fabrizio. "Why Grades Engender Performance-Avoidance Goals: The Mediating Role of Autonomous Motivation." *Journal of Educational Psychology*, Vol. 103, pp. 683–700, 2011. https://doi.org/10.1037/a0023911.

Rademacher, Tom. *It Won't Be Easy: An Exceedingly Honest (and Slightly Unprofessional) Love Letter to Teaching*. University of Minnesota Press, 2017.

Range, Melissa. "A Skiff of Snow," *Birmingham Poetry Review*. The University of Alabama at Birmingham, posted 2014, www.uab.edu/cas/englishpublications/bpr/archive/bpr-41-2014/a-skiff-of-snow.

Rekdal, Paisley. *Appropriate: A Provocation*. W.W. Norton and Company, 2021.

Reyes, Barbara Jane. "Others Would Tell Me Nothing is Mine: Talking With Barbara Jane Reyes." Interviewed by Ire'ne Lara Silva. September 8, 2020. https://therumpus.net/2020/09/08/the-rumpus-interview-with-barbara-jane-reyes-2/.

Roberts, Judith C. and Roberts, Keith A. "Deep Reading, Cost/Benefit, and the Construction of Meaning: Enhancing Reading Comprehension and Deep Learning in Sociology Courses." *Teaching Sociology*, Vol. 36, pp. 125–40, 2008.

Roozen, Kevin. "Writing Is Linked to Identity." In *Naming What We Know: Threshold Concepts of Writing Studies* (pp. 50–52), edited by Linda Adler-Kassner and Elizabeth Wardle. Utah State University Press, 2015a.

Roozen, Kevin. "Texts Get Their Meaning from Other Texts." In *Naming What We Know: Threshold Concepts of Writing Studies* (pp. 44–48), edited by Linda Adler-Kassner and Elizabeth Wardle. Utah State University Press, 2015b.

Row, Jess. *White Flights: Race, Fiction, and the American Imagination*. Graywolf Press, 2019.

Salesses, Matthew. *Craft in the Real World: Rethinking Fiction Writing and Workshopping*. Catapult, 2021.

Shaughnessy, Brenda. "Blueberries for Cal," Poets.org, Academy of American Poets, 2019. https://poets.org/poem/blueberries-cal.

Sharpe, Christina. *Ordinary Notes*. Knopf Canada, 2023.

Smith, Zadie, *Changing My Mind*. Penguin Books, 2010.

Sondheim, Stephen. "Sondheim Teaches Send In the Clowns." Posted March 8, 2007 by AllanWo, YouTube, 2007. 4 min., 3 sec. www.youtube.com/watch?v=8-VXXZLh2a0.

Stanfield, Brian. *The Art of Focused Conversation: 100 Ways to Access Group Wisdom in the Workplace*. New Society Publishers, 2020.

Stevens, Wallace. *Harmonium*. Knopf, 1923.

Stommel, Jesse. *Undoing the Grade: Why We Grade and How to Stop*. Hybrid Pedagogy Inc., 2023.

Sword, Helen. *Air & Light & Time & Space*. Harvard University Press, 2017.

Tinberg, Howard. "Metacognition Is Not Cognition." In *Naming What We Know: Threshold Concepts of Writing Studies* (pp. 75–76), edited by Linda Adler-Kassner and Elizabeth Wardle. Utah State University Press, 2015.

Vandermeer, Jeff. *Wonderbook: The Illustrated Guide to Creating Imaginative Fiction*. Abrams Image, 2013.

Warrener, Sheryda (Ed.) *The Provocation Collection*. www.theprovocationcollection.com/.

Weiss, Robert S. *Learning from Strangers: The Art and Method of Qualitative Interview Studies*. Free Press, 1995.

Wiggins, Grant and McTighe, Jay. *Understanding by Design*, 2nd ed. Association for Supervision and Curriculum Development, 2006.

William, Dar. *How to Write a Song that Matters*. Hachette, 2022.

Wright, C. D. "The Art of Revision." Poets.Org. 2014. https://poets.org/c-d-wright-art-revision.

Yancy, George. *Look, A White! Philosophical Essays on Whiteness*. Temple University Press, 2012.

Youn, Monica. "Generative Revision. Beyond the Zero-Sum Game." *The Sewanee Review*, Spring, 2023. https://thesewaneereview.com/articles/generative-revision-beyond-zero-sum-game.

Yu, Timothy. "From Poet to Critic and Back Again." Poetry Foundation. October 9, 2022. www.poetryfoundation.org/featured-blogger/85602/the-poet-as-critic.

Index